SENSE AND NONSENSE about CRIME

A Policy Guide

2nd Edition

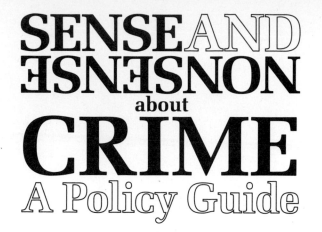

SENSE AND NONSENSE about CRIME

A Policy Guide

2nd Edition

Samuel Walker

University of Nebraska, Omaha

Brooks/Cole Publishing Company
Pacific Grove, California

Consulting Editor: *Roy Roberg*

Brooks/Cole Publishing Company
A Division of Wadsworth, Inc.

Printed in the United States of America

10   9   8   7   6   5   4

Library of Congress Cataloging in Publication Data
Walker, Samuel
  Sense and nonsense about crime.

  Includes index.
  1. Criminal justice, Administration of—United
States.   2. Crime prevention—United States.
I. Title.
HV9950.W34   1988   364.4'0456'0973   88-8120
ISBN 0-534-09120-2

Sponsoring Editor: *Claire Verduin*
Marketing Representative: *Henry Staat*
Editorial Assistant: *Gay C. Bond*
Production Editor: *Penelope Sky*
Production Assistant: *Marie DuBois*
Manuscript Editor: *Barbara Salazar*
Permissions Editor: *Carline Haga*
Interior and Cover Design: *Kelly Shoemaker*
Art Coordinator: *Lisa Torri*
Interior Illustration: *John Foster*
Cartoons: *Michael Kim*
Typesetting: *TCSystems, Inc., Shippensburg, Pennsylvania*
Printing and Binding: *Malloy Lithographing, Inc., Ann Arbor, Michigan*

Foreword

Through the Contemporary Issues in Crime and Justice Series, students are introduced to important topics that until now have been neglected or inadequately covered and that are relevant to criminal justice, criminology, law, political science, psychology, and sociology. The authors address philosophical and theoretical issues, and analyze the most recent research findings and their implications for practice. Consequently, each volume will stimulate further thinking and debate on the topics it covers, in addition to providing direction for the development and implementation of policy.

How can crime be reduced? That is the question. During the last several decades, extensive changes in crime control policy have been sought, first from a liberal perspective and more recently from the conservative point of view. At the same time, the amount of empirical research into crime and the criminal justice system has increased dramatically. Given these developments, it now should be possible to take a realistic look at the effectiveness of various crime control policies throughout the system. Of course, to achieve a realistic view of such policies we must take political ideologies into account. Yet few attempts have been made to assess the actual impact of crime control policies in this country, either in reducing crime or in effecting policy changes. Without such analyses it is impossible to know how close we are to reducing and controlling crime, or to recognize where our efforts should be directed now.

In *Sense and Nonsense about Crime*, Sam Walker takes a hard look at the prospects for crime control from the perspective of actual results. He offers a straightforward discussion of practices that have not worked and continue to be unproductive (the "nonsense"), and of those that appear to be working or at least have some potential for success (the "sense"). In this second edition Walker again offers serious challenges to many of the conservative and liberal prescriptions for crime reduction, and provides additional insight derived from the latest research data and court interpretations.

The first edition was widely acclaimed for its realistic and insightful assessments of the contemporary criminal justice system and its institutions. The major conclusion to be drawn from this second review reinforces his original premise: continual tinkering with the system will not produce significant reductions in serious crime. Walker forces us to face the reality that if we are to reduce crime we must be willing to overhaul our economic policies. Unfortunately, most of us in the criminal justice and criminology profession have little influence on the economic policies of the government. All is not lost, however, as Walker reminds that the criminal justice system has two goals: crime control and justice. He suggests that we have paid too much attention to the former and not enough to the latter. I suspect he is right, and that if we are willing to pay attention to the lessons to be learned from his examples we can participate effectively in the pursuit of justice within the system. In the final analysis, this may be the most important goal within our reach.

Roy Roberg

Preface

So what's new? Is there any justification for a second edition of *Sense and Nonsense about Crime*, apart from wanting to sell more books? The answer is yes, because things have changed in criminal justice during the four years since the first edition was published. The changes are not enormous, but they are important. One of my main goals is to help people think clearly about crime, to cut through the myths and the political rhetoric, and in order to do this we must remain aware of changing circumstances.

The most significant change is the steady deterioration of the theoretical foundations of conservative thinking about crime control. Ideas that were fresh ten years ago are already exhausted. Many have been tried and found wanting. This collapse, however, is on a purely intellectual level. In terms of public policy, several major conservative tactics have never been more popular, with legislators and the general public alike: preventive detention, imprisonment for deterrence and incapacitation, and the death penalty.

For the student of crime policy, there is a valuable lesson here. The current situation demonstrates how policies can continue to have powerful appeal despite the fact that their intellectual and theoretical underpinnings have eroded. Along the same lines, it is striking to note that public fear of crime remains extremely high although real crime rates continue to decline. This is a paradox that students will be wise to ponder at some length.

Although most conservative crime control policies are no longer valid, liberals have been unable to offer credible alternatives. Students may well wonder what is at the root of this rather remarkable failure. Why have liberals been able to offer only the same old ideas?

This edition of *Sense and Nonsense* ends far more pessimistically than the first, not necessarily because the situation is worse now, but perhaps because I am less reluctant to face the implications of my own thinking. The material examined throughout the book led me to the somber conclusion that discussing criminal justice policy may be irrelevant if our goal is to reduce crime. Perhaps you will diagree. If *Sense and Nonsense about Crime* inspires you to think seriously about crime control policy it will have served its purpose.

The first edition was very well received by teachers and students alike. I have received many favorable responses, most of them clearly spontaneous and thoughtful. I thus decided not to change either the basic structure or the theme of the book. I made a serious effort to add the most recent and important research in the field. On some issues I substantially revised my thinking in light of new evidence. My comments about probation, for example, are much less enthusiastic than they were. In the first edition I offered a suggestion for improving police–community relations. Soon after the book appeared, a Police Foundation study offered persuasive evidence that the idea didn't work. I have revised that section accordingly.

The structure of the book remains basically unchanged. In the first section I discuss general points about the administration of justice in the United States. No new research has caused me to change my interpretation here. In subsequent sections I again review conservative and liberal crime control policies. Although I have revised my treatment of particular issues, no new evidence has challenged the original interpretation.

Acknowledgments

Once again I want to thank a number of people for their help. Claire Verduin is an extremely able editor, a joy to work with. I have found that everyone else at Brooks/Cole is committed to producing quality books in an efficient and humane manner that has made the entire process a pleasure. Several people offered suggestions that helped me revise the text. I would like to thank Roy Roberg, Diana Gordon, Herman Goldstein, and George Cole in particular, as well as the following reviewers: Tom Bernard, Pennsylvania State University; Michael Meyer, University of North Dakota; Joel Samaha, University of Minnesota; Tom Schade, Arizona State University; and Thomas Winfree, New Mexico State University.

I dedicated the first edition to a small group of close friends. Four years later, waddaya know, most are still here and still good friends. Some people moved away, some dropped out, but new friends have appeared. Once again I dedicate this book to those who help make my life enjoyable.

Samuel Walker

Contents

──────────── PART FIVE ────────────

CONCLUSION 267

Propositions

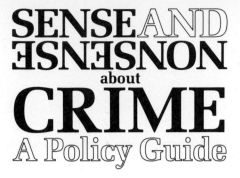

SENSE AND NONSENSE

about

CRIME

A Policy Guide

2nd Edition

PART ONE

THINKING CLEARLY ABOUT CRIME

Chapter 1

The Paradox of Crime in the 1980s

T he paradox of crime in the 1980s lies in the stark contrast between the public hysteria over crime and the steady decline in crime rates. Crime is down but fear is up.

Evidence of public fear of crime is everywhere. Public support for the death penalty is at an all-time high. In 1986 71 percent of Americans supported capital punishment; only 23 percent opposed it. Twenty years earlier only 40 percent supported the death penalty; by 1976 its supporters numbered 60 percent. The death penalty issue was the primary reason that in 1986 California voters removed three judges from the state supreme court, including Chief Justice Rose Bird. Draconic anticrime laws have been passed by Congress and by virtually every state legislature. In 1984 Congress passed a tough anticrime bill that included the denial of bail to dangerous offenders. Only a handful of liberal members of Congress were willing to oppose the bill. Most feared to be thought "soft" on crime in an election year. Similar preventive detention laws have been enacted in thirty-four states.

Prisons are bursting at the seams. As a result of tougher sentences by judges, mainly in response to public pressure, the number of people in prison is at an all-time high. By 1985 the "cage count" of prisoners in state and federal institutions reached 481,616, an astounding 50 percent increase just since 1980. The imprisonment rate had more than doubled, from 96 per 100,000 in 1973 to 201 per 100,000 in 1985. At the same time, local jails are jammed. The total jail population increased by 41 percent, from 158,394 in 1978 to 223,551 in 1983.

Yet crime is not increasing. In fact, the crime rate has been falling steadily for over a decade. According to the National Crime Survey (NCS), the rate of violent crimes declined by 13.6 percent between 1973 and 1986. Even more significant, rapes were down by 30 percent and robberies down by 23.7 percent. Household burglaries, meanwhile, declined by 33 percent.[1]

But wait a minute, what about the drug/gang problem that is in the news so much? Hasn't this produced a new crime epidemic? One of the main themes of this book is that we should not let our thinking be distorted by a special situation or a sudden new crisis. We need to look at the facts carefully.

The current problem is indeed serious. Gangs have virtually taken over entire neighborhoods of New York and Los Angeles. Members have Uzis and other automatic weapons. There are reports of senseless random shootings of innocent people ("drive-bys"). Homicides have suddenly increased in Detroit, Los Angeles, and Washington.

Terrible as this situation is, it is only part of the total crime problem. Gang violence is directed primarily at other gangs and limited to their immediate neighborhoods, in only a few cities. Victims tend to be law-abiding people who live in these areas. For most Americans the risk of victimization continues to decline. My generalization about crime trends still holds. The real tragedy is that an acceptable quality of life is a privilege instead of a right today more than ever. Those who are at the bottom, the "underclass," are worse off; the rest of us are a little better off, both economically and in terms of our feeling safe from criminal victimization.

How do we explain the paradox of increasing fear of crime while the crime rate is falling?

Part of the problem lies in the conflict between the two different estimates of the national crime rate published by the Justice Department. The National Crime Survey is a victimization survey that has been conducted annually since 1973. The more well-known and far more publicized figures on crime are those developed by the FBI Uniform Crime Reports (UCR) system. The UCR reports a very different trend over the past fifteen years. According to the FBI, violent crime rose 29.7 percent between 1977 and 1986 (down 17.1 percent, according to the NCS, in the same period). According to the UCR, rapes were up 27.6 percent; robberies increased 18 percent while burglaries declined by 5.3 percent.[2]

Public attitudes are more heavily influenced by the FBI's UCR figures, which have been the "official" crime data since 1930. The conflict between the two sets of crime data poses an important issue for the student of criminal justice. In any attempt to design effective crime control policies, it is important to know whether serious crime is increasing or decreasing. We examine the merits of the two systems in detail on pages 14–15.

Nothing better illustrates the gap between public fears and the actual risk of victimization than the celebrated case of Bernard Goetz. In December 1984 Goetz shot four young men who he claimed were attempting to rob him of $5 in a New York City subway. The shooting became a focal point of racial tensions in New York, as Goetz was white and the four youths were black. For many whites, Goetz became a hero—the "subway vigilante" who finally "did something" about crime. Controversy continued to rage over the case until Goetz was convicted on the lesser charge of weapons possession in 1987.

The Goetz case symbolized the issue of crime in the city—in this case, the specific problem of crime on the New York City subways. In the minds of many people, the subways are a dangerous, crime-ridden place. The reality is very different. When Dennis Kenney attempted to evaluate the impact of the Guardian Angels—a group of volunteers organized to provide additional protection on the subways—he found it impossible because there was so little crime on the subways to begin with. Less than 3 percent of all the crime in New York City occurs in the subways (only 9 of the 1,422 murders in 1984). In the areas Kenney selected for his study, the victimization rate for violent crimes was only 4 per 100,000. The national victimization rate is 30 per 100,000. The subways are in fact the safest area in New York City!

Crime Control: A Plague of Nonsense

The good news is that the crime rates are declining; the bad news is that the United States still has far more serious crime than any other "civilized" country. Crime afflicts our daily lives like a plague, affecting the way we think, the way we act, the way we respond to one another. Fear of crime has a corrosive effect on interpersonal relations, making us wary of small acts of friendliness toward strangers. Like creatures at the bottom of a polluted lake, Americans have adapted to this environment. No other industrial society has crime rates comparable with ours. We murder each other eight to twelve times as often as do people in Europe or Japan. The figures for robbery are even worse. New York City's robbery rate is five times greater than London's and, incredibly, 125 times higher than that of Tokyo.[3]

The threat of crime overwhelms our thinking. Instead of considering the problem realistically, we grasp at any new proposal. People react to the threat of crime the same way they do to being overweight. They desperately grasp at some new miracle diet—one that promises to take off pounds without effort. And every year a new miracle diet captures the public's attention. So it is with crime control. Every year an amazing new program promises to cut crime by 30 percent, 50 percent, or more. Criminal justice policy is given to fads: one year it is selective incapacitation, the next year intensive probation. Yesterday's fad is soon forgotten.

Our crime policies are intellectually bankrupt. We do not have a credible set of policies to reduce our persistently high levels of crime. Instead we are offered a series of desperate nostrums promising quick and easy solutions. Virtually none of them work and many are positively dangerous. In the past twenty years we have seen three "wars" on crime, one launched by Lyndon Johnson in the mid-1960s, one initiated by Richard Nixon in the late 1960s, and the third a massive effort in the 1980s. All three failed to reduce crime and only created unrealistic expectations about the nature of the task. The public was left even more angry and frustrated than before. The slow but steady reduction in serious crime since 1973 is due primarily to demographic trends—the decline in the number of people in the high crime age group of 14- to 24-year-olds.[4]

This book is about crime control policy. It is a search for sensible answers to an urgent question: What can we do to reduce crime? Our inquiry focuses on one simple question: *What works?* We will review all the major crime control proposals and weigh them against evidence of their effectiveness. Fortunately, we have learned a lot about crime and criminal justice in the past fifteen years. The "research revolution" in criminal justice offers a substantial and growing body of literature on how the criminal justice system works. Implementation of many currently popular crime control proposals has in fact been attempted, and some of those efforts have been rigorously evaluated. Most of that valuable evidence remains buried in obscure government reports and academic journals. This book presents the highlights of the best of the most recent research.

The Ground Rules

Let us establish the ground rules for this inquiry. We will focus on the crimes of robbery and burglary. These two predatory, high-fear crimes are a major source of public concern. We do not underestimate the significance of other serious crimes. Murder takes nearly 20,000 American lives each year. Rape victims often suffer twice, first from the brutal crime and again from the insensitive processes of investigation and prosecution. White-collar crime costs us at least ten times as much in pure dollar terms as robbery and burglary combined. Employees steal far more than shoplifters.

Concentration on two crimes imposes some needed discipline on our thinking. It allows us to compare systematically the impact of different crime control proposals. It also prevents us from dodging the hard questions by changing the subject. Too often the advocates of one policy or another shift the discussion from one crime to another. Liberals evade hard questions about robbery and burglary by digressing to so-called victimless crimes (gambling, marijuana use, unconventional sexual behavior, and so on). As Elliott Currie points out in *Confronting Crime,* liberals have had a difficult time facing up to the reality of serious crime. It's a subject they would prefer to avoid.[5] Conservatives are just as bad. They often concentrate on special cases (particularly mass murders and other heinous crimes) that have little to do with the routine felonies of robbery and burglary. Conservatives refuse to discuss the costs of their crime-fighting proposals. They talk tough about locking up more criminals but don't discuss the taxes that must pay for their incarceration. We will not allow ourselves to shift the terms of the debate here.

From time to time, to illustrate particular points, we will consider other crimes. An entire section is devoted to drunk driving, for example, because it illustrates many of the problems involved in deterrence as a crime control

"How about a crime control policy that works!"

strategy. We will focus primarily on crimes committed by adults. Juvenile crime and delinquency are serious problems and I have no wish to slight their importance. The world of juvenile justice is a very special realm that deserves a lengthy critical inquiry of its own.

A second ground rule involves a single-minded focus on crime control. By "crime control" I mean any policy or program aimed at reducing the level of serious crime. Such policies include programs designed to catch and punish more criminals as well as those designed to reduce crime by rehabilitating offenders or reforming society.

Questions of justice, fairness, and decency form a third ground rule. One of the hallmarks of a democratic society under the rule of law is the principle that there are limits to government authority. Effective crime control proposals must not violate this principle. As much as we would like to control crime, we do not want to turn the United States into a totalitarian society. We could summarily execute narcotics dealers. Or we could imprison all juveniles convicted of a felony. Such policies would shock the consciences of most Americans. As they are not acceptable to the majority of Americans, they are not realistic by our ground rules.

As this inquiry proceeds, I shall set forth my major ideas in the form of concise propositions. The first of these propositions establishes the basic thrust of this inquiry:

───────────────────── **PROPOSITION 1** ─────────────────────
Most current crime control proposals are nonsense.

Most of the crime control proposals advanced by politicians and criminal justice experts won't work. They fail the basic pragmatic test: they won't reduce robbery or burglary. Most crime control proposals are wishful thinking. Many are simply irrelevant: they cannot be implemented and would have no noticeable effect on crime rates. Some proposals entail serious risks. They might succeed in reducing crime, but only at an unacceptably high price. In a few cases the political price is high enough to guarantee that they will never be seriously tried in the first place. Some proposals have merit, but for reasons unrelated to crime control: they might improve the quality of justice, but that aim, important as it is, is a different goal from controlling crime.

The more we have learned about crime and criminal justice in the past twenty years, the more we have learned what *doesn't* work. In 1970 Norval Morris and Gordon Hawkins published a short book titled *The Honest Politician's Guide to Crime Control*. They began with the confident assertion that "we offer a cure for crime—not a sudden potion nor a lightning panacea but rather a legislative and administrative regimen which would substantially reduce the impact of crime."[6] Events of the past twenty years have exposed the foolishness of such extravagant claims. They would not make such a claim today, nor would any other sensible expert in the field of criminal justice. Morris and Hawkins are liberals. Conservatives have been guilty of the same kind of extravagance. In 1975 James Q. Wilson endorsed a tough sentencing policy that he claimed would reduce serious crime by one-third. Eight years later, when he wrote the second edition of *Thinking about Crime*, he had to back away from this extravagant promise. The accumulating evidence clearly indicated that there was no quick fix to the crime problem.[7]

The "research revolution" has taught us to be wary of cures for crime. Unfortunately, not everyone has learned this lesson. Indeed, the current predicament seems to produce just the opposite effect. Frustration over crime and the failure of highly advertised reforms increases the public's appetite for extravagant promises. New crime control measures have been enacted in most states. Other measures are currently under consideration. This inquiry is designed to show why they don't work. As is the case with other matters of public policy, political partisanship colors the debate. Crime is a salient political issue, and each side attempts to use it against its opponents. The sad fact is that neither side has anything very useful to say about crime control. My second proposition is:

───────────────────── **PROPOSITION 2** ─────────────────────
Both liberals and conservatives are guilty of peddling nonsense about crime.

For the last fifteen years conservatives have held the political initiative. Their ideas have been enacted into law and upheld by the Supreme Court: modification of the exclusionary rule, preventive detention, mandatory

"First we put all the good people in the world
on one side, and all the bad on the other. Then
we build this huge wall separating them."

prison sentences, and so forth. The current hegemony of conservative
thinking should be seen in the context of the ebb and flow of criminal justice
policy in this century. Liberal reform held sway from 1900 to World War I. A
conservative law-and-order reaction prevailed through the 1920s and 1930s.
Liberalism reasserted itself in the 1950s and completely dominated the field
through the 1960s. Conservative ideas regained the initiative in the 1970s.
They appeared fresh and exciting, while liberal ideas seemed exhausted.
The parallel with economic policy is striking. On that subject, some
observers have quipped, liberals have no ideas, while conservatives have
dangerous ideas.

The categories of "liberal" and "conservative" are admittedly crude.
Inevitably, subtle distinctions are blurred. Nonetheless, certain common
assumptions are shared by members of both groups. Conservative crime
control proposals seek to strengthen the machinery of justice. We can reduce
crime by catching more criminals, convicting more of them, and subjecting
the convicted to more severe punishment. Deterrence and incapacitation are
the two most important theoretical assumptions underlying conservative
crime control policy. The machinery of justice is weakened by various
"technicalities" of criminal procedure; the conservative agenda calls for
their removal.[8]

Liberal crime control policy calls for the reshaping of individual
offenders, of the criminal justice system, or of society as a whole. Rehabilita-

tion, the core theory underlying liberal policy, informs a wide range of programs designed to alter the behavior of individual offenders and mold them into law-abiding citizens. Social reform, meanwhile, proceeds from the assumption that much criminal behavior is rooted in social injustice. Expanded educational and economic opportunities would allow people to choose constructive lives and reject the temptations of deviant and criminal activity.[9]

In practice the distinction between liberal and conservative crime control policies is often difficult to discern. What, after all, is a prison? Official bureaucratic jargon labels it a "correctional facility," but most judges, much of the public, and probably all prisoners recognize it as a place of punishment. Does the prison then represent liberal or conservative policy? One of the first steps in thinking sensibly about crime is learning to penetrate popular slogans and official rhetoric.

The ambiguity of the prison suggests an important point: the real world does not necessarily conform to our assumptions. The fact that the prison was invented to rehabilitate does not mean that it accomplishes this task. The same can be said for parole. Likewise, the fact that some people think that prison terms serve as a deterrent does not mean that criminals are deterred from committing crimes. In the real world the gap between theory and result is very large. This insight will prove very useful as we proceed to examine why most crime control proposals do not work.

The labels "liberal" and "conservative" create further problems because prominent experts do not always fit neatly into one category or the other. Nor do their ideas remain static. James Q. Wilson, one of the more prominent conservatives, is a former liberal who has confessed the "error" of his ways. Former Chief Justice Warren Burger represents an even more curious phenomenon. One of the most outspoken conservatives through the 1970s, especially in some of his more intemperate opinions, he emerged in the early 1980s as the leading advocate of prison reform, championing the old liberal idea of vocational programs for prisoners.

Yet despite its limitations, the liberal-conservative classification scheme serves a useful purpose. It helps us think systematically about the various crime control ideas by directing our attention to the assumptions that underlie them. Proposals we label conservative do share a common set of assumptions, and they differ substantially from the assumptions on which liberals base their proposals.

One of my main arguments is that both groups begin with erroneous assumptions. Let us see where they go wrong.

Crime Control Theology

The basic problem with most crime control thinking is that faith triumphs over facts. For both liberals and conservatives, certain ideas acquire lives of their own and become, literally, articles of faith. This is the realm of crime control theology.

PROPOSITION 3

Most crime control proposals rest on faith rather than on facts.

Ideas about crime and crime control are often based on deeply held beliefs that resemble religious conviction. They cannot be proven or disproven by argumentation over factual evidence. Better to try to prove the existence of God. Over 70% of Americans today support the death penalty because they believe it will deter criminals. This belief persists despite the absence of conclusive evidence to support it. Many liberals continue to endorse rehabilitation in the face of considerable evidence that existing programs do not work.

Conservative Theology

Crime control theologies have compelling power because they imply idealized worlds that reflect the deepest hopes and fears of their adherents. Described in the simplest terms, believers in conservative crime control theology envision a world of discipline and self-control in which people exercise self-restraint and subordinate their personal passions to the common good. It is a world of limits, and the criminal law marks one important set of boundaries. Criminals lack self-control. Their passions get the better of them and they break the rules. They kill because they cannot curb their anger. They steal because they cannot control their desire to possess what they do not have or they cannot defer gratification until they have earned the right to possess something legitimately. Poverty is no excuse. If they are poor, it is only because they refuse to exercise enough self-discipline to get an education and a job that will lift them out of poverty. James Q. Wilson and Richard J. Horrnstein's conservative theory of criminal behavior holds that crime is essentially a matter of choice: "at any given moment, a person can choose between committing a crime and not committing it."[10]

Individual responsibility reigns in the idealized conservative world. People who break the rules should be punished. Punishment works, for an unpleasant sanction teaches a useful lesson. Criminals learn to obey the rules and others learn by their example that crime does not pay. In criminological jargon these processes are known as specific and general deterrence. There is also an important moral element to punishment. There are rules, and rules are terribly important. To break a rule is to strike at the very foundation of civilized society. Such a transgression deserves an appropriately serious response. We used to call this theory "retribution"; in recent years the term "desert" has become more fashionable, probably because it sounds less biblical. In James Q. Wilson's oft-quoted phrase,

"Wicked people exist. Nothing avails except to set them apart from innocent people."[11]

Conservatives are deeply ambivalent, often contradictory about the role of government in the control of crime. Wilson makes a strong argument that government policies cannot affect the basic social conditions that cause criminal behavior. He cites the failure of the liberal social programs of the 1960s. What he really means is that he doesn't like *liberal* programs: the ones related to job training, income maintenance, family assistance, and so on. Yet he bases his whole approach to crime control on the imposition of tougher penalties that will deter criminals from breaking the law. In short, he is saying that some government policies do influence human behavior while others do not. The real difference between conservatives and liberals is a

---

A Word about Rules

Conservatives are not alone in their concern about rules. Liberals attach great importance to them as well. Civil libertarians put special emphasis on the rules of procedure. The criminal law is a set of rules that govern everyone: don't kill, don't steal. Criminal procedure is a set of rules that applies specifically to criminal justice officials. It tells them what they *must* do (bring the arrested person before a magistrate "without unnecessary delay") and what they must *not* do (conduct an unreasonable search). For liberals, the rules of procedure define the boundaries of a civilized society. Even the slightest violation threatens its collapse. The point here is that, in certain respects, conservatives and liberals have the same attitude toward rules. It is largely a matter of which rules are in question.

Both sides are ambivalent about rule breaking. Conservatives who are outraged by violations of the criminal law are quite willing to excuse violations of the rules of procedure—and much of the conservative agenda calls for relaxation of those very rules. Liberals, for their part, are willing to tolerate minor law breaking by individuals but express outrage at violations of procedures by public officials. These responses are, of course, subject to some limitations. Conservatives neither endorse nor condone gross abuses by police or other officials. Nor do liberals endorse or condone crime. Their differences are a matter of priorities. Conservatives are willing to overlook minor official wrongdoing for the greater good of producing a society with less crime. Liberals are willing to tolerate a little more crime in the name of a society in which officials honor the principles of procedural regularity.

SOURCE: Herbert Packer, "Two Models of the Criminal Process," in Packer, *The Limits of the Criminal Sanction* (Stanford: Stanford University Press, 1968), chap. 8.

basic political choice between different government policies. As we shall see shortly, liberals are just as ambivalent on the question of individual responsibility.

The world of conservative crime control is modeled on an idealized image of the patriarchal family. Criminal sanctions resemble parental discipline. Minor misbehavior is greeted with a gentle warning; a second misstep earns a sterner reprimand. More serious wrongdoing is answered with severe punishment. The point is to teach the wisdom of correct behavior by handing out progressively harsher sanctions and threatening even more unpleasant punishment if the behavior continues. Communication of this message is the essence of deterrence theory. Many people were raised in this way and raise their own children in the same manner. Their personal experience tells them it works, and they assume that society should work the same way. Conservative thinking about crime is closely related to conservative ideas about the problem of "permissiveness" in child rearing.

The real world, unfortunately, does not work this way. It is filled with some very incorrigible children who not only don't get the message but don't accept the legitimacy of the "parent's" authority. The light sanctions for early misconduct fail to prevent more serious criminal activity. Even harsh punishment fails to deter.

Conservatives then have to explain why their idealized world is not reflected in the real world of criminal justice. Their answer is that the structure of discipline has broken down and it can be repaired in two ways. First, the certainty of discipline has been undermined by a series of procedural technicalities. The conservative agenda puts great emphasis on eliminating the loopholes that allow criminals to beat the system: the exclusionary rule, the Miranda warning, the insanity defense, plea bargaining, and so on. If we could just ensure the absolute certainty of punishment, the message would get through and people would be deterred from crime. The second remedy is to raise the level of punishment. If current punishments fail to deter, then a stronger dose will surely do the job. Mandatory imprisonment, longer prison terms, and the death penalty are means to this end.

The idea that innumerable criminals "beat the system" and "get off easy" is an article of faith in conservative crime control theology. As we shall see, the evidence does not support this view, but the faith remains unshaken. The conservative agenda calls for strengthening the hand of the criminal justice system, which is imagined as the hand of a stern parent, to increase its ability to mete out swift, certain, and severe punishment.

Liberal Theology

Liberal crime control theology is not as different from its conservative counterpart as you might expect. It also posits an idealized world and

Who Do You Trust?
The Debate Over Crime Statistics

The differences between the data provided by the FBI's Uniform Crime Reports (UCR) and the victimization figures yielded by the National Crime Survey (NCS) demand our attention. This is not simply an academic dispute. When crime control policy is formulated, it makes all the difference in the world whether crime is increasing or decreasing. Are we in the midst of a crime wave or are we witnessing a long-term decline in criminality? Perceptions of the crime problem have a major influence on the political debate. Finally, meaningful evaluation of specific crime control programs requires reliable measures. If one crime data system is inherently superior to another, it should form the basis of all evaluations.

The FBI's UCR system was developed in 1930, and though it has undergone minor adjustments, it has remained basically unchanged ever since. It is based on reports of "crimes known to police" and forwarded to the FBI by local law enforcement agencies. From the moment the UCR system was created, criminologists recognized serious problems with it. Among its shortcomings are these:

1. It takes no account of unreported crimes;
2. the Crime Index includes only eight crimes and does not offer a picture of the total crime problem (it does not measure white-collar crime or organized crime, for example);
3. the police may at their discretion (a) fail to file a crime report even though they know that a crime has been committed, (b) report a crime as a lesser offense (e.g., write up a robbery as a larceny from the person, or a rape as an assault), (c) change the recorded offense at some later time;
4. police department record keeping is unaudited and crime reports may be "lost" through simple inefficiency or a deliberate effort to keep the crime rate low;
5. all Index crimes are treated equally, so that one murder equals one larceny;
6. when an offender commits numerous crimes more or less simultaneously, the system records only the most serious crime (thus if a man robs, rapes, and murders his victim, only the murder is recorded).

The victimization survey was developed in the mid-1960s to deal with some of the problems inherent in the UCR. It is essentially a "proactive" system by which the data collector surveys a random sample of the population to determine if they have been victimized. The survey may be conducted by phone, by mail questionnaire, or by personal interview.

Through the victimization surveys we have learned that only about half of all felonies are reported to police. The reporting rate varies in accordance with the crime: the more serious the crime, the more likely it is to be reported. Thus robberies with injury are heavily reported, whereas larcenies have a low reporting rate. Because of insurance coverage, commercial burglaries and robberies are more frequently reported than household burglaries or personal robberies. The survey also develops useful data on why victims do not report crimes, yielding valuable insights into public attitudes and behavior. The NCS system has also produced richly detailed information about crime victims (income, race, age, sex, etc.), giving us a far more detailed picture of crime in the United States. It also produces useful data on public attitudes toward the police.

For all these reasons, many criminologists (and this author) regard the NCS system as being far more reliable than the FBI's UCR system. The victimization survey, for example, has been applied with great success in such landmark studies as the Kansas City Preventive Patrol Experiment.

The victimization survey is not perfect, of course. Citizens are subject to lapses of memory. They may simply forget about a crime. Or they may "telescope" it, reporting a crime that occurred a year and a half ago even though they were asked about crimes only in the past twelve months. Finally, they may choose not to report a crime. They may be embarrassed about a domestic assault committed by a member of the family, for example.

Other sources of crime data have been used. Self-reports by offenders have been widely used in studies of juvenile delinquency and, more recently, in surveys of prisoners. In response to criticisms of the UCR system, the Police Executive Research Forum developed the Crime Classification System (CCS). This system measures *harm* by weighting crimes according to seriousness. The CCS was tested in an initial experiment but has not been widely adopted.

SOURCES: FBI, *Crime in the United States,* annual; U. S. Department of Justice, *Criminal Victimization in the United States,* annual. Police Executive Research Forum, *Crime Classification System: Three Month Summary Report for Hampton, Virginia* (Washington, D. C., 1984); Joseph Weis, "Crime Statistics Reporting Systems and Methods," in *Encyclopedia of Crime and Justice,* ed. Sanford Kadish (New York: Free Press, 1983), p. 392.

sustains its faith in the face of abundant evidence to the contrary. Liberals and conservatives disagree most sharply on the explanation of criminal behavior. Whereas conservatives attribute it to individual moral failure, liberals see it in terms of social influence. People do wrong because of bad influences in the family, the peer group, or the neighborhood, or because of broader social factors, such as discrimination and lack of economic opportunity. This assumption points in two directions with respect to policy: reshaping individuals and reforming society.

If conservatives view the world as a large family, liberal crime control theology views it as a big classroom. Rehabilitation, the core liberal policy, involves instructing the criminal offender in the ways of correct behavior. Parole, for example, was invented to teach prisoners that they could earn early release by behaving properly. Supervision under probation or parole is designed to guide the offender in the proper direction. Other correctional programs, such as basic education and vocational training, are even more obviously a form of schooling. Liberals and conservatives disagree fundamentally on the questions of both the social factors in criminal behavior and the proper role of government. Whereas conservatives emphasize individual responsibility, liberals stress the impact of unemployment and racial discrimination. Liberals argue not only that government has a responsibility to reduce these problems but that properly designed programs can work.

Elliott Currie goes even further on the question of government responsibility. He argues that we have actually had a "pro-crime" policy. Government economic policies designed to promote economic growth have undermined neighborhoods and families, which, virtually everyone agrees, are the most important influences in promoting stable, law-abiding lives. These economic policies have encouraged millions of people to migrate from farms to cities and have allowed large employers to close plants with no regard for the impact of their actions on the community. Government plays a major role in shaping these economic policies. Currie argues that more attention should be given to the impact of such policies on families, neighborhoods, and crime. In short, government policies affect crime, but in the wrong way.[12]

The emphasis of liberal crime control theology on the social environment also underlies its views on the prison. Originally the prison was invented as a controlled environment, one that would cut the inmate off from corrupting influences in the real world. Total isolation was soon abandoned as basic prison policy, but the original assumption remained unchallenged. Prison reform over the course of 150 years has sought merely to reengineer the prison environment. Environmentalism also points liberal crime control policy in the direction of social reform. If people have adequate opportunities for advancement through legitimate means, they will be less tempted to choose illegitimate activities.

A fundamental article of faith in liberal crime control theology is the belief that people can be reshaped. Much liberal thinking in this area is directed toward a search for an effective rehabilitation program. The history of prison and correctional reform is the story of a continuing search for the Holy Grail of rehabilitation. The prison was launched with great hopes. When it had obviously failed, parole and the indeterminate sentence became the magic keys that would make it work. Successive reforms included individual diagnosis and classification, group counseling, and intensive supervision. Faith continues to survive in the face of repeated failure. Programs are questioned but their underlying assumptions are not.

Liberals are as ambivalent on the question of individual responsibility as conservatives are on the role of government. While liberals emphasize the importance of social conditions in causing crime and reject the conservative obsession with individual responsibility, they do not and cannot completely ignore the role of individual choice. Rehabilitation programs, in fact, are designed to influence individuals to make different (and better) choices. In the realm of the public policy debate, however, they soft-pedal the entire issue of individual responsibility.

Thinking of crime control policy as theology helps us explain the tenacity of various ideas. If liberals have been proposing variations on the theme of correctional treatment for more than 150 years, conservatives have argued the value of swift and certain punishment for just as long. Conservatives have been advocating repeal of the exclusionary rule for more than twenty-five years, while for the same length of time liberals have been urging community-based alternatives to prison. These policy recommendations flow from deeply held and unexamined assumptions.

Notes

1. U. S. Bureau of Justice Statistics, *Criminal Victimization in the United States, 1986* (Washington, D. C.: U. S. Government Printing Office, 1987).
2. United States Department of Justice, *Crime in the United States* (Washington, D. C.: Government Printing Office, 1987), p. 41.
3. Dane Archer and Rosemary Gartner, *Violent Crime in Cross-National Perspective* (New Haven: Yale University Press, 1984). The comparative figures on New York and Japan are found in David Bayley, *Forces of Order* (Berkeley: University of California Press, 1976), chap. 1.
4. Samuel Walker, *Popular Justice: A History of American Criminal Justice* (New York: Oxford University Press, 1980).
5. Elliott Currie, *Confronting Crime: An American Challenge* (New York: Pantheon, 1985), p. 227.
6. Norval Morris and Gordon Hawkins, *The Honest Politician's Guide to Crime Control* (Chicago: University of Chicago Press, 1970).
7. James Q. Wilson, *Thinking about Crime* (New York: Basic Books, 1975; 2nd ed. 1983).
8. Walter B. Miller, "Ideology and Criminal Justice: Some Current Issues," *Journal of Criminal Law and Criminology* 64 (June 1963): 141–162.
9. Lyndon Johnson's "war on poverty" in the 1960s was closely linked to his

concurrent "war on crime," as represented by his President's Crime Commission report. See Walker, *Popular Justice*, pp. 232–235.

10. James Q. Wilson and Richard J. Herrnstein, *Crime and Human Nature: The Definitive Study of the Causes of Crime* (New York: Simon & Schuster, 1985), p. 44.

11. Wilson, *Thinking about Crime* (1975), p. 209.

12. Currie, *Confronting Crime*, p. 226.

Chapter 2

Models of
Criminal Justice

The triumph of faith in crime control requires a willful inattention to the realities of crime and criminal justice. Because the machinery of justice is so very complex, the realities are not hard to overlook. The mechanics of the system are intricate enough; we have fifty state criminal justice systems, each with its own criminal code, along with one federal system. There are 19,691 separate law enforcement agencies. The rules of criminal procedure, meanwhile, are terribly complicated. But the formal mechanics are only the beginning of the problem. The crucial decisions about who gets what are made in a series of informal, low-visibility procedures: the street encounter between police officer and citizen, the negotiated plea of guilty. These events are not witnessed by outsiders and leave no written records. Even many experts are mystified by much that goes on in our criminal justice system. There is considerable debate, for example, over the important question of whether there is systematic racial discrimination in American criminal justice. It is only comparatively recently that we have begun to probe the hidden realms of police discretion and plea bargaining. In the absence of good information, myth and misunderstanding prevail. So our next proposition is:

PROPOSITION 4

Most crime control ideas are nonsense because they are based on false assumptions about criminal justice.

Two attitudes dominate public thinking about the administration of criminal justice: the Old Idealism and the New Cynicism. Neither is very helpful in explaining how the system works.

The Old Idealism is the civics-book image of the administration of justice. It is a vision of law, order, and justice in which hard-working officials diligently handle each case on the basis of its merits. A person who commits a crime is duly arrested and prosecuted. If convicted, the offender receives a punishment commensurate with the crime. The Old Idealism also posits an adversarial system of justice, wherein questions of guilt and innocence are determined through a public contest between prosecution and defense, overseen by an impartial judge. This version of the criminal process expresses an ideal, but no one mistakes it for a description of reality.

The New Cynicism is essentially a mirror image of the Old Idealism and isn't very useful either. It portrays a criminal justice system awash in arbitrary and irrational decision making. Police officers often do not arrest offenders, even when they have probable cause; then they arrest people with no justification. Prosecutors plea-bargain wildly, dropping charges or recommending sentences of meaningless leniency in return for guilty pleas. Meanwhile, some defendants are railroaded through overcharging. Judges exercise virtually unchecked discretion in sentencing. Prisons are a hidden world the public hears about only when inmates riot or escape. Parole boards grant or deny release with no rational basis for their decisions. In this chaotic world there is neither law, order, nor justice.

The New Cynicism comes in two varieties. Conservatives see irrational decision making as undermining effective crime control. Criminals do not pay for their crimes because the police do not arrest them, prosecutors trade away charges, judges are too lenient, and parole boards release inmates too early. The rules of criminal procedure, meanwhile, are easily used by crafty defense attorneys to hamstring officials.

Liberals find systematic injustice in the pattern of irrational decision making. The entire system treats the "respectable" offender with kid gloves and reserves the harshest treatment for the poor—especially the young, black poor. Police arrest selectively. White-collar criminals are barely prosecuted at all. Sentencing favors the offender with financial means. Class and race bias pervades the entire administration of justice, according to the liberal version of the New Cynicism.[1]

Both of these versions contain some element of truth. Much criminal justice decision making is irrational. Vast numbers of offenders do escape punishment, even when they have been caught. Discrimination does pervade the system. But neither of these views adequately explains the routine operations of American criminal justice on a day-to-day basis. Decision making is arbitrary, but broadly consistent patterns can be seen as well. There are gross disparities in the outcomes of apparently similar cases. Convicted murderers in Philadelphia, for example, get either two years in prison or twenty. Rape defendants in New York City can expect either a dismissal of their case or twenty-five years in prison. These are obviously gross disparities. As our inquiry proceeds, we will attempt to discover why they exist. For the moment, we can say that they illustrate Frank Zimring's comment on the paradox of American criminal justice: "The problem is not that our system is too lenient, or too severe; sadly, it is both."[2]

The implications of this point for policy making are enormous. Too many reforms are nonsense because they attack the wrong problem. All too often they are based on exceptional cases that have little to do with the general flow of cases through the system. These exceptional cases nourish the faith but do little to reform the system.

The Crime Commission's Model

To help us understand how the administration of justice works, social scientists have constructed models of the system. The first and most famous model (figure 2.1) was developed fifteen years ago by the President's Crime Commission. It has since appeared in virtually every criminal justice textbook and dominates public and professional thinking about criminal justice.

The Crime Commission developed its model to emphasize the "systemic" nature of the administration of criminal justice. Before the mid-1960s we rarely heard the term "criminal justice *system*." The public and professionals alike conceived of separate agencies that had only a limited relationship with each other. The systemic nature of criminal justice was first recognized in the late 1950s in the course of the American Bar Foundation Survey, a major research project that also focused attention on the pervasive exercise of discretion.[3] The systems approach emphasizes the interrelationship among agencies (we now commonly refer to them as the "components" of the system) and the flow of cases through the system. It also directs research toward the various decision points (arrest, charging, plea bargaining, sentencing, and so on) at which cases are channeled to different parts of the system.

The Crime Commission's flow-chart model is prescriptive as well as descriptive because it focuses attention on certain problems and suggests certain reforms. It identifies fragmentation and the lack of coordination among the components of the system as a major problem. Some experts are fond of referring to a *non-system* of justice. Little coordination exists among the 19,691 separate law enforcement agencies, which are divided among three levels of government. Police, prosecutors, judges, and correctional officials, meanwhile, jealously guard their respective turfs, often competing rather than cooperating. The flow-chart model also emphasizes efficiency and cost-effectiveness as primary goals. When cases are conceptualized as a flow, emphasis is placed on inputs and outputs, and policy makers are encouraged to keep an eye on efficient management of work load and productivity. This model assumes that efficiency (as opposed to justice or some other value) is the most important consideration.[4]

The Crime Commission's model was a quantum leap forward in our understanding of American criminal justice. It accomplished exactly what models are designed to do: it provided a conceptual framework that helped identify general patterns, define major problems, and focus both research and policy planning. After twenty years, however, we can see the limitations

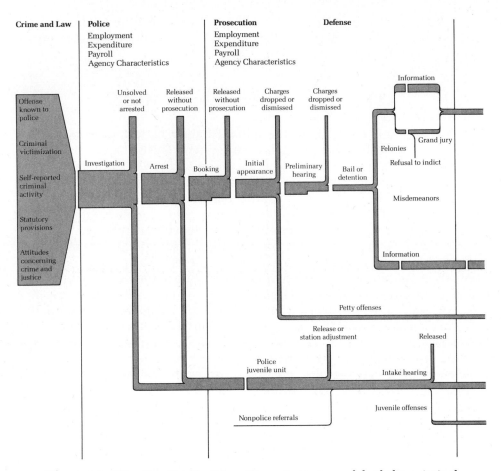

Figure 2.1 The President's Crime Commission's model of the criminal justice system (President's Commission on Law Enforcement and Administration of Justice, *Task Force Report: Science and Technology* [Washington, D.C.: U. S. Government Printing Office, 1967], pp. 58–59).

of this model. A new model is necessary, one that takes into account the results of recent research.

The Criminal Justice Wedding Cake

The major limitation of the Crime Commission's flow chart is that it portrays a *single* system. The day-to-day administration of justice is more complex, in two ways. First, we have fifty-one different criminal justice systems (one federal and fifty state systems). Second, and more important, each of these

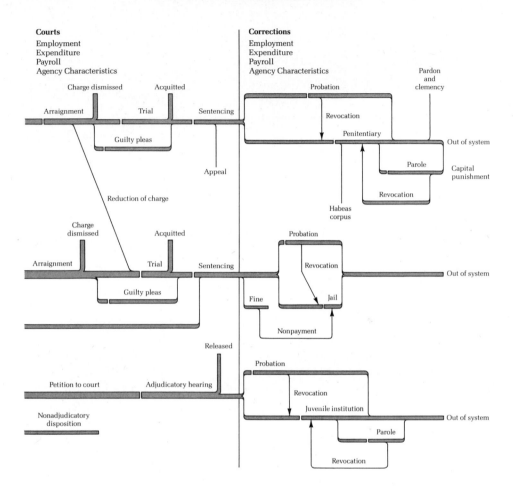

systems is divided into several layers. Our alternative model is the four-layer criminal justice wedding cake.

The wedding-cake idea was first proposed by Lawrence Friedman and Robert V. Percival in *The Roots of Justice*, a history of criminal justice in Alameda County, California. Additional support based on contemporary evidence is found in Michael and Don Gottfredson's *Decision-Making in Criminal Justice*.[5]

The wedding-cake model recognizes the fact that criminal justice officials respond to different kinds of cases in very different ways. They exercise great discretion in deciding how important a case is. The result is

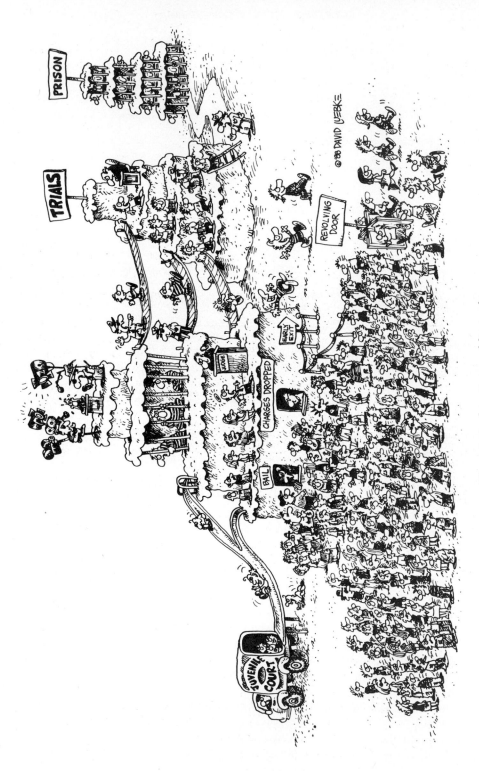

The criminal justice wedding cake

great disparity between cases at different levels but—and this is an extremely important point—there is a high degree of consistency within each layer. The major contribution of the wedding-cake model lies in its distinction between different categories of cases. Too many crime control proposals are inappropriate because they are based on perceptions of special cases that are not representative of the general run of cases. Reforms based on exceptional cases do little to improve the basic operations of the system.

Celebrated Cases: The Top Layer

The small layer at the top of the wedding cake includes what Friedman and Percival call the "celebrated cases." They are exceptional by virtue of being celebrated. These are the cases that make the news. Examples in recent years include the cases of Bernard Goetz, John Hinckley, and Claus von Bulow. Their most important characteristic, of course, is the enormous amount of publicity they receive. The trials are like national soap operas, with the public eagerly awaiting each day's episode. (Will Bernie get off? Did Claus really put the needle in Sunny? Tune in tomorrow.) These cases are also extraordinary in that they involve the full criminal process, including that rarest of events, the jury trial. We get to see all the controversial issues contested in public view: the sanity of the defendant, the admissibility of the evidence, the probity of the witnesses, and the competence of prosecutor, defense attorney, and judge. Public fascination is aroused in part because these issues are so seldom viewed publicly. Most cases are disposed of quietly in a negotiated settlement. Finally, the celebrated cases almost inevitably result in extended appeals, offering us a glimpse at yet another part of the criminal process.

There are really two types of celebrated cases. One includes the rich and famous (or, in the case of John Hinckley, someone whose intended victim is famous). The other usually involves people who are at the other end of the social and economic spectrum but whose cases involve a "landmark" Supreme Court decision. Dolree Mapp, Ernesto Miranda, and Danny Escobedo are famous not for what they did but because of the mistake some official made in handling their case and the way the Supreme Court ruled on that mistake.

Celebrated cases exist at the local level as well. Each community has its highly publicized crimes each year. Usually they involve a particularly grisly murder or a crime committed by someone just released from prison, on parole, or out on bail. According to the journalist Linda Ellerbee, Houston television stations covered murders in the black community only when there were three or more victims.[6]

Because of the publicity they receive, celebrated cases have an enormous effect on public perceptions of criminal justice. People assume that the system ordinarily functions as it does in those instances—that Ernesto Mirandas are "beating the system" every day because of "technicalities" or

"Today, Marvin Weinbar was honored with his own star on Hollywood's walk of fame, by virtue of being the most celebrated defendant in criminal history . . ."

the insanity defense. These celebrated cases, however, are extremely atypical and do not reflect the way the system routinely operates. Our concern in this inquiry is with the vast number of routine robberies and burglaries. To understand how those cases are handled, we need to turn our attention to the second and third layers of the wedding cake.

Felonies: The Second and Third Layers

In their original model, Friedman and Percival put all felony cases in one layer. The Gottfredsons refined this scheme by identifying two separate categories of felonies, which we may place in the second and third layers of the wedding cake.

The Gottfredsons' principal insight is that three basic factors affect the response of criminal justice officials: (1) the seriousness of the crime, (2) the prior record of the suspect, and (3) the relationship between the victim and the offender. When we say "the system," we really mean the accumulated decisions of individual officials—police officers, prosecutors, judges. Essentially they all ask, "How much is this case worth?" Generally, "serious" cases end up in the second layer while "not-so-serious" cases fall into the third layer.

The operating rule of thumb is a common-sense judgment about the facts of the case. Serious crimes include most but not necessarily all violent crimes: murder, robbery, rape, and assault. The relationship between the victim and the offender is a major countervailing factor. We think of robbery as a particularly violent crime, but about one-third of all robberies involve people who know each other. These crimes are often a means of settling a private dispute—a disagreement about some borrowed money or tools, for example—in which the "offender" is simply trying to recover property he believes is rightfully his. Donald Black calls such crimes a form of "self-help." People are taking care of their problems in the most direct—albeit illegal—way.[7] Criminal justice officials look at these facts and devalue the case, deciding that it is really a private matter and just not "worth" very much. Informally, they assign it to the third layer. If the offender has a prior record of arrest and/or conviction and/or imprisonment, however, the case retains its seriousness. Let us say that a robbery involves two people who know each other and originates in a dispute over some borrowed property. Normally this case would fall into the third layer; but if the offender has a substantial criminal record, officials tend to view him or her as a genuine threat to public safety and treat the crime as a second-layer case.

The same phenomenon can be seen in the case of burglary. As a property crime, burglary is generally regarded by officials as less serious than robbery (especially if the dollar value of the stolen property is small). About a third of all burglaries involve people who know each other. This factor further diminishes the seriousness of the offense in the eyes of officials. But if the offender has a long criminal record or if the burglar stole a great deal of valuable property, they treat it as a serious crime and process it as a second-layer case.[8]

The importance of prior relationships is most dramatically evident in the case of rape. About half of the sexual assaults on adult women in the United States are committed by men who know the victim. The Vera Institute found the figure to exceed 80 percent. Sixty percent of the prior-relationship rape cases it studied were dismissed and another 20 percent ended with a guilty plea and virtually no punishment. Yet all of the stranger rapes went to trial. Three-quarters of those cases resulted in conviction and imprisonment and two-thirds of the convictions resulted in prison terms exceeding twenty-five years.[9]

Susan Estrich has called into question the traditional practice of using prior relationship as a criterion. In her book *Real Rape* she argues that all sexual assaults should be prosecuted vigorously. Rapes between people who know each other should not be devalued; the woman was sexually assaulted, no matter what their prior relationship was. Estrich describes her conversation with a local prosecutor who explained that he used this criterion in all criminal cases. She argues that this is not a valid criterion, at least for rape.[10] But what if she is right? Then we should disregard prior relationship in all criminal cases. Right or wrong, the effect on the criminal justice system would be enormous. Many more cases would be prosecuted, and many of the charges would be major felonies.

The everyday language of police and courthouse officials expresses their judgment about the relative importance of crimes. They routinely refer to "heavy" cases and "real" crimes as opposed to the "garbage" or "bullshit" cases. These distinctions are a basic part of the routine administration of justice. They permit officials to classify cases quickly and dispose of them swiftly and impersonally.[11]

The practical result is that "serious," or second-layer, cases are treated seriously. The suspects are generally charged, prosecuted, convicted, and given relatively severe sentences. As our inquiry proceeds, we shall see considerable evidence in support of this point. The less serious, third-layer cases are another matter altogether. These defendants are routinely treated with leniency. When we recognize the distinction between the second and third layers, we can resolve Zimring's paradox that the system is simultaneously both harsh and lenient. The Vera Institute's study of felony arrests in New York City documents the tremendous impact of the relationship between the offender and the victim.

Figure 2.2 indicates that 88 percent of the stranger robberies resulted in conviction. Moreover, prosecutors were not lenient in plea bargaining; 77 percent of those convictions (68 percent of the original arrests) were on felony charges. Nearly three-quarters (74 percent) of those convicted were incarcerated, and half of them did a year or more. This is hardly a picture of a system soft on crime. The prior-relationship robberies are a completely different story. Only a third (37 percent) of the suspects were convicted and only 13 percent of them (5 percent of the number originally arrested) were convicted on felony charges. Slightly more than half (56 percent) of those convicted were incarcerated, but none did a year or more.

The same pattern prevails in burglary cases, although the punishment is generally less severe than for robberies. Most of the stranger burglaries (89 percent) resulted in conviction. Very few of those burglars (8 percent) were convicted on felony charges. Prosecutors, in other words, generally bargained these cases down to misdemeanors. Slightly more than half of those convicted were incarcerated, but none did more than one year. Meanwhile, convictions were obtained in only 53 percent of the prior-relationship burglaries, and only 11 percent of these convictions resulted in incarceration.

Is the system hard or soft on crime? With respect to robbery and burglary, it depends on the facts of the case. The system is clearly hard on stranger robberies and clearly soft on prior-relationship burglaries. The situation in regard to the other two categories is more ambiguous. The system is somewhat hard on stranger burglaries and perhaps less so on prior-relationship robberies. As Zimring argues, the debate between the so-called hard-liners and soft-liners is tiresome and sterile. Our criminal justice system is simultaneously very harsh and very soft.[12]

We might be skeptical of the Vera Institute's data for several reasons. We could ask whether New York City's criminal courts are a special case, unrepresentative of court systems elsewhere. In many respects they are, but this does not necessarily invalidate these findings. If anything, the New York courts have a reputation for being overly lenient because they are swamped with cases. The fact that they appear to be quite hard on serious crime

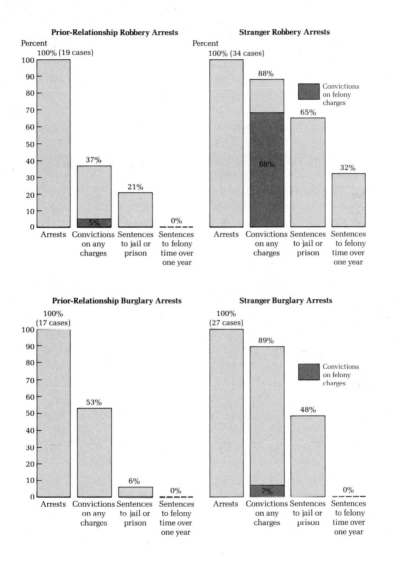

Figure 2.2   Outcomes of stranger and nonstranger robberies and burglaries, New York City (Vera Institute, *Felony Arrests*, rev. ed. [New York: Longman, 1981], pp. 68, 86. Reprinted by permission.)

suggests that courts in other cities are even more punitive. The Vera Institute's data are now fifteen years old. Have processing patterns changed? Generally speaking, yes, but in most areas they have changed in the direction of increased severity. In response to public pressure to do something about crime, judges sent more people to prison in the 1970s than they had before, and for longer terms.[13] The 1973 data, then, probably understate the current harshness of the system.

Additional support for the multitiered model of criminal justice can be found in the career-criminal prosecution programs. The idea behind those programs, which we shall examine in detail later, is to concentrate prosecutorial resources on a special class of hard-core or career criminals. The object is to guarantee that they are convicted and sentenced to prison. The San Diego Major Violator Unit did succeed in convicting 91.5 percent of the career criminals it handled. But 89.5 percent of the career criminals were being convicted before the program began. Under the program, 100 percent of the convicted career criminals were incarcerated, but the rate was 95.3 percent beforehand. Similar results were found in other cities that sought to get tough with career criminals. In other words, crimes and criminals deemed "serious" by common-sense criteria are generally handled in a serious fashion. Or, as Diana Gordon, former director of the National Council on Crime and Delinquency, puts it, "Being tough doesn't work because being lenient is not the source of the problem."[14] We shall explore this proposition in detail later as we examine the various "get tough" proposals.

The idea that our criminal justice system is already fairly tough on serious crime comes as a surprise to many people. Part of the reason is that crime statistics are normally aggregated into either one or a few gross categories, so that the very great differences in the treatment of cases of different kinds are obscured. The genuinely "soft" approach to most criminal cases reflects their degree of seriousness. Offenders who receive rather harsh handling are relatively few: those who commit violent crimes against strangers. Violent crimes represent only 10 percent of all felonies reported to the police. Larceny, the least serious of felonies, accounts for 54 percent of the total.

The common-sense distinction between serious and less serious cases is facilitated by the informal operations of the criminal justice system. In the jargon of criminal justice, proceedings are *administrative* rather than *adversarial*. Cases are rarely contested in a formal sense but are usually settled informally. Few administrative procedures are so well known as plea bargaining, but all stages of the criminal process operate in a similar manner. A police officer walks into a domestic disturbance; a physical assault has occurred. Even though there is probable cause to arrest the offender, the officer concludes that the complainant will not press charges in the morning and decides not to make an arrest. The decision is neither contested nor reviewed. A judge gives a convicted offender probation on the basis of a gut feeling that he is not a danger to the community.

Informal notions about what a case is "worth" are not entirely an individual matter. Officials are constrained by the expectations of the other officials with whom they work. Each criminal court system is maintained by a work group of officials who handle cases week in, week out. The work group establishes the "going rate"—an informal consensus on the worth of various cases. We shall examine the work-group and going-rate phenomena in Chapter 3. Before we get to them, however, we need to complete the picture of the wedding cake.

The research reviewed by the Gottfredsons demonstrates that outcomes in the second layer are highly consistent. Police discretion to arrest or not to arrest is more predictable than people believe. The more serious the crime, the more likely an arrest. If it is a serious crime between strangers, the probability of arrest is very high. Plea-bargaining outcomes are also very consistent, reflecting judgments about the seriousness of the case and the strength of the evidence. Crime victims share the same assumptions and report serious crimes far more frequently than less serious ones. They report 55 percent of all robberies (and 62 percent of robberies that result in injuries) but only 23 percent of larcenies that have involved no personal contact with the offender.[15]

Outcomes in the third layer are much less predictable. Officials generally agree that these cases are not worth much and the primary goal is to dispose of them as quickly as possible. Returning to the Vera Institute data in figure 2.3, for example, we find that only 37 percent of the prior-relationship robberies resulted in conviction. The other 63 percent of robbers got off without any criminal record. Most of those cases were probably dismissed because the victim would not press charges (or because the prosecutor thought the victim to be an unreliable witness in his or her own behalf). The difference between a conviction, even for a misdemeanor, and no conviction is substantial. A third of these people have a criminal record and two-thirds do not. Outcomes in stranger robberies are much more consistent. The same is true for burglary cases. Only half of the prior-relationship burglaries resulted in conviction. (One suspects that the conviction rate is higher here than for prior-relationship robberies for the simple reason that the prosecutor could rely on mute evidence, the stolen property, instead of just the testimony of the victim, as is usually the case with robbery.)

The Lower Depths: The Fourth Layer

The fourth layer of the wedding cake is a world unto itself. The lower courts handle all of the misdemeanors in most jurisdictions. The volume of cases is staggering; such cases far outnumber all felonies, and violent felonies are still fewer. The eight Index crimes account for only 20 percent of all arrests each year (2.4 million out of 11.9 million in 1985; only 497,000 involved violent Index crimes). About half of the misdemeanors are "public order" offenses: disorderly conduct, breach of the peace, drunkenness, and so on.

Only about a third involve crimes against persons or property, and most of those involve minor theft.

Using the same standards they apply to cases at the other levels, officials readily conclude that most of these cases are not worth much at all. Although some distinctions are made between more serious offenses and the general run of cases, few offenders at this level are regarded as real threats to public safety.

Most lower courts operate according to their own standards of due process. Because of the huge volume of cases and their relative lack of seriousness, no one gets terribly excited about the niceties of constitutional standards. In an excellent study of the lower courts of New Haven, Connecticut, Malcolm Feeley concludes that these institutions remain virtually untouched by the due-process revolution of the last twenty-five

---

System? Which System?
Broadening Our Perspective on Social Control

Criminal justice agencies are only one part of a broader system of social control. The criminal law is one of many influences over our behavior, along with family, religious training, peer groups, and so on. Our efforts to understand the criminal justice system require us to broaden our horizons and examine its relationship with other institutions.

Changes in the criminal justice system may be offset by changes in another social control system—in mental health policy, for example. An important illustration of this complex interrelationship is found in recent research on the changing populations of juvenile institutions.

In the 1960s this country embarked on a major shift toward "deinstitutionalization." Policy makers in the fields of criminal justice and mental health argued that many clients could be treated more effectively in the community than in large institutions. The populations of state institutions for the mentally ill and the mentally retarded dropped substantially. The populations of both adult and juvenile criminal justice institutions declined during the 1960s. While adult prison populations have dramatically increased since then, the effect on juvenile institutions has been lasting. This change was encouraged by the 1974 Juvenile Justice and Delinquency Prevention Act, which required states to remove "status" offenders from secure juvenile facilities (reform schools, training schools, etc.). Ira Schwartz and his colleagues found that the rate of admission to juvenile detention facilities declined by 12.3 percent between 1974 and 1979 (most of the decline represented a drop in female admissions). Yet they discovered that at the same time admission to private facilities— especially psychiatric hospitals for drug- and alcohol-related problems—

years. To enter the lower courts is to step back in time eighty years. They function as our higher criminal courts did at the turn of the century.[16]

None of the defendants in the 1,640 cases examined by Feeley insisted on a jury trial. Half of them never had an attorney; for the rest, the contribution of the lawyer was decidedly minimal. Even more shocking to our sensibilities, defendants were arraigned en masse. In assembly-line fashion, the lower courts meted out extremely light sanctions. Half of the defendants received a fine of $50 or less; only 4.9 percent were sentenced to jail.

Feeley concludes that the "process is the punishment": simply being brought into the lower courts is punishment enough. Insistence on your "rights" only costs you more. A private attorney, for example, would charge $200 to handle your case. The fee would be four times the fine if you simply

---

nearly doubled in the late 1970s and early 1980s.

Schwartz refers to this network of private facilities as a " 'hidden' system of juvenile control." This research raises several important questions regarding criminal justice. Have we simply replaced one form of control (state reform schools) with another (private hospital care)? Many of these hospital facilities are, for all practical purposes, run like prisons—the "patient" is not free to walk out the door. Schwartz raises the question of the obvious impact on the cost of medical care, since these juvenile treatment programs are generally covered by private health insurance. If there is a replacement effect, are these the same kids? Are the juveniles who were formerly sent to reform school now sent to a hospital psychiatric ward? Or is this a different group of kids? Are the lower-class kids who used to go to reform school out on the streets while middle-class kids are being sent to the hospital programs? Since most of the hospital programs are paid for through private insurance programs, it seems logical that the patients are more likely to be middle-class kids.

Many questions remain unanswered, but Schwartz and his colleagues have identified an important aspect of American criminal justice. The "system" involves more than criminal justice agencies. We need to think in terms of a social control system that includes private and public agencies that have no formal connection with criminal justice. There is an obvious warning here for would-be reformers: A dramatic change in criminal justice policy may be offset by compensating changes in unrelated agencies.

SOURCES: Barry Krisberg and Ira Schwartz, "Rethinking Juvenile Justice," *Crime and Delinquency* 29 (July 1983): 333–364; Ira Schwartz, Marilyn Jackson-Beeck, and Roger Anderson, "The 'Hidden' System of Juvenile Control," *Crime and Delinquency* 30 (July 1984): 371–385.

copped a plea at the earliest possible moment. Moreover, since most lower-court defendants are wage earners rather than salaried professionals (who can take time off), lost wages exceed potential fines. In Feeley's study, cases averaged about three court appearances. If we assume that each appearance cost half a day's work, the lost wages would more than exceed the possible fine. Insistence on one's "rights" only increases the number of court appearances and the cost in lost wages.

The closer we look, however, the more complicated the picture becomes. A recent study of the Philadelphia lower courts challenges Feeley's view and illustrates the hazards of generalizing about American criminal justice. Stephen J. Schulhofer found that in Philadelphia's two lower courts—Municipal Court and the Court of Common Pleas—about half (48%) of the cases went to trial, virtually all defendants had legal counsel, and the punishments meted out to the guilty were relatively significant (that is, worth contesting). Nearly a quarter (22%) of the convicted offenders received a jail sentence and 17.4% received fines (which ranged as high as several hundred dollars). Schulhofer's most important point is that Feeley overstated the "process" costs of contesting a case in the lower courts. The price of the likely penalty makes the case worth fighting. The main reason appears to be that penalties are significantly stiffer in Philadelphia than in New Haven.[17]

The different conclusions reached by Feeley and Schulhofer highlight an extremely important point about the American criminal justice system: there is no one system. In addition to the various layers of the wedding cake, we find extreme variation from jurisdiction to jurisdiction. Clearly, the New Haven and Philadelphia lower courts operate in very different ways. The difference can be explained in part by each city's local political culture and by the traditions observed by each criminal court work group. The beginning of wisdom in any discussion of criminal justice is sensitivity to the special quality of the particular jurisdiction you happen to be discussing.

Notes

1. For the best analysis of the issue of race, see Joan Petersilia, *Racial Disparities in the Criminal Justice System* (Santa Monica, Calif.: Rand Corporation, 1983). But see also William Wilbanks, *The Myth of a Racist Criminal Justice System* (Pacific Grove: Brooks/Cole, 1987).
2. Franklin Zimring, Sheila O'Malley, and Joel Eigen, "Punishing Homicide in Philadelphia: Perspectives on the Death Penalty," *University of Chicago Law Review* 43 (Winter 1976): 252.
3. Donald J. Newman, "Sociologists and the Administration of Justice," in *Sociology in Action*, ed. Arthur B. Shostak (Homewood, Ill.: Dorsey Press, 1966), pp. 177–187.
4. President's Commission on Law Enforcement and Administration of Justice, *Task Force Report: Science and Technology* (Washington, D. C.: U. S. Govern-

ment Printing Office, 1967), pp. 58–59. See also Daniel L. Skoler, *Organizing the Non-System* (Lexington, Mass.: Lexington Books, 1977).

5. Lawrence M. Friedman and Robert V. Percival, *The Roots of Justice: Crime and Punishment in Alameda County, California, 1870–1910* (Chapel Hill: University of North Carolina Press, 1981); Michael R. Gottfredson and Don M. Gottfredson, *Decision-Making in Criminal Justice: Toward the Rational Exercise of Discretion* (Cambridge, Mass.: Ballinger, 1980).

6. Linda Ellerbee, *"And So It Goes:" Adventures in Television* (New York: Berkley, 1987), p. 22.

7. Vera Institute of Justice, *Felony Arrests*, rev. ed. (New York: Longman, 1981), p. xiii; Donald Black, "Crime as Social Control," in *Toward a General Theory of Social Control*, ed. D. Black (Orlando: Academic Press, 1984), 2:1–28.

8. Vera Institute, *Felony Arrests*, pp. 81–95.

9. Ibid., pp. 42–43.

10. Susan Estrich, *Real Rape* (Cambridge: Harvard University Press, 1987), p. 20.

11. David Sudnow, "Normal Crimes: Sociological Features of the Penal Code in a Public Defender Office," *Social Problems* 12 (Winter 1965): 255–276.

12. Zimring et al., "Punishing Homicide," p. 252.

13. Jonathan D. Casper, David Brereton, and David Neal, *The Implementation of the California Determinate Sentencing Law: Executive Summary* (Washington, D. C.: U. S. Government Printing Office, 1982).

14. Diana R. Gordon, *Towards Realistic Reform: A Commentary on Proposals for Change in New York City's Criminal Justice System* (Hackensack, N. J.: National Council on Crime and Delinquency, 1981), p. 16.

15. On police discretion, see Donald Black, *Manners and Customs of the Police* (New York: Academic Press, 1980). On plea bargaining, see Lynn Mather, "Some Determinants of the Method of Case Disposition: Decision-Making by Public Defenders in Los Angeles," *Law and Society Review* 8 (Winter 1974): 187–216. On citizen reporting, see U. S. Bureau of Justice Statistics, *Criminal Victimization in the United States, 1985* (Washington, D. C.: U. S. Government Printing Office, 1986).

16. Malcolm M. Feeley, *The Process Is the Punishment* (New York: Russell Sage Foundation, 1979).

17. Stephen J. Schulhofer, "No Job Too Small: Justice without Bargaining in the Lower Criminal Courts," *American Bar Foundation Research Journal* 1985, no. 3 (Summer 1985): 519–598.

Chapter 3

The Going Rate

We can now turn our attention to the basic questions about the administration of criminal justice: How effective is the system in controlling crime? How successful is it in catching, prosecuting, convicting, and punishing dangerous criminals? What is the "going rate" for crime? Is the system fair? Is there a pattern of racial discrimination?

Evaluating the performance of our criminal justice system is a difficult task. The leading experts disagree on some of the most elementary facts. Part of the problem is the lack of decent statistics. Although we have made tremendous improvements in recent years, many important questions still remain unanswered for want of reliable data. Even when such figures exist, there is substantial and legitimate disagreement as to what they mean. An additional problem arises from the variations among our fifty-one criminal justice systems. Los Angeles and Salt Lake City, for example, handle cases very differently.[1] With these caveats in mind, let us consider some general features of American criminal justice.

Many people believe that our criminal justice system fails to catch, prosecute, convict, and sufficiently punish dangerous criminals. Conservatives take this failure as their ideological starting point: crime flourishes because the risks are so low. James Q. Wilson and Richard Herrnstein's theory that crime is a matter of choice rests heavily on their belief that the risk of punishment is very low in comparison with the immediate rewards of crime. Not everyone agrees, however. Charles Silberman and Diana Gordon argue that we are surprisingly effective in punishing the criminals we catch—an important qualification—and extremely harsh in the punishments we dole out.

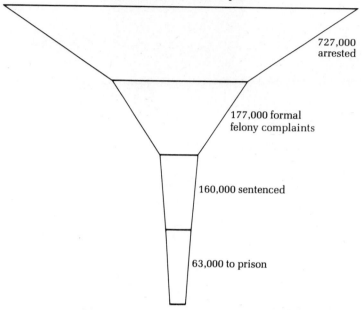

2,780,000 Index Crimes Reported

727,000 arrested

177,000 formal felony complaints

160,000 sentenced

63,000 to prison

Figure 3.1 The funneling effect of the criminal justice system (The President's Commission on Law Enforcement and Administration of Justice, *Task Force Report: Science and Technology* [Washington, D. C.: U. S. Government Printing Office, 1967], p. 61).

The Funnel

To sort our way through this debate, let us begin with the data compiled by the President's Crime Commission. Figure 3.1 represents a 1967 analysis of the annual flow of cases through the system. The bottom-line figure of 63,000 people sent to prison represents only 1 percent of the estimated 5.5 million Index crimes committed each year (because half of all Index crimes are not reported to the police, the actual number is twice the official figure). This ratio leads many people to conclude, with great outrage, that only 1 percent of all criminals go to prison.

Because it fails to differentiate among Index crimes, the funnel represented in figure 3.1 is highly misleading. We need to take into account several complex factors. First, only about half of all crimes are even reported, so the situation is in some respects even worse than the funnel suggests (that is, if we look at it from the offender's perspective on the risk of punishment). Yet officials can hardly be held responsible for failing to impose sanctions on crimes that are never brought to their attention in the first place.

Charles Silberman argues persuasively that the Crime Commission's analysis is "grossly misleading."[2] His reanalysis of the same data yields a

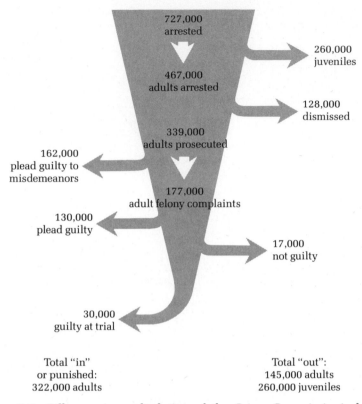

Figure 3.2   Silberman's recalculation of the Crime Commission's funnel (Charles Silberman, *Criminal Violence, Criminal Justice* [New York: Random House, 1978], pp. 257–261).

picture of a rather effective and quite punitive system (figure 3.2). He begins by pointing out the obvious: the most serious problem is our inability to catch criminals. The official FBI clearance rate for all Index crimes is about 26 percent. The "true" rate, when unreported crimes are taken into account, is half that figure. We shall examine in detail various crime control proposals designed to improve clearance rates.

Silberman then attacks the Crime Commission's argument that 75 percent of cases are "lost" between arrest and the felony complaint stage. About 260,000 (35.7 percent) of the original 727,000 arrests involve juveniles whose cases are transferred to juvenile court. (This is a separate issue, which is discussed on pp. 39–40). For the moment, let's concentrate on the adults. When the juveniles are subtracted, we have 467,000 adult arrestees. Silberman argues that this is the proper baseline from which the performance of the adult criminal courts should be assessed. About 27 percent of these cases (128,000) are dismissed for one reason or another, leaving 339,000 prosecuted adults. A prosecution rate of 73 percent is not exactly a sign of softness on crime. Nearly half (48 percent) of these adults plead guilty to a misdemeanor. We can legitimately debate whether this is a proper disposition and whether these people are getting off too easily. Nonetheless, these cases are not "lost," and the defendants are in fact punished and end up with a criminal record, albeit for a misdemeanor rather than for a felony.

We are now left with 177,000 adult felony complaints. An impressive 90 percent of these arrestees are convicted: 130,000 by a guilty plea and 30,000 by trial. When we combine the felony and misdemeanor convictions, we have a total of 322,000 adults convicted and punished, which represents 69 percent of the adults arrested and 95 percent of those prosecuted. This is a very different picture from the one drawn by the President's Crime Commission.

Some comments on Silberman's analysis are in order. He overstates his case a little. The fact that 87 percent of all crimes do not result in arrest cannot be ignored. The risk of apprehension is indeed very low, and in this respect the system is terribly weak. There are two ways of calculating the risk of arrest, however. The risk is particularly low if it is calculated in terms of a single crime by a single person. The more crimes you commit, the greater your chances of being arrested. In fact, it appears that career criminals are almost certain to be caught sooner or later.

This observation takes us back to the wedding cake. Silberman's analysis

---

A Few Words about Those Juveniles

We need to say something about all those juveniles who are arrested each year. There is substantial controversy over the relative severity or leniency of the juvenile courts. Many critics charge that they are excessively lenient, letting repeat offenders off with only a slap on the wrist. You will have no trouble finding a "celebrated case" involving an offender who has committed a very serious crime and who has a long record of juvenile crime. This point is extremely important because recent research has substantiated the conventional wisdom that adult career criminals usually had juvenile records or gave other early indications of later criminality (e.g., noncriminal antisocial behavior or school problems). Recent reexamination of the performance of the juvenile courts challenges the charge of leniency. Peter Greenwood found that juveniles who had committed serious crimes in California and who also had prior criminal records were incarcerated about as often as were comparable young adults. Moreover, the California juvenile justice system has become more punitive in recent years. Detention of juveniles in secure facilities increased 23 percent between 1978 and 1981. The juvenile justice system appears to be lenient because most of the kids arrested have not committed serious crimes.

(continued)

A Few Words about Those Juveniles
(continued)

Over 60 percent of the juveniles arrested never went to juvenile court. Most received informal counseling or were referred to some other agency. The system did respond effectively to serious crime. Greenwood found that "juvenile arrests for more serious crimes such as burglary or robbery were filed and settled in court about as often as were adult arrests."

Ira Schwartz and his colleagues found similar evidence of increasing severity when they examined national data. They were initially struck by the apparent contradiction between declining admissions to secure juvenile institutions and increasing populations in such institutions. Between 1977 and 1982 new admissions declined by 15 percent while one-day population counts increased by 19 percent. The explanation lies in the fact that the average length of stay increased from twelve to seventeen days—a 42 percent increase. In other words, fewer juveniles were being locked up, but for longer terms. For all practical purposes this is a de facto selective incapacitation policy. Contrary to popular impression, the juvenile justice system is far from lenient. In a review of the literature, Patricia M. Harris concludes that the charge of juvenile justice leniency is "not clearly substantiated."

SOURCES: Joan Petersilia, Peter W. Greenwood, and Marvin Lavin, *Criminal Careers of Habitual Felons* (Washington, D. C.: U. S. Government Printing Office, 1978); Peter W. Greenwood, "Differences in Criminal Behavior and Court Responses among Juvenile and Young Adult Defendants," in *Crime and Justice: An Annual Review of Research,* ed. Michael H. Tonry and Norval Morris, vol. 7 (Chicago: University of Chicago Press, 1986), pp. 151–187; Ira M. Schwartz et al., "Juvenile Detention: The Hidden Closets Revisited," *Justice Quarterly* 4 (June 1987): 219–235; Patricia M. Harris, "Is the Juvenile Justice System Lenient?" *Crime and Delinquency Abstracts,* 18 (March 1986), 104.

lumps all adult felonies in a single category. When the more serious felonies are isolated, it becomes clear that we are extremely punitive toward the serious offender—even more so than Silberman suggests. Data from the Institute for Law and Social Research (*INSLAW*) on robbery and burglary cases (See figure 3.3) indicate that the criminal justice system in Washington, D. C., performs reasonably well once it has an adult in custody. About 90 percent of the adult robbers are prosecuted, although only slightly less than half are convicted. All of the adult burglary suspects were prosecuted and between 30 and 40 percent of them were convicted. If *INSLAW* had distinguished between stranger and nonstranger offenses, the conviction rates for stranger crimes would undoubtedly be much higher.[3]

The *INSLAW* data also help to explain what happened to the cases that were prosecuted but did not result in conviction. Very few of those defendants won formal acquittal; most had their cases dismissed. Why?

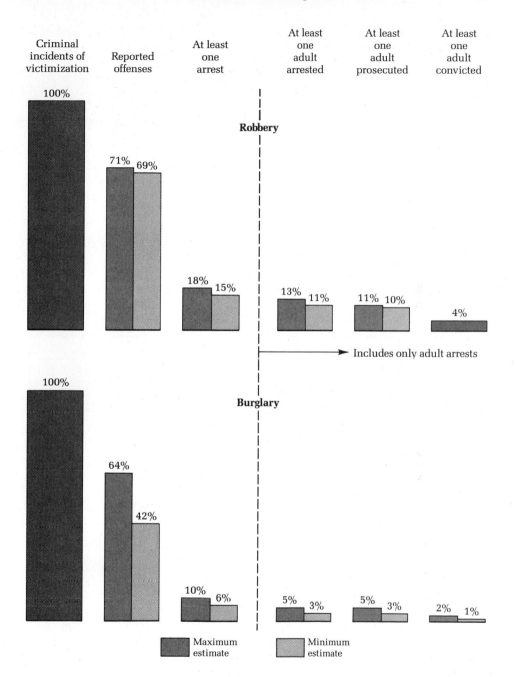

Figure 3.3 Outcomes of robbery and burglary cases in Washington, D. C., 1973 (Kristen M. Williams and Judith Lucianovic, *Robbery and Burglary* [Washington, D. C.: INSLAW, 1979], p. 8).

Table 3.1   Reasons given by prosecutor for rejecting arrests at initial screening, 1974, by major offense group

	Crime group					
Rejection reason	Robbery	Other violent	Nonviolent property	Victimless	Other	All crimes
Witness problem	43%	51%	25%	2%	5%	25%
Insufficiency of evidence	35%	18%	37%	40%	41%	34%
Due-process problem	0%	0%	2%	20%	3%	5%
No reason given	0%	0%	1%	0%	1%	1%
Other	22%	30%	36%	38%	50%	36%
Total rejections	100%	100%	100%	100%	100%	100%
Number of rejections	242	876	1,257	654	621	3,650
Number of arrests	1,955	3,176	6,562	3,659	2,182	17,534
Rejection rate	12%	28%	19%	18%	29%	21%

SOURCE: Brian Forst, Judith Lucianovic, and Sarah J. Cox, *What Happens after Arrest?* (Washington, D. C.: *INSLAW,* 1977), p. 67.

Table 3.2   Reasons given by prosecutor for dismissing cases initially accepted, 1974, by major offense group

	Crime group					
Dismissal reason	Robbery	Other violent	Nonviolent property	Victimless	Other	All crimes
Witness problem	20%	33%	12%	2%	5%	13%
Insufficiency of evidence	2%	1%	1%	1%	2%	1%
Due-process problem	0%	0%	1%	3%	4%	1%
Completion of diversion program	1%	5%	30%	56%	13%	28%
Private remedy	0%	1%	2%	0%	1%	1%
No reason given	39%	34%	32%	26%	38%	32%
Other	38%	27%	22%	13%	37%	24%
Total dismissals	100%	100%	100%	100%	100%	100%
Number of dismissals	568	858	1,940	1,329	421	5,116
Number of arrests	1,955	3,176	6,562	3,659	2,182	17,534
Dismissal rate	29%	27%	30%	36%	19%	29%

SOURCE: Brian Forst, Judith Lucianovic, and Sarah J. Cox, *What Happens after Arrest?* (Washington, D. C.: *INSLAW,* 1977), p. 69.

Tables 3.1 and 3.2 present the *INSLAW* data on reasons for dismissal at two points. At the initial screening stage (table 3.1), before formal charges are filed, problems with the witness and insufficiency of the evidence are the major causes for dismissal. These factors continue to be important for cases dismissed after charges are filed (table 3.2), though more so for robbery than for burglary (combined here with other property offenses).[4]

Several comments should be made about the data in the two tables. First, due-process problems are relatively insignificant. We shall explore this issue in greater detail when we discuss proposals to abolish the exclusionary rule and the *Miranda* warning. We should note in passing that the category "insufficiency of evidence" refers to whether or not the evidence itself could convict the defendant, whereas "due-process problems" refers to the manner in which that evidence was gathered. Second, most of the witness problems undoubtedly involve victims who are acquainted with the offenders. The suspect probably committed the crime but the victim does not really wish to pursue the case. Third, the number of dismissals in the categories of "no reason given" and "other" is disturbing. We would like to know more about the exact circumstances of those dismissals.

To summarize our discussion of the "going rate" so far, we can draw three general conclusions. First, most crimes do not result in arrest. Second, most arrests result in dismissal rather than prosecution. But most of the dismissals involve less serious crimes, crimes whose victims know the offenders, or crimes in which the evidence is weak. These facts lead us to our third point: when a serious crime is committed by a stranger and the evidence is reasonably solid, the system appears to do an effective job of convicting and punishing. For the crimes that count the most, the system is fairly strong.

A Trickle-Up Effect?

Finally, we have to take note of the trickle-up effect. Reforms designed to "get tough" are irrelevant because we are already tough with people deemed to be serious offenders. These reforms have the unanticipated side effect of raising the level of punishment imposed on *less* serious offenders, including people convicted of such property offenses as burglary and persons with no prior record. Reforms that consist of provisions for mandatory actions (mandatory imprisonment, for example, or prohibition of plea bargaining) close off the avenues by which less serious cases are settled with a relatively light penalty. In effect, such provisions force officials to treat these cases as second-layer rather than third-layer cases. The net result is one not intended by the reform measure. While serious crimes carry the same relatively severe penalties, punishments are escalated for the less serious crimes. We call such escalation the trickle-up effect. It has been found in connection with both Michigan's gun-crime law and Alaska's ban on plea bargaining. Conservative crime control policies are not the only ones that have unanticipated and undesirable consequences. Many liberal rehabilitation programs have the effect of "expanding the net," of bringing more people under some form of social control. We shall examine the expanding-net phenomenon in detail in chapter 11.[5]

The Courtroom Work Group

The going-rate phenomenon has another dimension in regard to the severity of punishment. We measure such severity in two ways: the likelihood of incarceration and the length of the prison sentence. In each jurisdiction there is a general consensus on the going rate for each offense. This is simply an expression of how much a case is worth. In Detroit, for example, crimes involving a gun are worth about five or six years in prison. In California, imprisoned robbers do an average of fifty months of actual time in prison. To understand why the going rate varies from place to place, we need to recognize how local criminal justice systems conduct their business. The determining factor is the courtroom work group.[6]

The administration of criminal justice is a human process, involving a series of discretionary decisions by people who work together day in and day out. We call them the courtroom work group. It is a sociological truism that such officials develop a shared need to get the work done. Consequently, they need to get along and develop informal understandings about how cases should be handled. Their everyday working language reflects these shared understandings. Prosecutors and defense attorneys agree on the distinction between "heavy" or "serious" cases and the "garbage" or "bullshit" ones. They also make the same evaluations of the strength of the evidence. They recognize the "dead-bang" cases, where the evidence is conclusive, and the "weak" cases. Their terminology is a form of shorthand that allows them to classify and dispose of cases quickly.[7]

These shared understandings generate a high degree of cooperation in the courthouse. Conflict between prosecution and defense is the exception rather than the rule. The absence of conflict has led most criminal justice experts to describe our system as administrative rather than adversarial. That is to say, the idea of a truly adversarial system, one in which the question of guilt or innocence is contested, is a notion expressed in the Old Idealism but not found in any American courthouse. Numerous studies document the prevalence of cooperation rather than conflict. Frederic Suffett found conflict in only 3 percent of all bail-setting decisions and disagreement in only another 9 percent. Lynn Mather found plea bargaining to be a highly routinized operation, with little actual bargaining ever taking place.[8] Many critics of plea bargaining argue that in a climate of cooperation the defendant is the primary loser. In this view, courthouse officials sacrifice the interests of the defendant for the sake of getting along with each other. Rather than aggressively push for the best possible deal, the defense attorney "sells" the deal to the defendant. This view underpins the recent calls for the abolition of plea bargaining.[9]

Frustrating Reform

Two aspects of the courtroom work-group phenomenon merit special attention. The first is the capacity of the work group to adapt to changes imposed by others. In his excellent study of court reform, Malcolm Feeley documents the ability of officials to roll with the punch, so to speak—to evade, absorb, or blunt reforms they don't like.

"Tell you what, Ted. You give me another week on the Hanson trial and me and Sally will take you and Pam to the Purple Penguin."

Feeley's point is most persuasive with respect to recent "speedy trial" legislation. The Congress and several states have enacted laws imposing strict deadlines on the disposition of criminal cases. If the deadlines are not met, the charges against the defendant are dismissed. Those laws were opposed by judges, prosecutors, and defense attorneys alike (although for somewhat different reasons). In the face of this hostility, the laws have had virtually no effect. Officials availed themselves of the various loopholes and exceptions that were written into the laws (for example, the ability to delay a case in the interest of "the ends of justice"). One judge was openly cynical: "Our court has figured out ways to deal with the [speedy trial] act that don't cause us to change our practices at all."[10]

The ability of the work group to frustrate reform has enormous implications for virtually all the proposals we shall consider in this book. The proposals represent attempts to get officials to change their behavior. For instance, preventive detention is intended to allow (or force) judges to deny bail to dangerous offenders. Mandatory sentencing is a scheme to require imprisonment of convicted offenders. As we shall discover, courtroom work groups have an amazing capacity to evade such requirements. We might add that the same problem affects most attempts to enhance fairness in the criminal justice system. The *Miranda* decision, for example, is an attempt to require police to advise suspects of their rights. Yet the police have ample opportunity to evade either the letter or the spirit of this requirement.

Most reforms are designed to change either the rules or the resources of the criminal justice system. We hear the same proposals repeatedly: "We ought to require . . ."; "If we only had more [judges, prosecutors, police], then we could . . ." Yet, as Feeley, Raymond Nimmer, and others have discovered, an externally imposed change is often futile. Meaningful change occurs not when the law is formally altered but when one or more members of the work group perceive the need for change and take steps to bring it about.[11]

Criminal Justice Thermodynamics

A second important aspect of the work-group phenomenon is the group's ability to control both its work load and the amount of punishment it metes out. It is able to exercise such control in the face of changes imposed by others, whether the changes take the form of new laws, court rulings, or other methods. This principle, which has been termed "the law of criminal justice thermodynamics," holds that local criminal justice systems maintain a steady state that adjusts and accommodates itself to any planned or unplanned change.[12]

The steady state is the product of the courtroom work group's informal consensus regarding the going rate, which simplifies their work by eliminating haggling over particular cases. Any significant new element threatens the established understandings. Malcolm Feeley observes that "the pace and manner of handling cases are part of the fragile balance of the courts. To alter them will set up a chain reaction throughout the entire system and precipitate new problems."[13] New laws requiring longer prison terms or mandatory prison terms, or no bargaining of felonies down to misdemeanors alter the "price" of particular cases. We shall find again and again that this kind of action produces an opposite reaction: members of courtroom work groups adjust their actions in such a way as to absorb and blunt the intended effect of the new law. For example, the severe penalties of New York's 1973 drug law were offset by a reduction in the number of drug cases fully processed through the system. A similar effect occurred in one county in Iowa where the local prosecutor stopped plea-bargaining drug cases. The Massachusetts Bartley-Fox law, which called for a mandatory one-year prison term for people who carried firearms without a permit, apparently induced Boston police officers to conduct fewer frisks. The officers did not want to find "otherwise law-abiding" people guilty of this offense. With respect to drunk-driving laws, we will find that public attitudes in regard to the appropriate penalties for "otherwise law-abiding" people are also a major constraint on strict enforcement.[14]

Our law of criminal justice thermodynamics states that:

An increase in the severity of the penalty will result in less frequent application of the penalty.

"Listen, chances of you getting the death
penalty are as likely as my being struck by
lightning right now."

The effect will be that the overall level of sanctions imposed remains about
the same. There is an important corollary:

*The less often a severe penalty is applied, the more arbitrary will be the
occasions when it is applied.*

These principles are best seen in action in the death penalty. Death is, quite
obviously, the severest sanction possible. Its potential application exerts
enormous pressure on the courtroom work group. A variety of devices are
used to evade its application (plea bargaining to a second-degree murder
charge, demand for a jury trial, use of the insanity defense, appeal on every
potential issue, request for pardon or commutation, and so forth). The
availability of these options to the defense places a burden on the
prosecution, which would prefer not to have to face a jury trial, endless
appeals, and so on. Thus the defense can raise the price for the prosecution
to offset the price faced by the defendant. The net result is that few criminal
defendants who are potentially eligible for the death penalty ever have to
face that reality. In the words of the U. S. Supreme Court in the landmark
case of *Furman* v. *Georgia* (1972), the actual application of the death penalty
is so rare as to be "freakish" and akin to being "struck by lightning."

Franklin Zimring and his colleagues describe the steady-state principle
in their study of death-penalty cases in Philadelphia. Officials easily
circumvented the law mandating a minimum term of life for certain types of
murders. They "responded to the mandatory minimum term by effectively
redefining the circumstances that mandate its use. In this sense the high
minimum sanction generates leniency by reducing the number of cases that

will result in convictions for the highest degree of murder." In effect, they made the crime fit the punishment. A similar process occurs in virtually all felony cases. Officials determine how much a case is worth and then fit it into a particular crime category that will yield the punishment they deem appropriate.[15]

Cross-City Comparisons

An important characteristic of the courtroom work-group phenomenon is its variation from city to city. Each work group establishes its own set of informal understandings, which are not necessarily the same as those of other jurisdictions. We have already noted the extreme variations in the lower courts in two cities. These variations make it difficult to generalize about American criminal justice.

Kathleen Brosi's study for *INSLAW* found tremendous differences in bail practices. In Washington, D. C., 99 percent of all felony defendants were released before trial. Yet in Salt Lake City only 59 percent were. In other words, 41 percent of all felony defendants were detained in jail, despite the presumed constitutional right to bail. Detroit resembled Washington in that virtually all (97 percent) of the defendants were accorded pretrial release, but generally by somewhat different means. Half (49 percent) of the Washington defendants avoided detention without having to post money or other financial security, while only 29 percent of the Detroit defendants were released without bail. These differences reflect the impact of the 1966 federal Bail Reform Act and its strong presumption in favor of nonmonetary release in the District of Columbia.[16]

The general pattern of outcomes of felony cases in different cities is seen in figure 3.4. The data indicate, for example, that the use of guilty pleas ranges from a high of 62 percent to a low of 17 percent. These figures can be deceptive, however. Practices in Los Angeles involve a somewhat disguised form of plea bargaining, referred to as a "submission on transcript," or "SOT." The defendant is in effect pleading guilty while going through the motions of a contested trial.[17] Thus, in this respect, Los Angeles is not so different from other cities as the comparison might suggest. Furthermore, figure 3.4 shows that 76 percent of all cases in Los Angeles are dismissed, a rate far higher than that of any other city in the study. Yet the context is important: the police arrest people at a far higher rate in Los Angeles than in most other cities (when arrests are considered as a proportion of population); thus the high rate of dismissals simply brings the overall sanction or punishment level down to a more typical proportion.[18]

Courtroom work groups also vary considerably with respect to sentencing. Indianapolis and New Orleans, for example, send 91 percent of convicted robbers to prison, while Detroit imprisons 73 percent and Los Angeles only 63 percent. Meanwhile, Indianapolis imprisons 81 percent of its convicted burglars, while the rates for New Orleans, Los Angeles, and Detroit are 59 percent, 49 percent, and 42 percent, respectively.[19]

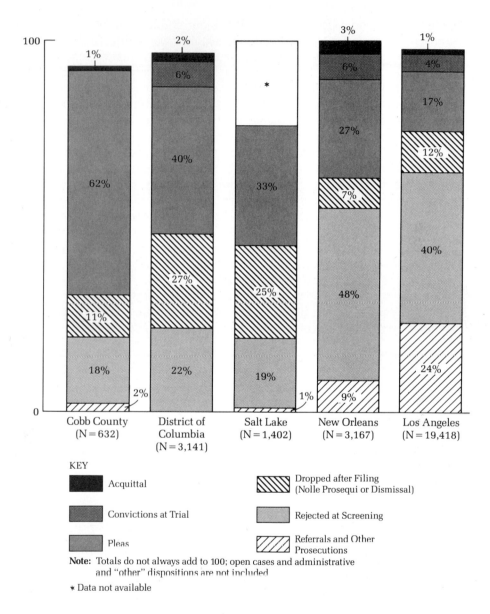

Figure 3.4   Disposition of felony cases from arrest to trial in five major cities, 1977 (Kathleen B. Brosi, *A Cross-City Comparison of Felony Case Processing* [Washington, D. C.: INSLAW, 1979], p. 7).

What Are We Talking about? A Note on Language

Language is often a barrier that frustrates our efforts to make sense of criminal justice. In his study of the Philadelphia lower courts, Stephen J. Schulhofer discusses the difficulty of specifying exactly what we mean by an "adversary" process. In conventional social science research, a case that goes to trial is classified as an adversarial proceeding, while one that is settled by a plea bargain is considered an administrative proceeding. This classification, however, does not necessarily reflect what really happens. Schulhofer found that in some cases that went to trial in Philadelphia's lower courts, the defense never challenged the core of the prosecution's case. How adversarial is such a proceeding? In many respects it is nothing more than a "slow plea." At the same time, some cases are settled by a bargaining process in which the defense attorney is extremely aggressive in challenging the core of the prosecutor's case, or at least in threatening to challenge it if the case goes to trial. Although we refer to such a case as an administrative proceeding, for all practical purposes it is highly adversarial. The defendant in such a case may be better represented than the defendant who goes to trial.

To understand the criminal justice process we have to look beyond the purely formal aspects of the proceeding and penetrate both everyday language and conventional social science classification categories.

SOURCE: Stephen J. Schulhofer, "No Job Too Small: Justice without Bargaining in the Lower Criminal Courts," *American Bar Foundation Research Journal* 1985, no. 3 (Summer 1985): 527–528.

Is the Going Rate Racist? The Debate Continues

Racism has been one of the most inflammatory issues in American criminal justice for at least twenty-five years. Some observers would argue that it is *the* main issue. The debate rages on, with new research adding fuel to the fire. Are there patterns of systematic racial discrimination in American criminal justice? Does the going rate reflect racial bias that results in harsher treatment for black offenders?

The Supreme Court confronted the issue in the 1987 case of *McCleskey* v. *Kemp.* In a highly controversial 5–4 decision, the Court ruled that statistical evidence of racial discrimination in the application of the death penalty was not sufficient cause to overturn Warren McCleskey's sentence or to rule the Georgia death-penalty statute unconstitutional. It should be noted that the Court did not refute the evidence of racial discrimination presented in McCleskey's brief. The justices held that statistical evidence per se was not sufficient to permit them to rule in his favor. The data themselves present a clear pattern of discrimination.

The debate over discrimination in criminal justice is apparent in two recent studies. William Wilbanks offers the provocative argument that systematic racial discrimination is a myth. Joan Petersilia of the Rand Corporation takes a somewhat more moderate view, finding evidence of discrimination in some parts of the criminal justice process but not in others. She found, for example, that while case processing followed a generally steady course, minorities were given longer sentences and thus were more likely to be sent to prison than to jail. Once in prison, moreover, minorities also served longer than whites.

How do we make sense of these conflicting interpretations? A historical overview of the research itself provides valuable perspective. The literature represents an ongoing dialogue in which findings are reexamined and the new findings are in turn challenged by further research. Over the years, as the methodologies have become steadily more sophisticated, research has yielded different findings.

The first generation of studies, conducted in the early 1960s, tended to find extreme patterns of discrimination. Nathan Goldman's 1963 study of police arrests of juveniles, for example, found that black juveniles were referred to juvenile court nearly twice as often as whites. The first studies of the use of deadly force by police found that black deaths by police gunfire outnumbered similar deaths of whites at rates that ranged from 6 to 1 to nearly 30 to 1. The second generation of research, beginning in the mid-1960s, controlled for more variables and tended to find far less extreme disparities between the races. Albert Reiss's study of police behavior, for example, found that "police brutality" was a rare phenomenon and that black officers were as likely as white officers to use unjustifiable physical force against black citizens. William Geller, meanwhile, found that the disparities between whites and minorities shot by the Chicago police disappeared after he controlled for participation in criminal activity (measured in terms of arrest rates for forcible felonies) by white, black, and Hispanic citizens. At the same time, however, extreme disparity remained between unarmed white and black persons who were shot and killed (11 whites and 70 blacks). James Fyfe found a similar pattern in Memphis police shootings.

Many observers were surprised at the findings that emerged from the second generation of research. Anticipating broad patterns of discrimination, they overreacted to the apparent narrowness or absence of disparities. This is part of what has led Wilbanks to announce that systematic racism is a "myth."

(continued)

Is the Going Rate Racist? The Debate Continues
(continued)

A third generation of research has used still more sophisticated methodology. Cassia Spohn and her colleagues, for example, took another look at the question of racial discrimination in sentencing. While they found that racial disparities generally disappeared after they controlled for seriousness of offense and prior record, some disparity remained: black offenders were about 20 percent more likely than whites to be incarcerated. One of the most important new lines of research involves the relationship between the victim and the offender. David Baldus and his colleagues examined death sentences in Georgia and found that a sentence of death was four times more likely when the victim was white than when he or she was black. In short, the criminal justice system was systematically devaluing the lives of black people. William Bowers and Glenn Pierce found an identical pattern in post-1977 cases in Florida, Georgia, Texas, and Ohio. The probability of receiving a sentence of death in Ohio, for example, was 1 in 4 for black persons who murdered whites. It was zero for whites who killed blacks. David Baldus's research received national attention when it formed the basis for the plaintiff's argument in *McCleskey* v. *Warren*. Gary LaFree, meanwhile, found that the racial mix of victim–offender relationships affected the handling of rape cases. Cases involving a black offender and a white victim were treated much more severely.

Are we then to conclude that there is racism in the criminal justice system? Of course there is some. Racial discrimination is deeply entrenched in American society. It would be naive to assume that somehow the criminal justice system was exempt from this problem. The exact nature and extent of discrimination, however, are complex matters. It does not necessarily follow that discrimination exists in *all* parts of the system, or that the disparities in the treatment of the races are extreme. Overall police shootings, for example, may not indicate discrimination, but shootings of unarmed suspects may. The debate over discrimination has forced us to examine the administration of justice with a more critical and sophisticated eye. The challenge is to avoid a simpleminded proclamation of either pervasive discrimination or no discrimination at all, to examine the criminal justice system with sensitivity, and to maintain the highest standards of research.

SOURCES: McCleskey v. Kemp, 481 U. S. _____, 95 L ed. 2d 262, 107 S.Ct._____ (1987); William Wilbanks, *The Myth of a Racist Criminal Justice System* (Pacific Grove: Brooks/Cole, 1987); Joan Petersilia, *Racial Disparities in the Criminal Justice System* (Santa Monica: Rand Corporation, 1983); Nathan Goldman, *The Differential Selection of Juvenile Offenders for Court Appearance* (New York: NCCD, 1963) (the deadly-force data are reviewed in William E. Geller, "Deadly

Force: What We Know," *Journal of Police Science and Administration* 10 [1982]: 152–177); Albert Reiss, *The Police and the Public* (New Haven: Yale University Press, 1971); William A. Geller and Kevin J. Karales, *Split-Second Decisions: Shootings of and by Chicago Police* (Chicago: Law Enforcement Study Group, 1981), pp. 115–140; James J. Fyfe, "Blind Justice: Police Shootings in Memphis," *Journal of Criminal Law and Criminology* 73 (1982): 707–722; Cassia Spohn, John Gruhl, and Susan Welch, "The Effect of Race on Sentencing: A Reexamination of an Unsettled Question," *Law and Society Review* 16 (1981–1982): 71–88; David C. Baldus, Charles Pulaski, and George Woodworth, "Comparative Review of Death Sentences: An Empirical Study of the Georgia Experience," *Journal of Criminal Law and Criminology* 74 (Fall 1983): 661–753; William J. Bowers and Glenn L. Pierce, "Arbitrariness and Discrimination under Post-Furman Capital Statutes," *Crime and Delinquency* 26 (October 1980): 563–635; Gary LaFree, "The Effect of Sexual Stratification by Race on Official Reactions to Rape," *American Sociological Review* 45 (October 1980): 842–854; Gary LaFree, "Variables Affecting Guilty Pleas and Convictions in Rape Cases: Toward a Social Theory of Rape Processing," *Social Forces* 58 (March 1980): 833–850.

Notes

1. Kathleen B. Brosi, *A Cross-City Comparison of Felony Case Processing* (Washington, D. C.: Institute for Law and Social Research (INSLAW), 1979).
2. Charles Silberman, *Criminal Violence, Criminal Justice* (New York: Random House, 1978).
3. Kristen M. Williams and Judith Lucianovic, *Robbery and Burglary* (Washington, D. C.: INSLAW, 1979).
4. Brian Forst, Judith Lucianovic, and Sarah J. Cox, *What Happens after Arrest?* (Washington, D. C.: INSLAW, 1977).
5. Colin Loftin and David McDowall, " 'One with a Gun Gets You Two': Mandatory Sentencing and Firearms Violence in Detroit," *The Annals* (May 1981): 150–167; Peter W. Greenwood, *Selective Incapacitation* (Santa Monica, Calif.: Rand Corporation, 1982); Michael L. Rubinstein, Stevens H. Clarke, and Teresa J. White, *Alaska Bans Plea Bargaining* (Washington, D. C.: U. S. Government Printing Office, 1980).
6. The concept of the work group is best elaborated in James Eisenstein and Herbert Jacob, *Felony Justice: An Organizational Analysis of Criminal Courts* (Boston: Little, Brown, 1977). But see the criticism of the concept in Thomas W. Church, "Examining Local Legal Culture," *American Bar Foundation Research Journal* 1985, no. 3 (Summer 1985): 449–518.
7. Lynn Mather, "Some Determinants of the Methods of Case Disposition by Public Defenders in Los Angeles," *Law and Society Review* 8 (Winter 1974): 187–216.
8. Frederic Suffett, "Bail Setting: A Study of Courtroom Interaction," *Crime and Delinquency* 12 (1966): 318–331; David Sudnow, "Normal Crimes: Sociological Features of the Penal Code in a Public Defender Office," *Social Problems* 12 (Winter 1965): 255–276; Lynn Mather, "Some Determinants of the Method of Case Disposition: Decision-Making by Public Defenders in Los Angeles," *Law and Society Review* 8 (Winter 1974): 187–216.
9. Abraham Blumberg, *Criminal Justice* (Chicago: Quadrangle, 1970).

10. Malcolm M. Feeley, *Court Reform on Trial* (New York: Basic Books, 1983), p. 173.
11. Raymond T. Nimmer, *The Nature of System Change* (Chicago: American Bar Foundation, 1978), pp. 20–26. See Feeley's observations on changes in the role orientation of judges as the key to speeding up the trial process, in Feeley, *Court Reform on Trial*, p. 163.
12. Alfred Blumstein, Jacqueline Cohen, and Daniel Nagin, "The Dynamics of a Homeostatic Punishment Process," *Journal of Criminal Law and Criminology* 67 (September 1976): 317–334.
13. Feeley, *Court Reform on Trial*, p. 184.
14. Michael H. Tonry, *Sentencing Reform Impacts* (Washington, D. C.: Government Printing Office, 1987), p. 98.
15. Franklin Zimring, Sheila O'Malley, and Joel Eigen, "Punishing Homicide in Philadelphia: Perspectives on the Death Penalty," *University of Chicago Law Review* 43 (Winter 1976): 227–252. On the idea of making the crime fit the punishment, see Boyd Littrell, *Bureaucratic Justice* (Beverly Hills, Calif.: Sage, 1979).
16. Brosi, *Cross-City Comparisons*, p. 29.
17. Mather, "Some Determinants."
18. Donald M. McIntyre and David Lippman, "Prosecutors and Early Disposition of Felony Cases," *American Bar Association Journal* 56 (1970): 1156.
19. Brosi, *Cross-City Comparisons*, pp. 138, 147. Differences in case processing are also examined in Eisenstein and Jacob, *Felony Justice*.

Chapter 4

The Career Criminal

The so-called career criminal has been the primary focus of crime control thinking in the past decade. The most important policy initiatives—preventive detention, major-offender prosecution programs, and selective incapacitation—are aimed at offenders who commit large numbers of serious crimes. Anticrime rhetoric has always conjured up images of the "hard-core" criminal or the "chronic recidivist"—images traditionally constructed out of myth, stereotype, and fear. We are indebted to Marvin Wolfgang and his associates at the University of Pennsylvania for giving us a more detailed profile of this person. Their landmark study *Delinquency in a Birth Cohort*, the single most important piece of criminal justice research in the last twenty-five years, has profoundly influenced thinking on crime policy.[1]

Wolfgang's Birth Cohort

Wolfgang and his colleagues discovered that a small number of delinquents are responsible for a majority of all crimes and for about two-thirds of all violent crimes. They define as chronic delinquents those juveniles who have had five or more recorded contacts with the police. These juveniles represent only 18 percent of the youngsters who have ever had any contact with the police and only 6 percent of all juveniles in the cohort. Subsequent research, following the lead of Wolfgang's initial insight, has indicated a similar pattern among adult criminals.

Wolfgang and his colleagues took as their cohort all males born in Philadelphia in 1945 and traced them through official records until their eighteenth birthday in 1963. They were able to reconstruct complete records on a final sample of 9,945 juveniles. Of this group, as table 4.1 indicates, 3,475 had at least one officially recorded contact with the police. Obviously,

Table 4.1   Wolfgang's birth cohort

	Number	Percentage of original sample	Total criminal offenses	Percentage of total offenses
Original sample	9,945			
Delinquents	3,475	34.9%	10,214	
One officially recorded contact with police	1,613	16.2	1,613	15.8%
Two to four contacts	1,235	12.4	3,296	32.3
Five or more contacts	627	6.3	5,305	51.9

SOURCE: Marvin Wolfgang, Robert M. Figlio, and Thorsten Sellin, *Delinquency in a Birth Cohort* (Chicago: University of Chicago Press, 1972).

the real delinquency rate was higher than 35 percent because an unknown number of the others did something wrong but were never caught. Of the 3,475 who were caught by the police, 46 percent were never caught again. Wolfgang referred to them as "one-time offenders." That label is not completely accurate; many of the boys undoubtedly committed another offense but were not caught. Nonetheless, it is safe to assume that they ended their law breaking sooner rather than later. We don't know exactly why. But whether it is the result of deterrence, rehabilitation, or simple maturation, we can say that about half of all delinquents will stop their law breaking.

Wolfgang divided the remaining 1,862 juveniles into two groups. Two-thirds (1,235) were arrested two, three, or four times. Wolfgang referred to these as the "nonchronic recidivists." The other 627 were "chronic delinquents" who had had five or more arrests before they were eighteen years old. They represent 6 percent of the original cohort and 18 percent of the 3,475 delinquents. Since Wolfgang first identified them, those 627 "career criminals" have inspired the most important thinking in criminal justice.

The significance of the 627 chronic delinquents or career criminals becomes even greater when we consider how much crime they commit. As table 4.1 indicates, the 3,475 delinquents committed 10,214 crimes. (Keep in mind that this figure includes only officially recorded crimes and that the actual total was much higher). The one-time offenders were responsible for only 16 percent of the total. The nonchronic recidivists, meanwhile, committed 32 percent of the group's crimes. The 627 chronic delinquents committed more than half (52 percent) of all the crimes. The picture looks even worse when we consider the distribution of serious offenses. The chronic offenders were responsible for 63 percent of all the Index crimes, 71 percent of the murders, 73 percent of the rapes, and 82 percent of all the robberies.

To no one's surprise, Wolfgang also found that offense rates were highest among low-income males and nonwhite males. IQ scores and relative success in school also were correlated with delinquency rates.

Wolfgang's original findings are supported by a follow-up study of juveniles born in 1958. The 1958 cohort was much larger (28,338 subjects)

"Your honor, my client objects to being referred to as a 'chronic recidivist,' especially
since the term is well outside the scope of his
limited vocabulary."

and more representative of the population in terms of race and sex. The chronic offenders represented nearly the same percentage of the total cohort (7.5 percent) and they were responsible for 68 percent of all the Index offense arrests. As might be expected, the overall rate of criminality, especially violent criminality, was much higher. The 1958 cohort committed murders at a rate three times higher than that of the 1945 group and committed robberies at a rate five times higher. These data simply confirm the great increase in violent crime since the 1960s. It is important to note that the percentage of juveniles in both cohorts who had any contact with the police remained about the same: 34.9 percent in the 1945 cohort, 33 percent in the 1958 group. Thus delinquency has not increased in prevalence. Juveniles who become delinquent, however, are committing more crimes, and far more serious ones.[2]

Policy Implications

Wolfgang's research initiated a new era in criminal justice. It stimulated an enormous body of sophisticated research[3] and influenced public policy. In place of wild rhetoric we now had a more precise estimate of the size of the career-criminal group and the amount of crime they committed. The policy implications were immediately obvious. Because these few offenders were responsible for such a large proportion of all crime, we could reduce crime substantially if we could somehow identify and control them. Moreover, Wolfgang's data arrived just as the country was becoming more receptive to the obvious implications of his research. By 1972 crime rates had been rising steadily for a decade in the greatest and most sustained "crime wave" in American history. The rehabilitation-oriented policies of the 1960s were exhausted and discredited and the public was searching for a new set of ideas on crime control. This conjunction of events set the stage for the recent emphasis on programs designed to control career criminals.

Given Wolfgang's findings, the appropriate crime control strategy seemed obvious: identify the career criminals and get them off the streets. In the pages that follow we shall examine the specific policies that have emerged in every facet of the criminal process. Police programs prescribe intensive surveillance of suspected career criminals. Preventive detention calls for denial of bail to persons with long criminal records. Prosecution programs assign more resources to cases involving career criminals. Finally, the most highly publicized concept, selective incapacitation, calls for long prison terms for career criminals.

Before going any further we should recognize the important distinction that has been made between "career criminals" and "criminal careers." All offenders have a criminal career, just as we all have an academic career. Some are short, some are long. The high school dropout has an academic career—a brief and unsuccessful one. The kid who engages in some minor vandalism just once in his life has a criminal career. The key issues are *participation* (the distinction between people who commit crimes and those who don't), *frequency* (the rate at which active criminals commit crimes), *seriousness* (the gravity of the harm done by the crime), and *career length* (the length of time a person is actively engaged in a life of crime). Attention has focused on the few career criminals—those individuals who commit many crimes over a period of years.[4]

The Rand Corporation report *Selective Incapacitation* is an excellent example of the impact of Wolfgang's original study. It addresses the two main questions that Wolfgang raised but left unanswered: Exactly how many crimes do career criminals commit, and how can we positively identify the members of this small group? To answer the first question, the Rand team interviewed prison inmates in three states—California, Texas, and Michigan—and asked them how many crimes they had committed between arrests. The investigators attempted to validate these self-reports by cross-checking them against official records. The net result was an extremely high estimate of criminal activity for incarcerated offenders—who were not necessarily career criminals, we might add. Imprisoned robbers in California averaged 53 robberies per year, while those in Michigan averaged 77 and those in Texas averaged only 9 per year. Nor was this the extent of their criminal activity. The Rand investigators concluded that criminals did not specialize in one type of crime. Thus California robbers also averaged 90 burglaries, 163 thefts or frauds, and 646 drug offenses each year.[5]

Imprisoned Texas robbers had a much lower annual rate because Texas judges incarcerated robbers more often. As a result, the Texas sample included a higher proportion of low-rate offenders than Michigan and

California. In other words, the latter two states were already practicing a form of selective incapacitation.

The difference between Texas and the other two states has immense practical significance. A furious debate is now raging among criminologists over the question of exactly how much crime career criminals commit. If the estimates are high, then selective incapacitation will yield substantial reductions in crime. But if so-called career criminals actually have low rates of offending, then the payoff will be much lower. A low payoff, in turn, raises the question of whether it is worth investing vast resources in targeting the career criminal in the first place. In a major challenge to the recent emphasis on career criminals, Michael Gottfredson and Travis Hirschi conclude that "the evidence is clear that the career criminal idea is not sufficiently substantial to command more than a small portion of the time and effort of the criminal justice practitioner or academic community."[6] Much of their argument is based on the conflicting estimates of annual rate of offending by career criminals. Other studies have produced much lower figures. When Alfred Blumstein and Jacqueline Cohen studied Washington and Detroit, for example, they estimated that adult arrestees committed an average of 3.4 robberies per year in Washington and 4.7 in Detroit. Arrestees averaged 5.7 and 5.3 burglaries in Washington and Detroit, respectively. The National Youth Survey, meanwhile, estimated that active offenders committed an average of 8.4 robberies and 7.1 burglaries per year.[7]

The question of annual offending rates is directly related to the second question: Who are the career criminals? All career-criminal strategies rest on the assumption that we will catch, prosecute, convict, and punish the few hard-core career criminals, and only them. Imprisonment of a low-rate offender yields no practical benefit—we are incapacitating someone who is not going to commit a lot of crimes—to say nothing about questions of social justice. Police and prosecutorial career-criminal programs face the same potential problem of wasting valuable resources on low-risk, low-rate offenders. Catching the career criminal late in his or her career is another problem. As criminologists have long known, criminal activity is highest among people fourteen to twenty-four years old. Incapacitating a career criminal relatively late (say at age 22 or 23) will yield a relatively small payoff in terms of crime reduction.

The ability to identify career criminals is the test on which career-criminal programs succeed or fail. As we shall see, the problem of identification is an enormous and probably fatal weakness. Wolfgang identified his career criminals after the fact—an easy enough task. If crime is to be reduced, however, the career criminal must be recognized early rather than late. The process of identification is in effect a prediction about the person's future criminal behavior, followed by a choice based on that diagnosis (arrest, refusal of bail, prosecution, incarceration). We shall encounter the prediction problem on several occasions during the course of our examination of various crime control proposals. For the record, we should note that prediction is as great a problem for many liberal programs as it is for conservative crime control proposals. Probation and parole decisions require the same kind of identification of who is and who is not suitable for release to the community.

The Rand inmate survey suggests that offense rates are even more unevenly distributed than Wolfgang indicated. In fact, the distribution of offense rates was so highly skewed that it is virtually impossible to talk about an "average" career criminal. Among the inmates surveyed, the median annual robbery rate was five per year. Yet the top 10 percent committed eighty-seven robberies per year. At first glance, this finding simply confirms what Wolfgang had already found. We have to remember that, unlike Wolfgang, the Rand team surveyed prison inmates. When we consider how few offenders actually go to prison, it is apparent that the Rand team surveyed a group of fairly serious offenders. The top 10 percent of their sample, in other words, are the hard core of the hard core. This group represents an extremely small proportion of all the people who are ever caught by the police and a minute fraction of the total population.

Notes

1. Marvin Wolfgang, Robert M. Figlio, and Thorsten Sellin, *Delinquency in a Birth Cohort* (Chicago: University of Chicago Press, 1972).
2. Paul E. Tracy, Marvin E. Wolfgang, and Robert M. Figlio, *Delinquency in Two Birth Cohorts* (Chicago: University of Chicago Press, 1985).
3. Alfred Blumstein, Jacqueline Cohen, Jeffrey A. Roth, and Christy A. Visher, eds., *Criminal Careers and "Career Criminals"* (Washington, D. C.: National Academy Press, 1986).
4. Ibid.
5. Peter W. Greenwood, *Selective Incapacitation* (Santa Monica, Calif.: Rand, 1982).
6. Michael Gottfredson and Travis Hirschi, "The True Value of Lambda Would Appear to Be Zero: An Essay on Career Criminals, Criminal Careers, Selective Incapacitation, Cohort Studies, and Related Topics," *Criminology* 24 (May 1986): 213–234.
7. Alfred Blumstein and Jacqueline Cohen, "Estimating Individual Crime Rates from Arrest Records," *Journal of Criminal Law and Criminology* 70 (1979): 561–585; Delbert Elliott et al., *The Prevalence and Incidence of Delinquent Behavior, 1976–1980* (Boulder, Colo.: Behavioral Research Institute, 1983).

PART TWO

"GET TOUGH": THE CONSERVATIVE ATTACK ON CRIME

Conservatives argue that we can reduce serious crime if we just get tough with criminals. According to conservative theology, crime flourishes because the criminal justice system fails to arrest, prosecute, and punish dangerous criminals. Conservatives identify five specific ways of getting tough with criminals. First, we should lock up people who are guilty of committing serious crimes. To be more specific, we should lock up more of those people and imprison them for longer periods. Keep those people off the streets and the crime rate will fall. We will examine three strategies for locking up more criminals. Second, conservatives believe that it is possible to deter criminals more effectively than we do at present. We will review two deterrence strategies. Third, conservatives believe that we could catch more criminals if we unleashed the cops and gave them more power and resources. We will look at four strategies for unleashing the cops. One of those strategies involves elimination of some procedural constraints on the police. This plan is related to the fourth conservative method of getting tough, which is to close the loopholes that allow criminals to "beat the system." We will probe four proposals aimed at closing loopholes in the criminal justice system. Finally, conservatives argue that the criminal justice system protects criminals at the expense of their victims. We will discuss various means proposed to reduce crime by protecting the rights of victims.

Chapter 5

Lock 'em Up

The primary objective of conservative crime control strategy is to get dangerous criminals off the street. Our inquiry begins with three "lock-'em-up" proposals: preventive detention, selective incapacitation, and mandatory sentencing. All three reflect the assumption that the criminal justice system turns dangerous criminals loose, allowing them to prey upon law-abiding citizens. The three proposals build upon Marvin Wolfgang's research by targeting a small number of dangerous repeat offenders.

Proponents of lock-'em-up strategies focus on two aspects of the criminal justice process. The first is judicial discretion. They believe dangerous criminals are set free because judges have unfettered discretion to release them on bail, grant them probation, or sentence them to inappropriately short prison terms. All three proposals, therefore, are attempts to limit the discretion of judges. The second problem, according to the lock-'em-up perspective, is excessive preoccupation with the rights of suspects, defendants, and criminals. Conservatives view judges as "bleeding hearts" who are more concerned with the rights of criminals than with the rights of crime victims and the protection of society as a whole. The lock-'em-up strategy represents an effort to reverse two of the major criminal justice reforms of the 1960s: the expanded rights of suspects under the due-process clause of the Constitution and the expanded use of nonprison alternatives to sentencing.

Preventive Detention

Provisions for preventive detention authorize judges to deny bail to defendants they decide are dangerous and likely to commit additional crimes. The Eighth Amendment to the U. S. Constitution has traditionally been construed to mean that all criminal defendants have a right to bail. The only exceptions are persons accused of "capital" crimes, which in practice means persons accused of murder. Advocates of preventive detention seek to reverse the long-standing principle in Anglo-American law that the sole purpose of bail is to ensure the defendant's appearance at trial, not to keep dangerous people off the street. Preventive detention has been a major goal of conservatives for twenty years.[1] At first glance, some data do seem to support the conservative view. The Washington, D. C., police department reported that 30 percent of all robbery defendants were rearrested while out on bail. Another study by the U. S. Attorney's Office found a rearrest rate of 70 percent for bailed robbery defendants.[2]

To a great extent the demand for preventive detention reflects a backlash against the bail-reform movement of the 1960s. The civil rights movement focused public attention on the plight of the poor criminal defendant who could not raise bail. The President's Crime Commission found that in 1967 52 percent of all people in jail were awaiting trial. Critics labeled America's jails the "new poorhouses." Pretrial detention had nothing to do with danger or risk of failure to appear at trial. Wealthy mobsters have no trouble raising high bail. Only the poor sit in jail. Research also indicated that people who could not achieve release on bail were more likely to be convicted at trial.[3]

The bail-reform movement helped establish nonmonetary alternatives to release. The only relevant criterion was the historic legal principle of guaranteeing the defendant's appearance at trial. The likelihood of flight was deemed to be slight for the person with a job, family, or other roots in the community. The landmark legislation of the reform movement was the 1966 federal Bail Reform Act, which directed federal courts to develop such nonmonetary procedures as "release on recognizance" (or ROR, as it is popularly known). Many states followed suit or developed "10 percent plans" that facilitated release on bail. Bail reform went a long way toward putting the traditional bail bondsman out of business.

The bail-reform movement achieved many of its goals. The percentage of people in jail who were being held for trial dropped from 52 percent in 1967 to 39 percent in 1983. In Washington, D. C., 99 percent of all defendants obtain pretrial release. Reform did not completely eliminate the problems with the bail system, however. New bail-setting procedures generally operated on the principle that employed defendants were better risks than the unemployed. Thus the system institutionalized a form of discrimination against unemployed or marginally employed persons. Nor did the reform efforts succeed in eliminating the judicial practice of setting impossibly high money bail for "dangerous" defendants.[4]

Despite the positive achievements of the bail-reform movement, a backlash set in almost immediately. The high point of the movement coincided with the great upsurge in the crime rate in the mid-1960s. Conservatives saw a connection between the two events, arguing that this was another of the softhearted, muddleheaded social experiments that only harm society at large. The backlash was first felt in Washington, D. C. In 1966 the Commission on Crime in the District of Columbia recommended preventive detention for the District. A minority of the Commission's members dissented, reflecting the sharp ideological division over the bail issue. A special Judicial Council Committee established to study the impact of the Bail Reform Act in the District recommended preventive detention by a narrow 6–5 vote. President Nixon endorsed the idea in 1969 and preventive detention became law for the District of Columbia in 1970.

Although no state followed the federal example immediately, in the last decade the advocates of preventive detention have been extremely successful in achieving their goal. Preventive detention has been popular with legislators and with voters, and has been sanctioned by the Supreme Court. By the mid-1980s, thirty-four states had adopted some form of preventive detention, either by statute or by amendment to the state constitution. A 1978 amendment to Nebraska's constitution allowed judges to deny bail to persons accused of sex offenses. California added preventive detention to its state constitution in 1982 as a part of Proposition 8. The Michigan constitution allows preventive detention in four kinds of crimes when the judge finds a possibility of "danger" if the defendant were to be released. Two presidential commissions under Ronald Reagan have recommended preventive detention: the Attorney General's Task Force on Violent Crime and the President's Task Force on Crime Victims. The Crime Victims Task Force recommended legislation to "allow courts to deny bail to persons found by clear and convincing evidence to present a danger to the community." The Supreme Court has upheld the principle of preventive detention in two decisions. In 1984 it permitted detention of juveniles without bail, and in 1987 it upheld the constitutionality of the 1984 federal preventive-detention law. In *United States* v. *Salerno* the Court held that preventive detention was a limited "regulatory" measure that was not inherently punitive, and that as long as elaborate procedural guidelines were provided, it did not violate a fundamental constitutional right.[5]

Preventive detention seems to offer an obvious solution to the crime problem: reduce crime by keeping repeat offenders off the street. Unfortunately, it is not quite that simple in practice. My position is:

PROPOSITION 5

Preventive detention will not reduce violent crime.

Preventive Detention in Washington

The law passed in Washington, D. C., in 1970 allows us to examine preventive detention in practice. Under that law, a person charged with a crime of violence or a dangerous crime can be held for up to sixty days without bail. A formal hearing is required to determine that substantial probability of guilt exists and that no other release procedure can guarantee public safety. Moreover, to qualify for detention, the defendant must have been convicted of a crime in the preceding ten years, be a narcotics addict, or currently be on pretrial release, probation, or parole. Finally, the defendant has a right to release on bail if the trial is not held within sixty days. In short, the law is circumscribed by several procedures designed to limit its application and ensure a measure of due process.

How does preventive detention work in Washington? It hardly works at all. Despite all the public uproar about crime in the streets, judges rarely resort to preventive detention. A study by Georgetown University and the Vera Institute found that only ten defendants were detained in the first six months after the law went into effect. Prosecutors filed detention motions against only 20 of the 6,000 felony defendants in that period. Those motions resulted in nine formal hearings and eight actual detentions. Another two defendants were detained through judicial initiative. But this is not the end of the story. Five of the ten detentions were reversed on appeal or reconsideration. Another was dismissed when the grand jury refused to indict the suspect on the original charge. Thus only four persons were fully detained during the entire ten-month period.[6]

The startling lack of recourse to preventive detention is easy to explain, and it has little to do with the soft hearts of judges. Prosecutors do not use the law because they don't need it. They can effectively detain a defendant simply by setting bail at a level comfortably beyond his or her financial means. It is not hard to do so, given the fact that most robbers have little or no income. James Eisenstein and Herbert Jacob found that bail for armed robbers averaged $3,075 in Detroit, $7,719 in Chicago, and an astounding $23,686 in Baltimore. These figures were considerably higher than the going rate for bail for murder suspects in all three cities.[7] By setting high bail, prosecutors in Washington kept offenders off the street and avoided all the time-consuming procedures required by the 1970 law.

The American criminal justice system has always practiced a covert form of preventive detention. Despite the Eighth Amendment and the legal principle that the purpose of bail is solely to ensure a defendant's appearance at trial, judges and prosecutors have always used money bail to keep people they think are dangerous off the streets. Frederic Suffet's study of bail setting found a high degree of cooperation among judges, prosecutors, and defense attorneys. Members of the work groups disagreed in only 12 percent of all cases (only a quarter of these cases, or 3 percent of the total, aroused serious conflict). One of the main functions of the bail-setting process is to spread the responsibility around just in case something goes wrong. If the bailed offender should immediately commit another crime, the judge does not have to shoulder sole responsibility.[8] The bail-reform movement did not eliminate this informal practice.

The impact of the federal preventive-detention law has not yet been evaluated. The initial evidence, however, indicates that it is being used far more extensively than the Washington, D. C., law. By the time the Supreme Court found the law constitutional, about 2,500 people had been denied bail as dangerous (730 were held because they were deemed dangerous to the community; 1,770 were held both because they were dangerous and to ensure their appearance at trial; another 2,300 were held without bail only because they might flee to avoid trial). The director of the U. S. Marshals Service said that the law was having "a dramatic impact on the entire Federal criminal justice system." The impact, of course, was on the already overcrowded jails. There is no evidence, one way or the other, of any impact on crime.[9]

The Prediction Problem

The debate over preventive detention has stimulated considerable research on the question of how well defendants "succeed" while they are out on bail. Since detention of suspects to prevent them from committing additional crimes entails a prediction about their future behavior, we now have to look at the prediction problem.

The "facts" about the success and failure of defendants released on bail can be presented in a variety of ways. It is possible to make the situation look much better or worse than it is by the way you juggle the figures. Basically, we want to know how often defendants out on bail commit another crime (although actually we mean "are *arrested* for another crime," since we cannot know about the crimes committed by people we don't arrest). We must deal with two sets of figures: the crimes for which defendants were originally arrested and released on bail and the crimes for which they were rearrested. One approach uses gross categories and includes *all* criminal defendants and rearrests for *all* kinds of offenses. A better approach is to look only at defendants originally arrested for felonies. After all, we are concerned primarily with serious crime, and a misdemeanor is hardly such a threat to public safety that it would justify preventive detention. A further refinement would be to consider only felony defendants who were arrested again for another felony. The best approach would focus on particular crimes—robbery and rape, for example—and determine how often those defendants were arrested for another violent crime.

When the first three approaches are used, the data indicate that relatively few defendants are rearrested while on bail. A 1970 study by the National Bureau of Standards, regarded by many experts as the most thorough of all the studies on this complex issue, found that only 11 percent of all defendants (charged with felonies and misdemeanors) were rearrested. The rearrest rate for felony defendants was higher (17 percent), but only about half of them were arrested for another felony. Thus 7 percent of all persons arrested for a felony and released on bail were arrested again for another felony.[10]

When we narrow our focus to specific crimes, the issue becomes more problematic. Certain types of defendants have extremely high failure rates. People arrested for possession of drugs have a very great tendency to go out and use (or deal in) drugs right away—and be rearrested. Sex offenders, on the other hand, have a rather low failure rate (despite the popular impression, fostered by the occasional celebrated case or horror story, that rapists are chronic and quick repeaters). Robbery is a special case. Failure rates are higher for robbery than for any other category of violent crime. In a sober assessment of the available data, Wayne Thomas concludes that about 30 percent of all robbery defendants out on bail will be rearrested for robbery.[11] If we expand the rearrest category to include other types of felonies, robbers fail more than 50 percent of the time.

The data on robbers out on bail are grim and pose a serious test of anyone's commitment to the principle of the right to bail. For conservatives, these figures clinch the case: lock up the few dangerous people and we will reduce the crime rate.

Translating this idea into practice is not so easily done. With preventive detention we encounter the prediction problem for the first but not the last time. The policy works only if we succeed in identifying and detaining the dangerous repeaters *and only those offenders*. Mistakes take two forms. First there are defendants whom we detain unnecessarily. We label them dangerous when in fact they will not commit violent felonies while they are out on bail. These people are referred to as "false positives." Then there are people who slip through our net. We fail to identify them as potentially dangerous when in fact they do commit more violent crime while they are out on bail. These are the "false negatives." In both cases the social cost is high. Not only does locking people up unnecessarily deny them their constitutional right to bail, but jailing them while they await trial imposes a tremendous financial cost. Jails are already overcrowded, and few people are prepared to pay the taxes necessary to build more cells. Failure to detain dangerous people, on the other hand, means that innocent people may be victimized.

Two studies of preventive detention independently found that only 5 percent of the criminal defendants who were potentially eligible for detention (that is, had committed a violent crime) would be rearrested for a violent crime while out on bail. The National Bureau of Standards study found that between 15 percent and 25 percent of those eligible under the Washington, D. C., law would be rearrested but only 5 percent of those rearrests would be for a violent crime. A similar study in Boston found that 14.5 percent of the potentially eligible would be rearrested but only 5.2 percent for another violent crime. Identifying the small dangerous group within the original group is difficult, if not impossible. Remember, all of the original group qualify by having committed a violent crime. One obvious solution is to cast a broad net and lock up a lot of people just to be safe. The Boston study concluded that in order to hold all of the actually dangerous people, we would have to detain nineteen nondangerous people for every dangerous one. In other words, there would be nineteen false positives for every dangerous person we correctly detained. The cost of such mistakes would be threefold. Not only would we violate the rights of those individuals needlessly detained, but the jail experience would encourage many of them toward more antisocial attitudes and behavior. Finally, the dollar cost of locking up so many people would be enormous.[12]

The truth is that we simply can't tell who is dangerous and who is not. Human behavior is too unpredictable and past behavior is not necessarily the best guide. Many people think they can spot the dangerous repeaters. The concept of the "career criminal" is, in many respects, very misleading. The people we call "chronic" offenders commit crimes in spurts. They go through periods of very active criminality, followed by periods of inactivity. They are not like white-collar workers who go to the office on time week in and week out. In short, it is impossible to predict what one convicted offender will do in the next few weeks or months. Judge Charles Halleck of the District of Columbia Court of General Sessions, an advocate of preventive detention, did think he could make successful predictions. The D. C. bail agency had the impertinence to compare Judge Halleck's track record with that of another judge of the same court. Halleck granted pretrial release to only 49 percent of the 200 defendants in his sample, while Judge Alexander released 80 percent of his defendants. The rearrest rates for the two judges were virtually identical: 8 percent of those released by Judge Halleck and 9 percent of those released by Judge Alexander were rearrested. In other words, while Judge Halleck detained two and a half times as many people as Judge Alexander, he was no more successful in spotting the truly dangerous.[13]

Unfortunately, we do not have a detailed study that focuses specifically on armed robbers. Although this group has the worst record of failure on bail, the prospects for reducing crime through preventive detention are not great. Even if the rearrest rate is 50 percent for this group, as Thomas estimates, we would still be wrong half the time. A rearrest rate of 30 percent, Thomas's low estimate, would mean that we would be wrong more than two-thirds of the time. Finally, there is another perspective on this problem. In most cities, armed robbers are already being detained through the use of high money bail. This is not the case in Washington, D. C., where 99 percent of the defendants obtain release, but it is certainly true in Salt Lake City and Omaha, two cities whose practices are more nearly typical of cities across the nation. In most jurisdictions relatively few armed robberies are committed by defendants out on bail. When such robberies do happen, they make the news; they are the exceptions and not the general rule.

Preventive detention is not a reasonable criminal justice policy. Most prosecutors and judges will simply avoid using the law and try to achieve the same ends by covert means. If the law were implemented, it would fail in one of two costly ways: detention of too many, at great dollar and constitutional cost, or detention of too few, and failure to reduce crime effectively. The case that reached the Supreme Court was brought by the reputed organized crime boss Anthony ("Fat Tony") Salerno. His detention illustrates the real uses of the law. Mafia bosses themselves do not commit crimes of violence (they hire others to do it for them) and have no trouble

"Mirror, mirror on the chamber wall. Who's
the most perceptive judge of all?"

continuing to run their criminal syndicates from jail or prison. Thus
detention of "Fat Tony" Salerno will in no way protect the community. He is
really being held for political reasons, so a federal prosecutor can project an
image of being tough on crime. In practice, prosecutors and judges will try to
strike a balance between the false positives and false negatives, leaving us
with the worst of both worlds.

Speedy Trial: A Better Way

A better solution is a speedy trial. All the bail studies confirm that the
likelihood of rearrest increases dramatically with length of time out on bail.
Table 5.1 compares the findings of two studies that demonstrate this pattern.
In the Boston study, 70 percent (29 out of 41) of the crimes committed by
people out on bail took place more than sixty days after their original release.
In the National Bureau of Standards study, 61 percent occurred after more
than sixty days. Other studies have found roughly similar patterns.

A speedy trial would solve several problems simultaneously. It would
preserve two important constitutional rights: the right to bail and the right to
a speedy trial (we might note that many advocates of crime victims' rights
see speedy trials as serving the interests of the victims as well). At the same
time it would reduce between 60 and 70 percent of the crime committed by
people on bail. Thus we can conclude with:

Speedy trials can reduce pretrial crime while preserving constitutional rights.

We should not be optimistic about the prospects of achieving speedy trials, however. Malcolm Feeley's study of the issue does not inspire hope. A federal speedy-trial law took effect in 1974 and several states have followed suit. Feeley found that the laws have had little if any direct effect on the speed with which criminal cases are processed. In fact, there appears to have been little serious effort to comply with even the formal requirements of the federal law. Judges, prosecutors, and defense attorneys alike had their reasons for opposing the provisions of the federal law. Together they have been able to negate its impact. Their success again illustrates the futility of trying to change the criminal justice process by means of an externally imposed requirement—particularly one that is not fully supported by the various members of the courtroom work group.[14]

It is possible to hasten the processing of criminal cases. When one of the key members of the courtroom work group, usually the judge with administrative responsibility for the particular court system, identifies delay as a problem, he or she can take specific steps to speed up the process. The point, according to Feeley, is that the effective force is the initiative of the presiding judge, not special legislation.

Incapacitation

Incapacitation rests on the same deceptively simple idea as preventive detention: we can reduce crime by locking up the few chronic offenders. Politically, incapacitation is currently one of the hottest ideas in criminal justice. James Q. Wilson gave it a strong endorsement in the first edition of his *Thinking about Crime* when he estimated that serious crime could be

Table 5.1 Cumulative percentage of crimes committed by entire pretrial release group

Days on pretrial release	Boston study	National Bureau of Standards study
1 30	19.5%	23.4%
31–60	29.3	38.3
61–90	48.8	46.8
91–120	61.0	61.7
121–150	68.3	70.2

SOURCE: "Preventive Detention: An Empirical Analysis," *Harvard Civil Rights–Civil Liberties Law Review*, 6 (1971). National Bureau of Standards, *Compilation and Use of Criminal Court Data in Relation to Pretrial Defendants: Pilot Study* (Washington, D. C.: Government Printing Office, 1970).

You and Me and the Prediction Problem: AIDS Testing and False Positives

The call for mandatory testing as a means of confronting the current AIDS problem illustrates the problem with false positives in a way that has direct implications for all of us.

In theory, AIDS testing identifies those people who have been exposed to this deadly disease and allows us to take measures to prevent it from spreading further. In practice, testing is highly unreliable and can seriously affect many "innocent"—that is, healthy—people.

The Congressional Office of Technology Assessment has estimated that the actual incidence of people carrying the AIDS virus in the general population—blood donors in your city, for example—is 10 per 100,000. The most reliable test available would correctly detect nine of those people. It would miss the tenth person (a "false negative"). Worse, it would incorrectly identify eighty-nine people as carrying the AIDS virus. Those eighty-nine "false positives" would be told that they carried the AIDS virus when in fact they didn't.

To put this matter in personal terms, imagine that you donated blood and, after testing, were informed that you carried the AIDS virus. Imagine the impact on your life and on the people close to you. Those of us who are law-abiding people discuss criminal justice programs in a detached manner—they involve things that will be done to them, not to us. The question of AIDS testing brings the problem of false positives home to us.

---

reduced by *one-third* if each person convicted of a serious crime received a mandatory three-year prison sentence. Wilson drew upon the research of Shlomo and Reuel Shinnar, who made the even more extravagant claim that the right dose of incapacitation could reduce crime by 80 percent.[15]

The most important statement on behalf of the policy is the 1982 report *Selective Incapacitation,* by Peter Greenwood of the Rand Corporation. With a properly fine-tuned sentencing policy, the report suggested, we could reduce robbery by 15 percent and at the same time reduce the prison population by 5 percent. This proposal seemed to offer the best of both worlds. The Rand study received enormous publicity, including lengthy coverage in the Sunday *New York Times* and in *Newsweek*. Selective incapacitation appeared in late 1982 to be an idea whose time had come.[16]

Incapacitation seems to be an easy policy to implement. Sentencing is one of the more visible decision points in the criminal justice system (compared, say, with the very low-visibility decisions of arrest and plea bargains) and is subject to direct control by legislatures. The best criminological research, meanwhile, supports the idea that a small number of career criminals are responsible for an extremely high proportion of violent crimes. A policy of *selective* incapacitation, as opposed to a gross lock-'em-up strategy, targets this small group of chronic offenders.

Selective incapacitation, however, is too good to be true; it fails on several points. My argument is:

--------------------------- **PROPOSITION 7** ---------------------------
Selective incapacitation is not a realistic policy for reducing serious crime.

The careful reader will note that I have cautiously qualified my proposition. I say that incapacitation is not a "realistic" policy for reducing serious crime. If we were not concerned about the practical consequences, we could probably reduce crime by locking a lot of people up. Totalitarian societies follow this practice, but it is not consistent with our ideals. Our goal is to develop policies that effectively reduce crime while preserving our standards of fairness and humanity—and policies that are politically feasible. Incapacitation fails on all these points.

Despite the publicity that *Selective Incapacitation* received, few people noticed its last paragraph. It begins: "In conclusion, this study does not attempt to prove the case for selective incapacitation or to provide unequivocal guidance for future sentencing policies."[17] Even its author claims to have offered only a "think piece," designed to stimulate further research. Greenwood is properly cautious because selective incapacitation as a policy is confronted with serious challenges. These include:

1. The difficulties of correctly estimating the amount of crime reduction;
2. the difficulties of accurately identifying the chronic offenders (the prediction problem again);
3. the monetary cost of increased prison populations and the political cost of reducing prison terms for low-risk offenders in order to offset increased prison terms for high-risk offenders;
4. the difficulty of implementing the policy without gross violations of constitutional rights; and
5. other unpredictable side effects.

Let us look at each of these problems separately.

How Much Crime Reduction?

Incapacitation specialists do not agree on the question of exactly how much selective incapacitation would reduce crime. The Shinnars promised a reduction of anywhere from 30 percent to 80 percent, but no one seriously accepts such a figure today. The Rand Corporation report envisions a more modest 15 percent reduction in robbery alone (and we should note that they anticipate a lower rate in certain states because of their prevailing sentencing patterns). Yet David Greenberg estimates a reduction of between 0.6 percent and 4 percent, while the Ohio State team of Stephen Van Dine, John Conrad, and Simon Dinitz projects a 1.7 percent reduction.[18]

The major source of these very different estimates is the question of how many crimes are committed annually by so-called career criminals. This is currently a matter of furious debate among criminologists, involving highly complex methodological questions. Obviously, a high estimate of annual offending rates will yield a large reduction in crime. A lower estimate produces a much lower crime-reduction effect. It is extremely important to point out that all estimates of annual offending rates by career criminals are just that—estimates. The leading experts are sharply divided over the methodologies used to produce these estimates. David Greenberg used an estimate of only one felony per year. The Shinnars and others used much larger estimates. James Q. Wilson summarizes the conflicting estimates and concludes that the average is somewhere in the vicinity of fourteen serious offenses per year.[19]

With all of these estimates we encounter a fundamental problem: it is meaningless to talk about *average* offense rates. There is no such thing as an "average" offender. Criminal activity is highly skewed. A very few criminals engage in crime at a very high rate. Others, even other "repeat" offenders, commit crimes at a much lower rate. Wolfgang's delinquency research provided some insight into this phenomenon. The Rand *Selective Incapacitation* report offers even greater detail. Rand found that imprisoned robbers in California committed an estimated fifty-three robberies per year, along with ninety burglaries and some other crimes. Imprisoned robbers in Michigan committed an estimated seventy-seven robberies per year. These figures are incredibly high and, at first glance, might seem to clinch the case for selective incapacitation. But they are deceptive. The high *averages* are inflated by the extremely high rates for a very select group of offenders. As the Rand report observes, "most offenders reported fairly low rates of crime."[20] Thus the median rate of robberies was only five per year, but the worst 10 percent of this group (or the 90th percentile) committed eighty-seven per year!

We should point out that the offenders in the Rand study (prison inmates in three states) are a pretty select group simply by virtue of being in prison in the first place. The tremendous difference between the worst 10 percent and the rest of those inmates means that an effective selective incapacitation policy would have to make fine distinctions among people who have already earned the label of serious offender. This is not a minor technical problem— in fact, it is a very large and fundamental obstacle for the incapacitation strategy. It is necessary, therefore, to explore the prediction problem again.

The Prediction Problem Revisited

We have already encountered the prediction problem in our discussion of preventive detention. Predicting who will and who will not commit multiple offenses is the essence of the selective incapacitation policy. The Rand Corporation's approach involves selecting out not just the high-risk offenders, who will receive long prison terms, but the low-risk as well. They are to receive shorter sentences in order to make room in the prisons for the high-risk, long-prison-term offenders.

A considerable amount of research has been invested in the quest for formulas that would allow us to predict the future behavior of criminal offenders. The initial impetus came from parole, since parole release decisions are, for all practical purposes, predictions about future behavior. (We will consider this aspect of the prediction problem when we discuss rehabilitation as a policy.) E. W. Burgess, one of the pioneers of American criminology, developed the first prediction table in 1928. Despite the advances in the social and behavioral sciences over the past half century, we are no closer to the original goal of successful prediction than Burgess was.[21]

There are basically three methods for predicting behavior. The first is anamnestic prediction. Norval Morris and Marc Miller explain this approach as follows: "This is how he behaved in the past when circumstances were similar. It is likely that he will behave in the same way now." The second method is actuarial prediction. Insurance companies use this approach to predict the risks associated with people who fit certain statistical categories (e.g., the risk of automobile accidents is very high for teenagers, low for middle-aged people). The Rand *Selective Incapacitation* report uses this approach. The third method is clinical prediction. Psychologists use this approach, combining analysis of information about the subject with professional judgment. As Morris and Miller point out, criminal justice officials have always based their decisions on predictions of the offender's future behavior. These predictions, however, have always been implicit. Usually they were nothing more than hunches, or at worst the products of bias. The challenge of contemporary policy making is to make them explicit and scientifically verifiable.[22]

The most widely cited research on predicting violent behavior is a study sponsored by the National Council on Crime and Delinquency. Ernst A. Wenk, James O. Robison, and Gerald W. Smith investigated a sample of 4,146 youths committed to the California Youth Authority and found that 104 members of that group subsequently became "violent recidivists." The researchers' task was to design a prediction device that would have identified those 104 violent recidivists in advance.[23]

The most obvious predictor of violence would be a record of previous violence. Unfortunately, only half of the 104 youths who were later to be violent recidivists had any previous history of violence. The other fifty-two

Table 5.2 Numbers of youths predicted to be violent and nonviolent who proved to be violent and nonviolent, California, 1972

	Predicted violent	*Predicted nonviolent*
Actual violent	True positives: Violent persons correctly identified as violent and incarcerated 52	False negatives: Violent persons incorrectly identified as nonviolent and not incarcerated 52
Actual nonviolent	False positives: Nonviolent persons incorrectly identified as violent and needlessly incarcerated 404	True negatives: Nonviolent persons correctly identified as nonviolent 3,638

SOURCE: Ernst A. Wenk, James O. Robison, and Gerald W. Smith, "Can Violence Be Predicted?" *Crime and Delinquency* 18 (October 1972): 393–402.

would have slipped through the net (false negatives) because we would not have predicted their subsequent violence. Wenk, Robison, and Smith asked some professional clinicians to develop indices of "violence-proneness" to help identify the potentially violent. The resulting indices used such obvious factors as previous violent behavior, evident emotional problems, and drug or alcohol abuse. The researchers' most optimistic hope was that an index could be devised to give accurate forecasts for half of the juveniles who actually became violent; but one that did so could succeed only by casting a wide net that would be wrong in 10 percent of the remaining cases. A 10 percent error rate may not sound too bad until we look at the results indicated in table 5.2.

The 10 percent error rate yields 404 false positives—people whom the index would incorrectly predict to be violent. If we were using it to apply an incapacitation policy, we would be incarcerating eight people unnecessarily for every violent person we correctly indentified and locked up. Meanwhile, the fifty-two false negatives remain. In other words, we lock up a large number of people, most of them unnecessarily, and still fail to prevent half of the violence.

The Rand *Selective Incapacitation* report uses a more sophisticated analysis of criminal histories but does no better at prediction. Its prediction device involves seven factors derived from the histories of the offenders in its inmate survey. Each factor is worth one point and offenders are classified as low risk, medium risk, or high risk, depending on their total number of points.

The Rand team then correlated inmates' scores with their self-reported criminal activity. As table 5.3 indicates, the prediction device was correct only 51 percent of the time. You and I could do as well by flipping a coin. We reach the 51 percent figure by adding the predicted low-risk offenders who

Table 5.3   Predicted versus self-reported offense ratio for robbery and burglary

Score on prediction scale		Self-reported offense rates			
		Low	Medium	High	Total
Low	(0–1)	14%	10%	3%	27%
Medium	(2–3)	12	22	10	44
High	(4–7)	4	10	15	29
Total		30%	42%	28%	100%

SOURCE: Peter W. Greenwood, *Selective Incapacitation* (Santa Monica, Calif.: Rand Corporation, 1982), p. 59.

proved to be low risks (14 percent), the predicted medium risks who proved to be medium risks (22 percent), and the predicted high risks who actually proved to be high risks (15 percent). The prediction device was grossly wrong in 7 percent of the cases: the sum of the 4 percent who were predicted to be high risks but who turned out to be low risks (false positives) and the 3 percent who were predicted to be low risks but proved to be high risks (false negatives). It follows that the device was only moderately wrong in the remaining 42 percent of the cases.

We can hardly expect this or any other system to be perfect. The relevant question is how its effectiveness compares with that of current sentencing practices. If it led to an improvement that was substantial, even though less than perfect, it would be useful. Greenwood took his sample of offenders and recategorized them as low, medium, or high risks according to a scale implied by their prison sentences, which indicated how the sentencing judges evaluated them. The judges' sentences/predictions were "correct" 42 percent of the time as compared with the 51 percent rate for the Rand device. Meanwhile, the judges were grossly wrong 12 percent of the time, as against 7 percent for the Rand device. In other words, the extremely sophisticated model developed by Rand was somewhat better than what judges are actually doing, but not a great deal better.

The truth of the matter is that human behavior is unpredictable. People are exactly as poets and novelists and philosophers have always said they were: quirky, individualistic, and highly idiosyncratic. Their behavior does not conform to the rigid correlates of scientific prediction devices. Some people with no record of violence commit acts of violence. Meanwhile, some people with histories of violence cease their violent behavior. Because so much criminal justice policy rests, implicitly or explicitly, on our ability to predict behavior precisely, we need to state this point as a general proposition:

--------------------------- **PROPOSITION 8** ---------------------------

The present state of the social and behavioral sciences does not allow precise prediction of violent or otherwise dangerous criminal behavior.

The Cost of Incapacitation

The idea of incapacitation won considerable initial support because so many people were fed up with crime. Locking up a lot of criminals seemed to be a simple, direct, and effective solution. The advocates of incapacitation, however, never discuss the dollar cost of this policy. They offer sophisticated estimates of crime reduction but never calculate the cost to taxpayers of locking up all those people. There is a reason: the cost is absolutely staggering. In today's economy it is politically prohibitive. No elected official (or serious candidate for office) in the United States today can seriously propose spending the amount of money required to implement any of the various incapacitation schemes.

The Rand Corporation report promised the best of both worlds: crime reduction *and* fewer people in prison. We shall examine this bit of wizardry in a moment, but first we'll look at some estimates of the costs of other incapacitation programs.

The Ohio State Dangerous Offender Project estimated that a mandatory five-year prison term for every person with a prior felony conviction would reduce violent crime by 26.7 percent. Such a policy would be far out of line with the prevailing going rate. According to Van Dine, Conrad, and Dinitz, this policy would increase the Ohio prison population by 500 to 600 percent. The number of prisoners would rise from 13,000 (the 1973 figure) to at least 65,000. David Greenberg projected similar increases for New York in his study of the effect of incapacitation.[24]

Let us project these figures onto a national scale. There were 299,134 prisoners in state penitentiaries on January 1, 1981. To simplify things, let's round that figure off to 300,000. If we assume only a "modest" 400 percent increase, there would be 1.5 million inmates in state prisons after five years. If the high estimate is correct, there could be 1.8 million or even 2.1 million prisoners. Even in 1981 the United States ranked third in the world in the number of prisoners per 100,000 population. The proposed incapacitation policies would have us leapfrog over the current world leaders, the Soviet Union and South Africa—not what you would call distinguished company.[25]

The prospect of an "American Archipelago" numbering anywhere from 1.5 to 2 million people hardly merits serious discussion. But since conservative advocates of incapacitation solemnly recommend this policy, let us take them at their word and look hard at the dollar cost. First we would have to build new prisons to house the additional 1.2 million prisoners (for the sake of argument, let's use the more modest estimate). The cost of prison construction varies greatly, depending on the type of facility, regional cost variations, and so on. The National Moratorium on Prison Construction found that the average cost of the 685 state and local institutions proposed or under construction at the time of its study was between $45,000 and $53,000 per inmate (a recent estimate puts the cost of New York City jails at $70,000

"We use it to keep track of the rising prison
population."

per inmate). We'll take $50,000 as a convenient figure. (Keep in mind that
the incapacitation policy involves locking up dangerous criminals; we
would therefore have to build the relatively more expensive maximum-
security facilities. Also, costs have risen since those figures were gathered.)[26]
The final bill for prison construction would come to $60 billion. To put this
in some context, remember that most people blanched when the Attorney
General's Task Force on Violent Crime proposed $2 billion in federal
assistance for prison construction. Congress, of course, never even considered the idea.

The tab would be even higher if we used the mid-range estimate. Given a
prison population of 1.8 million, the construction costs would come to $75
billion. We can make a separate estimate for each state. Ohio, for example,
would add 42,000 new prisoners at a construction cost of $2.1 billion.

The cost of building new prisons is only the first installment on the bill.
Operating costs are equally staggering. Estimates of the cost per inmate to
run a prison also vary widely, depending on the type of institution, the
region, and the method used to calculate administrative overhead. Estimates
range from a low of $8,000 per year to a high of $50,000. If for the sake of
argument we take the relatively low figure of $10,000, the aggregate national
bill for operations comes to $12 billion. (If the correct figure is $20,000 per
year, the total is $24 billion.) These are, of course, annual and recurring
operating costs, which will rise each year. Even without any increase, the
five-year total would be $60 billion (again on the basis of the low estimate).

Thus over five years we would incur combined construction and
operating costs of $120 billion to achieve an estimated 26.7 percent reduc-
tion in violent crime. Is any elected official prepared to make such a
proposal? The failure of incapacitation advocates to discuss the dollar costs

is utterly irresponsible. We might note in passing that such neoconservatives as James Q. Wilson are fond of making fun of liberal "social experiments" that promise great reforms with no acknowledgment of the cost. It seems that liberals do not have a monopoly on "social engineering."

The New York City jail crisis dramatically illustrates the cost of "getting tough." The population of the city's jails doubled, from 7,000 to 14,000, in ten years. The jails were bursting at the seams. The city announced plans to build facilities with 2,000 more beds. One plan even called for holding jail inmates on boats. The reason for the increase was not a rise in crime but the fact that more detainees were being held for longer periods of time. Judges and other officials were worried about being seen as "soft" on crime. Yet getting tough only brought more problems. The jails became so overcrowded that in 1983 a federal court imposed a cap on the population in the House of Detention for Men on Rikers Island. Another reduction was ordered by the courts in 1987. The immediate result was the release of 611 pretrial detainees. A similar kind of "forced release" occurs in many state prisons. Seventeen states have emergency release laws that place a cap on prison populations and mandate release of some current inmates before new ones can be admitted. This practice raises an obvious question: If these people can be released so suddenly, why were they being held in the first place? Overcrowding only aggravates the already terrible conditions in the jails. Robert Gangi, director of the Correctional Association of New York, points out that thirty-five violent incidents are reported each day in the New York jails (and probably many more are unreported). Finally, the cost of this heavy use of incarceration is frightful. The Correctional Association estimates that the cost of constructing a jail cell in New York City is $71,000 and that the cost of operating it is $40,000 a year. Thus 2,000 more jail inmates would cost the city $142 million to construct facilities to hold them and $80 million to operate them.[27]

The Rand Corporation, taking into account the cost-based criticism of incapacitation, promised to reduce crime and reduce prison populations. It would achieve this two-pronged goal by balancing longer prison terms for high-risk offenders with shorter terms, or no prison sentences at all, for low-risk offenders. The report projects a 5 percent reduction in the prison population because the "savings" in terms of low-risk offenders will exceed the added costs of locking up high-risk offenders for longer terms. These savings are to be achieved through one of three sentencing strategies: (1) sentencing all low-risk offenders to county jails rather than state prisons, (2) sentencing low-risk offenders to jail and cutting prison terms for medium-risk offenders in half, and (3) sentencing both low- and medium-risk offenders to jail.[28]

Perhaps the most remarkable aspect of this "savings" approach is that it is precisely what liberal prison-reform advocates have been proposing for years. The National Council on Crime and Delinquency, the National Moratorium on Prison Construction, Alvin Bronstein of the National Prison

Project of the American Civil Liberties Union, and many other experts have long maintained that we lock up many people unnecessarily. Many observers believe that at least 30 percent of our current inmates are not dangerous. They committed property offenses and do not represent a threat to life and limb. The main objective of liberal proposals for prison reform has been the development of nonprison alternatives for such offenders.[29]

Three flaws—political, technical, and financial—can be discerned in the Rand Corporation's estimated "savings." The political problem, as I have suggested, is that at the moment there is no political support for the idea of getting people *out* of prison. This political problem has two aspects. First, judges are simply reluctant to exempt certain offenders from prison. Keep in mind that the Rand approach calls for a change in current sentencing practices. Somehow, judges would have to be convinced that it is safe to do something different with convicted criminals they are accustomed to sending to prison. In the present climate few judges are likely to take this step. Much of the recent increase in prison populations can be traced to the fact that judges are sending to prison some offenders who previously would have gotten probation. Second, sentencing alternatives would have to be created. Yet, despite years of work, liberal prison reformers have not been able to garner support for such alternatives.

If alternatives were created, there is good reason to expect that they would not produce the anticipated reductions in the number of prisoners. On the contrary, their numbers might increase on account of the so-called expanding-net syndrome. The availability of less severe alternatives does not reduce the severity of sentences. Instead, new and less restrictive alternatives are applied to very low-risk people who are not now subjected to any punishment at all. Rather than having their cases dismissed, or receiving probation or a suspended sentence, these people are sentenced to the new "less drastic" treatment programs. Thus more people are brought into the system and the punishment net expands. It is likely that this problem would afflict the Rand proposal. Judges would indeed sentence the high-risk offenders to longer terms and maintain their current practices with respect to low- and medium-risk offenders. The projected savings would not be achieved.

The technical problem with the projected "savings" is simply another aspect of the prediction problem. The policy assumes that we can correctly identify the low-risk offenders, who will then receive alternatives to prison. The difficulties of identifying them are exactly the same as those of identifying the high-risk offenders. In practice, we could not fine-tune the system to be precise in either respect.

The final problem with selective incapacitation is a financial/administrative one. Here the Rand report engages in sleight of hand. The "savings" are to be achieved by the sentencing of low- and possible medium-risk offenders to jail rather than prison. They are simply to be incarcerated in a different place, although admittedly for shorter periods of time. Yet many of our jails are already overcrowded. Also, the cost of providing sufficient jail cells is the same as the cost of building additional prison cells. So there are really no dollar savings at all. Moreover, corrections experts agree that jails are not designed for long-term incarceration. Few have even the minimal level of recreational, educational, or vocational programs. The staffs of most jails are altogether unprepared to treat mental and physical problems. Shifting 30 percent of our current prison inmates to local jails would only aggravate the already serious conditions in jails.

Due-Process Problems

Perhaps the most shocking aspect of the Rand *Selective Incapacitation* report is the use of employment history as a criterion for sentencing. An offender would acquire one point for having been unemployed for more than half of the two preceding years. On the seven-point scale, unemployment is as serious as a prior conviction for the present offense or as incarceration for more than half of the two preceding years. Under the proposed Rand formula, each point carries major consequences. A second point, for example, transforms the person from a low-risk to a medium-risk offender and thus means the difference between jail and prison.

It is outrageous that anyone should seriously recommend the imposition of criminal penalties for unemployment. But that is precisely what the Rand formula does. The policy would take us back two hundred years, to the days of imprisonment for debt. Fortunately, we are not likely to be called upon to endure this policy. In every legislature voices would be raised to point out the reactionary nature of this idea and vigorously oppose it. Even many law-and-order conservatives would hesitate to criminalize unemployment. And even if such a policy were to become practice somewhere, it would immediately be challenged in court. It is safe to say that most lower federal courts would throw such a case out on due-process grounds (current case law already forbids the criminalization of such conditions as vagrancy, drug addiction, and chronic alcoholism), and even the current Supreme Court is likely to agree.

Before we leave this issue, let me emphasize that the assignment of a point for unemployment was not an arbitrary decision by the Rand experts. Their sophisticated analyses determined that unemployment was one of only seven factors that were highly correlated with future criminal behavior. Take any one of those seven away and the entire formula begins to crumble; that is, their "success" rate would fall below the 51 percent they currently propose. They would then be doing no better than judges currently do, using a combination of presentence investigations and pure hunch.

The Rand data are undoubtedly correct: unemployment is highly correlated with criminal activity. The way to deal with that problem—the rational, effective, and humane way—is to provide employment.

Unforeseen Consequences

We now come to a final problem that probably would undermine the selective-incapacitation policy. A substantial alteration to current sentencing practices would disrupt the operations of our criminal courts. Modifying the sentences for one group of offenders would unsettle the established "going rate." Recall that the hypothetical mandatory five-year prison term discussed by Van Dine, Conrad, and Dinitz is way out of line with current practice. This new policy would send shock waves through the courtroom work group. After all, most convictions for burglary and virtually all of those for theft result in probation. Suddenly the "price" of these convictions would rise astronomically.[30]

The system would not "break down" or "collapse," as some alarmists predict. Instead, the courtroom work group would simply adapt. The most likely result would be a new set of rules for plea bargaining. Prosecutors would be under great pressure to dismiss charges or reduce them to misdemeanors (anything, in other words, to avoid the terribly penalizing effect of a felony conviction), especially for first offenders. This downward pressure would undermine the ultimate effect of the policy. Many people who would have received felony convictions in the past would no longer get them. In short, a policy designed to "get tough" would produce the opposite effect.

One of the most significant consequences is not unforeseen at all but has become a matter of public policy. At least seventeen states have passed emergency (or "safety valve") laws to deal with prison overcrowding. These laws place a cap on prison populations and mandate early release of current prisoners before new ones can be admitted. Inmates' parole dates are moved forward so that they can be released early. (The same result occurs when judges order limits on prison populations, as happened with the New York City jails.) This approach successfully manages the prison population but of course completely undermines the purpose of incarceration. Suddenly to grant early release to a prisoner is to make a mockery of the goals of incapacitation, deterrence, and punishment.[31]

In the end, incapacitation does not offer a solution to our crime problem. Gross incapacitation is financially and politically prohibitive. The more refined policy of selective incapacitation is subject to a number of technical problems and may not be significantly better than current practice. Van Dine, Conrad, and Dinitz, in a report that is extremely critical of incapacitation, do concede that "if there is a case to be made for incapacitation as a goal for the criminal justice system, then the strongest case can be made for robbery." Robbery is indeed a violent crime, and even most prison reformers agree that it merits imprisonment. Robbers also have very high rates of recidivism. Yet the fact is that we already practice selective incapacitation with armed robbers who have prior records. Most go to prison and are sentenced to rather long terms. Much of the rhetoric about incapacitation merely describes current practice. As a new policy designed to reduce crime, incapacitation has little to offer. In fact, the advocates of incapacitation have retreated in the face of the mounting evidence that the idea is unworkable. Wilson loudly proclaimed a 30 percent reduction in crime in the first edition of *Thinking about Crime*. In the second edition, published eight years later, he backed away from any extravagant claims. Another recent study, *Dangerous Offenders*, also found the evidence so complex and ambiguous that its authors could not make a clear case for incapacitation as a crime-reduction strategy.[32] *Dangerous Offenders* can be read as the unintended obituary for the incapacitation movement. After conceding point after point to the critics in an intellectually responsible fashion, the author could no longer make any credible case for incapacitation.

Conservatives may reply by pointing to the reduction in crime since 1973—the same NCS figures I cited at the beginning of this book. Look! Hasn't increased imprisonment brought the crime rate down? It is true that crime rates have declined since the mid-1970s and that the prison population has increased dramatically. The cause-and-effect relationship, however, is not so obvious as it may seem to be. The crime rate was already declining before imprisonment rates began to increase significantly. The great increase in prison populations did not really begin until 1980. The real reason for the steady decline in the crime rate is one that experts were predicting all along: demography. According to some estimates, about half of the total crime increase in the 1960s was a product of the "baby boom," the disproportionate number of young men in the high-crime age group of 14 to 24 years. In the 1970s this group began to pass into the low-crime years. In fact, James Q. Wilson predicted this effect back in 1975. Demography, not imprisonment, is primarily responsible for the steady decline in the crime rate.

Mandatory Sentences

The third strategy for locking up more criminals is mandatory sentencing, which really means mandatory imprisonment. More than thirty states have adopted some form of mandatory sentencing in the past ten years. Its current popularity flows from the assumption that softhearted judges place too many dangerous criminals on probation, thereby undermining both the deterrent and incapacitative effects of the criminal sanction. Mandatory sentencing represents an effort to restrict the discretion of judges and eliminate probation as a sentencing option. It is an extremely popular reform because it appears to be a way for "the people," speaking through the legislature, to impose their will on an otherwise independent and uncontrollable judiciary. It appears to be a quick and direct solution to the crime problem.

My view, however, is that the remedial effects of mandatory sentencing are largely illusory. Not only are the "mandatory" aspects surprisingly easy to evade but the policy itself does not produce the anticipated deterrent or incapacitative effects.

PROPOSITION 9

Mandatory sentencing has no significant impact on serious crime.

The first issue to consider is whether the basic premise of mandatory sentencing is correct. Is it true that the system is basically weak and that dangerous criminals do not go to prison? The analysis in Part One of this book led to the conclusion that the system appears weak when we aggregate all felony cases. This is what the President's Crime Commission did, and it came up with the alarming statistic that only 1 percent of all criminals go to prison. When we disaggregate the data and focus on particular crimes, a very different picture emerges: we are quite punitive toward offenders who have committed violent crimes.

Most convicted robbers go to prison. The *INSLAW* data indicate that 91 percent of the convicted robbers in Indianapolis and New Orleans are imprisoned. Even Detroit, which incarcerates felons at a generally low rate, locks up 73 percent of its robbers. In Los Angeles the rate drops to 66 percent. Your response to these figures is a matter of interpretation. Are you reassured that 66 percent are imprisoned or outraged that 34 percent are not?[33]

Sentencing Reform: Sorting Out the Options

Criminal sentencing in the United States is a terribly complex and confusing subject. The fifty-one separate jurisdictions have fifty-one different sentencing systems. A criminal sentence includes three separate components: the options open to the sentencing judge; provisions for reducing the sentence through "good time"; and parole release. Moreover, many states have special provisions for particular offenses.

Sentencing reform is no less complex, since it usually involves manipulation of one or more of the three basic components for one or more types of crime. Even the term "mandatory" has a variety of meanings when it is applied to sentencing. To bring some order out of this confusion, let us establish some general definitions.

"Mandatory sentencing" can mean either of two things: (1) mandatory imprisonment, which eliminates probation and suspended sentences as a sentencing option, and (2) a mandatory minimum sentence, so that the offender must serve a certain number of years in prison before becoming eligible for release. Confusion arises from the way these two provisions are combined and/or modified by other provisions. "Mandatory" can mean different things. You can have mandatory imprisonment without any control over the minimum. Accordingly, the convicted offender might be sentenced to only a one-year term and then have the year reduced in ten months (or

"This court would like to remind the defendant that there is a distinct difference between
plea bargaining and begging."

less) through good time. Or state law can establish mandatory minimums
without necessarily requiring imprisonment in the first place. Thus offenders are subject to the minimum only if they are sentenced to prison. Even if
the judge does impose a prison sentence, the law may or may not control the
release date. Many of the new laws specify no parole, or no parole before a
certain minimum term is served. Other laws "mandate" a minimum term but
then allow for reduction of that minimum through good time.

The greatest weakness in all mandatory sentencing schemes is plea
bargaining.[34] Hardly any of the new laws address this critical point. The
loophole is both large and obvious. In a state that combines mandatory
imprisonment with a mandatory minimum sentence, those mandates apply
only if the offender is *convicted* of the relevant offense. This reality creates
intense pressure to plea-bargain a charge down to a lesser offense to which
the mandatory provisions do not apply. We shall see how this requirement is
evaded when we investigate the mandatory suspension or revocation of
drivers' licenses in Wisconsin. The Massachusetts gun-control law and the
New York drug law are among the few attempts to control plea bargaining.

Another loophole is found in the various habitual-criminal statutes.
Virtually every state has some form of habitual-criminal sentencing law.
Such laws typically provide for either mandatory imprisonment or a long
prison term for a second or third conviction. In most states, however, the
application of these provisions is not automatic. The prosecutor must file
habitual-criminal charges. In Nebraska, where the habitual-criminal pro-

vision can add ten to sixty years to the sentence upon a third conviction for a felony, prosecutors in Douglas County (Omaha) exercised this option in only 3.6 percent (three out of eighty-two) of the possible cases.[35] The frightening habitual-criminal provisions are generally a bargaining chip in the plea negotiations, used most often as a threat. The point here is that a habitual-criminal statute that promises to lock up criminals for a long period of time may offer more illusion than reality.

Flat-Time, Determinate, and Presumptive Sentencing

In the early 1970s sentencing reform was the hottest fad in criminal justice. The movement to establish systems of "determinate," "flat-time," or "presumptive" sentencing received wide support. There was, and still is, a great deal of confusion over these approaches. They are not all the same. They are not necessarily the same things as "mandatory" sentencing, although some have mandatory elements. In theory, "flat-time" and "determinate" sentencing involve a formula whereby a particular crime carries a fixed single sentence; for example, the sentence for robbery might be five years. This approach eliminates both the judge's discretion to choose the exact number of years and the parole board's discretion to release the offender. Some proposed plans have involved the elimination of sentence reductions for good time. "Presumptive" sentencing is a plan that permits the judge to choose the sentence from a narrow and specific range of options. The present California law is a presumptive system despite the fact that it is officially labeled "determinate." The federal sentencing guidelines that went into effect in November 1987 are also a form of presumptive sentencing.

The Impact of Mandatory Sentencing

Despite its popularity, there is no evidence that mandatory sentencing reduces crime. A report by the Justice Department concluded that "It is difficult, perhaps fundamentally impossible, to substantiate the popular claim that mandatory sentencing is an effective tool for reducing crime."[36] The wording of this statement is appropriately cautious. It may be impossible to ascertain the effects of various sentencing practices *one way or the other.* So many factors affect criminal behavior that we may never be able to isolate the effect of only one small element: criminal sentences. We will again encounter the problem of determining effectiveness when we consider the question of the deterrent effect of capital punishment.

The Justice Department report was based on an evaluation of two of the most widely publicized mandatory sentencing innovations of the 1970s: the 1973 New York drug law and the 1976 Massachusetts gun-control law (they will come up again in our discussion of gun-control strategies). Both of these laws have been closely evaluated. Let us look at the evidence.

"The nation's toughest drug law"   In 1973 Governor Nelson Rockefeller sponsored a revision of the New York criminal code designed to deter and incapacitate dealers in hard drugs. Because its new sentencing provisions were so draconian, it quickly became known as "the nation's toughest drug law." The law contained three major provisions of interest to us here: mandatory and long prison terms for heroin dealers, restrictions on plea bargaining for heroin dealers, and mandatory prison terms for certain categories of repeat offenders.

The prescribed prison terms were truly awesome. The law established three categories of heroin dealers:

1. Class A-I included major dealers, defined as people who either sold one ounce of heroin or possessed two ounces. The law mandated minimum prison terms of fifteen or twenty-five years and a maximum of life imprisonment for offenders in this class.
2. Class A-II included middle-level dealers, defined as those who sold one-eighth of an ounce of heroin or possessed one to two ounces. The law mandated prison terms of at least six to eight and one-third years and a maximum of life for offenders in class A-II.
3. Class A-III included minor or "street" dealers, defined as those who sold less than one-eighth of an ounce of heroin or possessed up to one ounce. The law mandated prison terms of at least one to eight and one-third years and a maximum of life for these offenders.

In short, anyone caught selling heroin would definitely go to prison and would face the possibility of life imprisonment.

The law also sought to close the plea-bargaining loophole. Arrested persons in either of the two highest categories (A-I or A-II) could plead guilty to an A-III charge, but people originally charged with an A-III offense could not plead to anything lower. Thus the law established a "floor" on plea bargaining designed to preserve the threats of both mandatory imprisonment and a potential life term. Finally, the law included a habitual-criminal provision, imposing mandatory prison terms on convicted felons who had a prior felony conviction. (Although we focus here on the 1973 drug law, we should note that New York added mandatory minimum sentences for certain crimes in 1978 and for handgun-related crimes in 1980.) To cope with the anticipated increase in the criminal courts' work load as a result of the law, New York added forty-nine new judges, thirty-one of them in New York City.

Despite the combination of harsh sentences and the enormous publicity surrounding its implementation, the law had little if any effect on the crime rate. Its impact has been examined from several angles:

1. Drug use: heroin use in New York City was as widespread in 1976 as it had been in 1973.
2. Crime: serious property crime, the kind generally associated with

heroin users, increased sharply (15 percent) between 1973 and 1975. Neighboring states had similar increases, an indication that New York was not unique.

3. Recidivism: the law did not appear to deter convicted felons from committing additional crimes.

A rigorous evaluation concluded that "the threat embodied in the words of the law proved to have teeth for relatively few offenders."[57]

What happened? Why did such a tough law have so little effect? The answer is that deterrence and incapacitation are wonderful in theory but do not necessarily work in the real world. As the evaluation of the New York drug law concluded, "mandatory sentencing laws directly affect only an end product of a long criminal justice process—the convicted offender."[38] The 1973 drug law did have some impact, but often the effect in one area was offset by the effect in another.

Following an arrest, three key decision points affect the outcome of the case: indictment, conviction, and sentence. If the law is to have either a deterrent or an incapacitative effect, there can be no serious "slippage" or "leakage" (attrition of cases) along the way. In New York there was considerable leakage. Between 1972 and 1976 the percentage of drug arrests that led to indictment declined from 39 percent to 25 percent. At the same time the percentage of indictments that resulted in a conviction fell from 86 percent to 80 percent. Thus, though 33.5 percent of all drug arrests in 1972–1973 led to conviction, only 20 percent did so in 1976. To put it another way, the conviction rate for drug offenses declined by one-third, thereby seriously undermining the intended effect of the law.

The rate of incarceration did go up under the new law and more long prison terms were imposed. By 1976, 55 percent of the convicted offenders went to prison (it seems that some loopholes in the "mandatory" sentencing provision remained), compared with only 33 percent in 1972–1973. Meanwhile, the percentage of convicted offenders who received a sentence of three years or longer rose from 3 percent of all those convicted to 22 percent. Judges imposed harsher sentences under the new law but they had only two-thirds as many convicted offenders to deal with. How do we explain the leakage between arrest and conviction?

The answer lies in the thermodynamics of the criminal justice process. As we have already noted, an increase in the severity of the potential punishment creates pressure to avoid its actual application. The new restriction on plea bargaining did not cause the system to collapse, but it had a noticeable impact on the normal order of business. Before 1973, only 6 percent of all defendants demanded trials; after the new law went into effect, 15 percent—two and a half times as many—went to trial. Since a tried case takes fifteen times as long to process as a nontried case, the addition of even a few trials significantly disrupts the process. As a result, disposition time for all drug cases doubled under the new law—despite the addition of the new judgeships (and for some unexplained reason the new courts were noticeably less efficient than previously established courts).

As the new law raised the stakes for drug defendants and their attorneys, they raised the stakes for the prosecution. Drug cases took twice as long and there were two and a half times as many trials. Prosecutors responded by reducing their own work load. They indicted only 25 percent of drug arrestees, rather than the 39 percent they had indicted under the old law. They were still able to convict a high percentage of the indicted defendants, but the percentage did drop slightly, from 86 percent to 80 percent.

In the end, little changed. In 1972–1973, 11 percent of the people arrested for sale or possession of heroin went to prison. In 1976 the figure was still 11 percent. By a series of minor adjustments the courtroom work group accommodated itself to a nominal change in the going rate. True, offenders who were convicted suffered harsher punishment, but much of the intended effect of the law was mitigated.

The net effect on drug use and crime in New York was nonexistent. Drug dealers were more cautious for a time after September 1, 1973, the day the law went into effect, but they soon returned to their normal routines.[39] The publicity that accompanies a "crackdown" on crime often produces what criminologists term the "announcement effect." But it soon vanishes.

Getting tough with drugs in New York did not reduce drug use or drug-related crime. Punishment became more severe but only for the same small percentage of arrested persons who were actually convicted. The mandatory provisions of the 1973 New York drug law did not produce the anticipated deterrent or incapacitative effects. The legislature itself had serious second thoughts and revised the law twice. In 1976 it relaxed some of the plea-bargaining restrictions, and then in 1979 it virtually abolished the special features of the law altogether.

The Massachusetts gun-control law   The 1975 Massachusetts gun-control law, popularly known as the Bartley-Fox law, mandated a one-year prison term for anyone who carried a firearm outside his or her home without the necessary permit. The law permitted no plea bargaining, no probation, and no parole. In the words of the accompanying publicity campaign, "If you are caught with a gun, you will go to prison for a year and nobody can get you out."

Bartley-Fox has been evaluated as closely as any sentencing law. It is an experiment in both mandatory sentencing and gun control. The law is designed to control crime by a secondary effect. It does not restrict the supply or ownership of guns but does influence their use, specifically affecting the decision to carry a gun outside the home. Substantial evidence indicates that many violent crimes are spontaneous, unplanned events. The offender does not leave home planning to commit a murder, robbery, or assault.[40] The presence of a gun, however, may embolden the individual to commit a crime or may transform a lesser crime into a major one (for example, turn an unarmed assault into an armed assault with serious injury, or turn an assault into a homicide).

The evidence suggests that crime patterns did change in Massachusetts between 1974 and 1976. Whether those effects were the result of Bartley-Fox is less clear. Here we confront one of the basic problems in efforts to evaluate criminal justice policies. Human behavior, including criminal behavior, is affected by many factors. Crime rates fluctuate. Individual behavior changes. It is difficult and perhaps impossible to determine with any scientific precision that a given change was the result of a specific modification of one particular criminal justice policy. Bartley-Fox illustrates this phenomenon.[41]

The law apparently had some effect on armed assaults. In Boston, gun assaults declined by 13.5 percent between 1974 and 1975 and by 11.7 percent between 1974 and 1976—more than in nine of the thirteen comparable jurisdictions. But four jurisdictions experienced greater reductions than Boston's. In the absence of a new gun law, armed assaults went down by 21.3 percent in Philadelphia and 26 percent in Chicago over the two-year period. The decline in gun assaults in Boston was paralleled by a sharp rise in assaults by people armed with weapons other than guns. An increase of 40.4 percent in such assaults between 1974 and 1976 suggests that people simply shifted to different weapons. A "substitution effect" may have been operating as a result of Bartley-Fox.

Gun robberies declined by a substantial 35.5 percent between 1974 and 1976 in Boston, while nongun armed robberies went up slightly. Again, however, we face the problem of determining the precise cause of these changes. During the same two-year period, gun robberies declined even more in Chicago (43.5 percent) and Philadelphia (36.7 percent) and almost as much in Baltimore (30 percent).

A similar pattern appears with respect to murder. Gun murders went down a whopping 55.7 percent between 1974 and 1976 in Boston, but this decline was part of a general trend across the country. While none of the comparison cities enjoyed reductions as great as Boston's, all had fewer gun murders and several experienced reductions between 30 percent and 45 percent.

Several thorough and cautious evaluations have concluded that, despite the ambiguity of the data, Bartley-Fox did have some impact on gun-related crime. How and why it occurred is difficult to say. Publicity may have played a major role. Gun crimes began to decline in the months just before the law took effect. Evaluations of other experiments have found evidence of the "announcement effect" before a new law or policy had taken effect.

Additional evidence suggests that criminal justice officials adjusted to the "mandatory" provisions of the new law in such a way as to undermine their consequences. Police officers became a little more circumspect about whom they frisked for guns. Seventy of the seventy-nine officers interviewed admitted being more selective under the new law. As they explained, they did not want to involve "otherwise innocent" persons by catching them with illegal guns. The term "otherwise innocent" is fascinating. It means that police officers make moral distinctions between "real criminals" and "law-abiding" people, judging that the latter do not really deserve to be punished even if they happen to violate the letter of some law. The police officer who does not frisk a suspect will not find a gun, and the suspect is saved the embarrassment of arrest. Because of the greater restraint by police officers, the number of police reports on gun incidents in Boston declined by 25 percent between 1974 and 1976.[42]

Meanwhile, people who were arrested under Bartley-Fox fared better than similar defendants had done beforehand. The percentage of cases dismissed went from 18 percent in 1974 to 38 percent in 1976 (the law imposed no restriction on outright dismissal of charges). Acquittals in the remaining cases increased from 16 percent in 1974 to 40 percent in 1975 and 33 percent in 1976. Finally, the number of people who appealed their convictions soared. Only 21 percent of gun cases were appealed in 1974 but 94 percent were appealed in 1976. The appeal rate undoubtedly had some effect on the willingness of prosecutors to drop cases at some earlier stage.

The net effect of these actions was that far fewer people were sentenced for carrying a gun. The percentage of defendants actually sentenced dropped by more than half, from 41 percent of all defendants in 1974 to only 17 percent in 1976. The pressure against punishment was even greater under Bartley-Fox than under the New York drug law.

A Final Comment

In the second edition of *Thinking about Crime*, James Q. Wilson wrote that he was still convinced of the deterrent effect of mandatory sentencing. The problem, he says, is that it has never really been tried.[43] Citing the New York drug law, he points out how officials undermined its intended effect. If we would only give mandatory sentencing a genuine test, he intimates, we might find that it deterred crime. He completely misses the point. Experience indicates that any significant alteration of the prescribed penalties disrupts the established going rate and the members of the courtroom work group adjust their actions to offset the new rules. Experience also suggests that we can do little to control the resulting leakage. Wilson's complaint about mandatory sentencing is identical to the argument often heard from liberals in regard to rehabilitation: that it hasn't really been tried, and gee whiz, it will work if you "just give us one more chance." This response ignores the point that rehabilitation may be inherently unworkable in a prison setting. Wilson, for his part, ignores the possibility that it is inherently unfeasible to dictate a substantial increase in the penalties imposed on criminals.

Notes

1. U. S. Department of Justice, Attorney General's Task Force on Violent Crime *Final Report* (Washington, D. C.: U. S. Government Printing Office, 1981); President's Task Force on Victims of Crime, *Report* (Washington, D. C.: U. S. Government Printing Office, 1982), p. 17.

2. Wayne H. Thomas, *Bail Reform in America* (Berkeley: University of California Press, 1976).

3. Ibid.

4. John S. Goldkamp, "Philadelphia Revisited: An Examination of Bail and Detention Two Decades after *Foote*," *Crime and Delinquency* 26 (April 1980): 179–192.

5. United States v. Salerno, 481 U. S. ____, 95 L ed. 2d 697, 107 S. Ct. ____ (1987). John S. Goldkamp, "Danger and Detention: A Second Generation of Bail Reform," *Journal of Criminal Law and Criminology* 76 (Spring 1985): 1–74.

6. Thomas, *Bail Reform in America*, pp. 231–232.

7. James Eisenstein and Herbert Jacob, *Felony Justice* (Boston: Little, Brown, 1977), p. 200.

8. Frederic Suffett, "Bail Setting: A Study of Courtroom Interaction," *Crime and Delinquency* 12 (1966): 318–331.

9. *New York Times*, May 27, 1987.

10. Thomas, *Bail Reform in America*, chap. 20.

11. Ibid., p. 237.

12. "Preventive Detention: An Empirical Analysis," *Harvard Civil Rights–Civil Liberties Review* 6 (March 1971): 289–396.

13. Thomas, *Bail Reform in America*, pp. 239–240.

14. Malcolm M. Feeley, *Court Reform on Trial* (New York: Basic Books, 1983), pp. 156–180.

15. James Q. Wilson, *Thinking about Crime* (New York: Basic Books, 1975), pp. 200–202; Shlomo Shinnar and Reuel Shinnar, "The Effect of the Criminal Justice System on the Control of Crime: A Quantitative Approach," *Law and Society Review* 9 (1975): 581–611. We should note that in the revised edition of *Thinking about Crime* (1983) Wilson is much more cautious in his discussion of the probable effect of incapacitation.

16. Peter W. Greenwood, *Selective Incapacitation* (Santa Monica, Calif.: Rand Corporation, 1982).

17. Ibid., p. 94.

18. David F. Greenberg, "The Incapacitative Effect of Imprisonment: Some Estimates," *Law and Society Review*, 9 (1975): 541–580. Stephen Van Dine, John Conrad, and Simon Dinitz, *Restraining the Wicked* (Lexington: Lexington Books, 1979).

19. Alfred Blumstein, Jacqueline Cohen, Jeffrey A. Roth, and Christy A. Visher, eds., *Criminal Careers and "Career Criminals"* (Washington, D. C.: National Academy of Sciences, 1986). The conflicting evidence is also reviewed in the revised edition of James Q. Wilson, *Thinking about Crime* (New York: Basic Books, 1983), pp. 147–151.

20. Greenwood, *Selective Incapacitation*, p. 44.

21. John Monahan, "The Prediction of Violent Criminal Behavior: A Methodological Critique and Prospectus," in *Deterrence and Incapacitation: Estimating the Effects of Criminal Sanctions on Crime Rates,* ed. Alfred Blumstein, Jacqueline Cohen, and Daniel Nagin (Washington, D. C.: National Academy of Sciences, 1978), pp. 244–269.

22. Norval Morris and Marc Miller, "Predictions of Dangerousness," in *Crime and Justice: An Annual Review of Research* vol. 6, ed. Michael H. Tonry and Norval Morris (Chicago: University of Chicago Press, 1985), pp. 1–50.

23. Ernst A. Wenk, James O Robison, and Gerald W. Smith, "Can Violence Be Predicted?" *Crime and Delinquency* 18 (October 1972): 393–402.

24. Van Dine et al., *Restraining the Wicked;* Greenberg, "Incapacitative Effect of Imprisonment."

25. National Moratorium on Prison Construction, *A Perspective on Crime and Imprisonment* (Washington, D. C., November 1975); Michael Sherman and Gordon Hawkins, *Imprisonment in America: Choosing the Future* (Chicago: University of Chicago Press, 1981), pp. 58–73.

26. *Jericho,* no. 31 (Spring 1983), p. 12; Joan Mullen and Bradford Smith, *American Prisons and Jails,* vol. 3, *Conditions and Costs of Confinement* (Washington, D. C.: U. S. Government Printing Office, 1980).

27. Diane Steelman, *New York City Jail Crisis: Causes, Costs, and Solutions* (New York: Correctional Association of New York, 1984); Robert Gangi, "The Jail Bomb Ticks Louder and Louder," *New York Times,* May 9, 1987.

28. Greenwood, *Selective Incapacitation.*

29. National Council on Crime and Delinquency, "The Nondangerous Offender Should Not Be Imprisoned: A Policy Statement," *Crime and Delinquency* 19, no. 4 (1973).

30. Jacqueline Cohen, "The Incapacitative Effect of Imprisonment: A Critical Review of the Literature," in *Deterrence and Incapacitation,* ed. Blumstein et al., pp. 216–218.

31. Edward E. Rhine, "Prison Overcrowding Emergency Powers Act: A Policy Quandary for Corrections," Cited in *Jericho* (Fall 1987), 12.

32. Van Dine et al., *Restraining the Wicked,* p. 97; Wilson, *Thinking about Crime* (1975), p. 201; Mark H. Moore et al., *Dangerous Offenders* (Cambridge: Harvard University Press, 1984).

33. Some studies have reported an even lower imprisonment rate for robbers in California. The problem arises from the practice of "split sentences," whereby the convicted offender spends some time in jail and then is placed on probation. Technically, the offender does not go to prison. If we count only prison sentences, we come up with a relatively low percentage. But if we combine jail and prison sentences, we get a much higher incarceration rate.

34. Albert W. Alschuler, "Sentencing Reform and Prosecutorial Power: A Critique of Recent Proposals for 'Fixed' and 'Presumptive' Sentencing," in U. S. Department of Justice, *Determining Sentencing: Reform or Regression?* (Washington, D. C.: U. S. Government Printing Office, 1978).

35. William J. Cook, "The 'Bitch' Threatens, but Seldom Bites," *Creighton Law Review* 8 (July 1975):893–919.

36. U. S. Department of Justice, *Mandatory Sentencing: The Experience of Two States,* Policy Brief (Washington, D. C.: U. S. Government Printing Office, 1982).

37. U. S. Department of Justice, *The Nation's Toughest Drug Law: Evaluating the*

New York Experience (Washington, D. C.: U. S. Government Printing Office, 1978, p. 18.

38. Ibid., p. 13.

39. Ibid., p. 8.

40. Joan Petersilia, Peter W. Greenwood, and Martin Lavin, *Criminal Careers of Habitual Felons* (Washington, D. C.: U. S. Government Printing Office, 1978), p. 63.

41. Glenn L. Pierce and William J. Bowers, "The Bartley-Fox Gun Law's Short-Term Impact on Crime," *The Annals* 455 (May 1981): 120–137.

42. U. S. Department of Justice, *Mandatory Sentencing*, p. 6.

43. Wilson, *Thinking about Crime* (1983), pp. 117–144.

Chapter 6

Deterrence

Deterrence is an article of faith among conservatives: if penalties were only swift, certain, and severe enough, we would have less crime. In this section we look at two policies designed to reduce crime. After examining the death penalty we will turn our attention to drunk driving. Although drunk driving is technically outside the scope of our inquiry into burglary and robbery, it merits our attention because campaigns against it illuminate the deterrence issue.

The Death Penalty: Sorting Out the Issues

No issue in criminal justice better reflects the tension between facts and faith than capital punishment. For the simple reason that it is literally a life-and-death matter, the death penalty arouses intense emotion. On one side are people convinced that execution is a morally justified punishment and an effective deterrent to criminals. On the other are those equally firm in their belief that it is both morally abhorrent and ineffective in controlling crime.

The death penalty can be debated in terms of three issues, separately or in combination. First, there is the question of the morality of capital punishment. The arguments here are as old as recorded civilization. A second and much more recent issue is the constitutionality of executions. The constitutional attack on the death penalty is barely twenty years old. In the 1972 *Furman* decision, the Supreme Court rejected the argument that executions are inherently "cruel and unusual" but did rule that they were administered in an unconstitutionally arbitrary and capricious fashion. Four years later, in *Gregg* v. *Georgia*, the Court upheld the constitutionality of the death penalty in jurisdictions where the sentencing statute circumscribes the discretion of judges. The third issue is a purely practical one: does capital punishment deter people from committing crimes?

Only the final issue concerns us here. Capital punishment occupies a prominent position on the conservative crime control agenda. For many people its deterrent effect is a matter of passionately held faith. For others it is a matter of fact. We shall review the recent evidence on deterrence. The debate over capital punishment is of course but one part of a broader revival of interest in deterrence as a crime control strategy.[1]

Our minimal attention to the first two issues does not mean they are unimportant. Indeed, they are vitally important and are worthy of extended discussion. The focus of this inquiry, however, is the control of serious crime, and it is to maintain that focus that we concentrate on the deterrence question.

Executions: Opinion and Practice

The dramatic shifts both in public opinion on capital punishment and in its practice provide the context for any serious discussion of the issue. The attitudes of Americans toward the death penalty have shifted twice in the past thirty years (see figure 6.1). In the early 1950s, 68 percent of Americans supported capital punishment. Thereafter support declined steadily to a low of 42 percent in 1966. Attitudes then reversed and support rose to its present level of 72 percent. These wide swings on such an important issue in a relatively short time are certainly remarkable. They suggest that attitudes are highly volatile and that the present high level of support may not be so firm as it seems.[2]

The rise in support for the death penalty in the late 1960s is not hard to explain. Public opinion shifted because of increased crime, riots, protests against the war in Vietnam, the increase in the use of drugs, and the emergence of a youth counterculture. "Law and order" became the most salient issue in the 1968 elections. By itself, the increase in violent crime could have provoked a change in attitudes toward capital punishment. The upturn in crime occurred in 1962–1963, and if we allow for a reasonable time lag, we could expect the effect to be felt by the late 1960s. In the context of that turbulent decade, crime became intertwined with the other social issues.[3]

When opposition to the death penalty reached its peak in the mid-1960s, it followed a massive legal attack on the death penalty waged by civil rights groups. This campaign resulted in a de facto moratorium on executions. No one was executed in the United States between 1967 and 1977. The moratorium happened to coincide with the increase in violent crime in the 1960s, and this circumstance led many people to conclude that the absence of executions "caused" the increase in crime. And as we shall see, a number of sophisticated analysts have attempted to document that causal relationship.

Question: "Are you in favor of the death penalty for persons convicted of murder?"

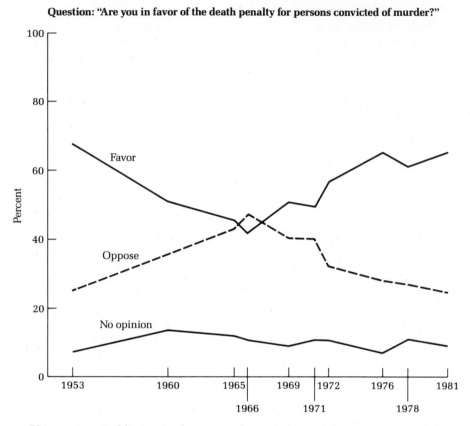

Figure 6.1 Public attitudes toward capital punishment, 1953–1981. (George H. Gallup, *The Gallup Poll* [Princeton, N. J.: The Gallup Poll. March 1, 1981]. p. 3. Figure constructed by Sourcebook staff. Reprinted by permission.)

My position is:

─────────────────────────── **PROPOSITION 10** ───────────────────────────
The death penalty does not deter criminals.

Dr. Ehrlich's Magic Bullet

The enfant terrible of deterrence theory is the economist Isaac Ehrlich. In 1975 he concluded that each execution prevented seven or eight murders.[4] This startling argument fell on extremely receptive ears in a nation that was increasingly frustrated by the crime problem. That responsive audience included a majority of the justices of the U. S. Supreme Court, who cited Ehrlich's evidence in their 1976 *Gregg* decision upholding the constitutionality of the death penalty where standards were established to guide sentencing decisions.

Deterrence theory has been around for a long time. Earlier, however, it had been an essentially intuitive argument. Frank Zimring and Gordon Hawkins puncture many of the prevalent common-sense theories in their book *Deterrence*. No one had ever given it such impressive statistical support as Ehrlich. His 1975 article reflected two important recent developments in the study of criminal justice. One was the general revival of deterrence theory within the academic community in the 1970s, a shift that paralleled political trends. For decades it was not a respectable criminological theory. The second development was the advent of the economists on the criminological scene. Employing sophisticated econometric formulas, economists began to examine many aspects of crime and criminal justice, including capital punishment.

A specific theory of human behavior underpins the econometric tools employed by Ehrlich and his colleagues.[5] The utilitarian "individual choice" theory holds that people's actions will be guided by efforts to enhance their gains and minimize their losses (or pain). Wilson and Herrnstein provide the most elaborate statement of this theory in *Crime and Human Nature*.[6] Human behavior can be shaped by manipulation of the various costs and benefits. Ehrlich's operating assumption is that "the propensity to perpetrate such crimes is influenced by the prospective gains and losses associated with their commission."[7] (We will encounter this theory, and Ehrlich, again when we consider the relationship of crime and unemployment.) Ehrlich set out to measure whether or not the diminution of the "prospective losses" (that is, the declining chance of being executed) had had any effect on the murder rate.

Ehrlich employed a highly sophisticated formula, one that most participants in the death-penalty debate could not begin to understand. But Ehrlich was on the right track. A statistic such as the murder rate is influenced by a number of subtle variables. Before the effect of one of those variables— execution—can be isolated, the analyst must control for all others. In Ehrlich's formula, the homicide rate is the product of the probability of apprehension, the probability of conviction for murder given apprehension, the probability of execution given conviction, the unemployment rate, the labor-force participation of adults, the real per capita income, and the proportion of the population between the ages of fourteen and twenty-four. The data covered the period from 1930 to 1969 (the period for which we have the most complete national figures on executions).

When Ehrlich finished crunching numbers, he concluded that each additional execution during this period might have resulted in seven or eight fewer homicides. In other words, he argued, capital punishment deters murderers by a factor of 8 to 1. Ehrlich's findings dominated the capital-punishment debate for a decade. The impressive weight of his numbers gives his argument a degree of power that has forced other analysts to respond.

"Used to be one of the top crime analysts until
a data error shot his theories to hell."

Measuring Deterrence

Ehrlich's great achievement is also his greatest weakness. The power of his
argument derives from the sophistication of his formula. Yet the more
sophisticated the formula, the more sensitive it is to such basic problems as
the reliability of the data, the precise mathematical technique applied, and
the interpretation of the results. A relatively small problem with the data, for
example, easily becomes amplified into a very large discrepancy in the final
results. Other analysts have used Ehrlich's own technique and concluded
that capital punishment does not reduce crime.

The most direct challenge to Ehrlich's argument focuses on the data from
the 1960s. Brian Forst, Peter Passell, and William Bowers and Glenn Pierce
found that if you exclude the years 1962–1969 from the analysis, the
deterrent effect vanishes. In other words, Ehrlich's formula does not indicate
that capital punishment reduced crime in the years from 1930 to 1961. Why
not?[8]

We have to recall that the 1960s were a very special period in the history
of American criminal justice. Two significant events coincided to produce
an apparent deterrent effect for capital punishment: the dramatic rise in the
rate of violent crime beginning in 1962–1963 and the de facto moratorium
on executions beginning in 1967. With these years included, a deterrent
effect appears; without them there is none. Brian Forst and others have
sharply criticized Ehrlich for his failure to use the 1960 cross-sectional data.
Ehrlich's explanation is inadequate, and Forst argues that he tended to select
for analysis only those data that demonstrated a deterrent effect. Forst's own
analysis of the 1960–1970 period found that executions did not reduce the
number of homicides. This is a classic example of how to use and misuse

statistics: simply select a particular time period or data set that conclusively "proves" the point you want to make.[9]

Data problems The reliability of basic criminal justice data is a major problem for all concerned. As we have already seen (p. 14), the FBI's Uniform Crime Report data are unreliable because they do not measure unreported crime. We do not know if crimes were even less frequently reported in the 1950s or 1930s than they are today, but if that were the case, we would have to revise our understanding of the recent increase in crime. We also know that police departments do a much more thorough job of maintaining crime data now than they did in the past. The practical effect of this improvement is that many of the official data from the 1930s, 1940s, and 1950s seriously undercount the amount of crime. In New York City alone there are at least two well-documented episodes (one in 1955 and the other in 1965) in which administrative changes in the police department produced large "increases" in crime. In the spring of 1983 the Chicago Police Department was found to be undercounting a substantial number of crimes, including robberies.

The unreliability of the data on the amount of crime undermines several key elements of Ehrlich's formula. If the amount of crime is artificially low, the apprehension rate will seem to be higher than it is. In other words, the declining certainty of apprehension between the 1930s and the 1960s may be only a statistical artifact produced by a more accurate count of crimes committed. By the same token, the increase in crime over the same period may be in part an artifact rather than a genuine increase. The declining number of executions may have had nothing to do with this increase.

The simultaneity problem Even if our data were perfect we would encounter the simultaneity problem. In the real world (as opposed to the neat and tidy world of econometrics), many factors are operating simultaneously to affect human behavior. Even if we isolate only two of them—crime and punishment, for example—we cannot specify how they interact.

Deterrence theorists believe that punishment affects crime. But in the real world, crime affects punishment as well. A good argument can be made for the proposition that judges and parole boards got tougher on crime in the 1970s in response to public pressure to "do something" about crime. Data from California support this view.[10] Similarly, research on the police and crime indicates not that an increase in the number of police lowers the crime rate but that a rise in the crime rate increases the number of police hired. High crime rates generate political pressure for additional police resources. Alfred Blumstein and Jacqueline Cohen, for example, have suggested a "stability of punishment" theory. The criminal justice system has a relatively fixed capacity: police, prosecutors, judges, and prisons can handle only so much business. As the amount of crime goes up, punishments are scaled down (through more plea bargaining, shorter sentences, earlier parole, and so forth) in order to keep the level of punishment fairly stable.[11] (Our earlier discussion of the "going rate" phenomenon and the tactics used by local court systems to cope with scaled-up penalties fits this general view.)

The difficulty of identifying causality, as opposed to correlation, in the real world of crime and justice is a serious and possibly insuperable problem.

Deterrence Theory Challenged

The first attempts to research the deterrent effect of capital punishment were undertaken by Thorsten Sellin in the 1950s. Sellin compared contiguous states, one with and one without the death penalty. As table 6.1 indicates, his comparisons failed to reveal any evidence of a deterrent effect. Michigan, without the death penalty, did not have consistently higher murder rates than neighboring Ohio and Indiana, which had it. Moreover, murder rates in all three states changed in roughly the same direction (decreasing from the 1930s to the early 1960s and then rising sharply), suggesting that social factors other than the death penalty were the primary causal factors. A variation of this approach involves a time-series analysis of states that abolished or restored the death penalty. Kansas restored the death penalty in 1935, yet the trend displayed by its homicide rate was nearly identical to those in Missouri and Colorado, where the law had not changed.[12]

Sellin's research did not conclusively demonstrate the absence of a deterrent effect. Geographically contiguous states are not necessarily similar with respect to all the factors that may influence the homicide rate. Ehrlich's efforts to account for such variables is precisely what makes his research so significant. The use of regression analysis is designed to control for the influence of a wide range of variables, all of which we know may have some effect on crime. Unfortunately, the most sophisticated formula is not enough to overcome the host of problems related to data analysis.

A more recent challenge to deterrence theory argues that, far from preventing crime, capital punishment may actually encourage it. Bowers and Pierce advance what they call the "brutalization" theory. They estimate that there may be as many as two or three more homicides than normal in the month following an execution. They found in three California counties a "slight but discernible" increase in the number of murders in the ten days following an execution (0.25 per execution). In Philadelphia there was a greater increase (1.6 per execution) in homicides within two months after an execution. Bowers and Pierce contend that the effect is felt among a limited group of people who, independently, have "reached a state of 'readiness to kill,'" in the sense of having an intended victim already in mind. The legal execution conveys the message that vengeance is justified. Bowers and Pierce concede that "there is room to quarrel" with their analysis, but Brian Forst reached a similar conclusion in his study of deterrence. Examining the

Table 6.1 Homicide rates in death-penalty states (Ohio, Indiana) and in a non-death-penalty state (Michigan), 1920–1974 (homicides per 100,000 population)

Quinquennia	Michigan	Ohio		Indiana	
		Rates	Number of executions	Rates	Number of executions
1920–1924	5.5	7.4	45	6.1	5
1925–1929	8.2	8.4	40	6.6	7
1930–1934	5.6	8.5	43	6.5	11
1935–1939	3.9	5.9	29	4.5	22
1940–1944	3.2	4.3	15	3.0	2
1945–1949	3.5	4.8	36	3.8	5
1950–1954	3.8	3.8	20	3.7	2
1955–1959	3.0	3.4	12	3.0	0
1960–1964	3.6	3.2	7	3.2	1
1965–1969	6.6	5.1	0	4.7	0
1970–1974	11.3	7.8	0	6.4	0

NOTE: After 1949, homicides caused by police intervention and legal executions have been deducted before rates were computed.

SOURCE: National Office of Vital Statistics, *Vital Statistics of the United States;* William J. Bowers, *Executions in America* (Lexington, Mass.: D. C. Heath, 1974), appendix A; Thorsten Sellin, *The Penalty of Death* (Beverly Hills, Calif.: Sage, 1980), p. 144.

years 1960 through 1970, Forst found no evidence that executions prevented crime and some evidence that they actually "provoked" homicides.[13]

The safest conclusion one can draw from the available research is that the deterrence argument has not been proved. Supporters of the death penalty reply that the deterrent effect has been undermined by the long delays in executions. Persons sentenced to death understandably exercise their right to appeal. And with their lives at stake, obviously they explore every possible angle. As a result, years elapse before they are actually executed. By 1987 more than 1,500 people were on the nation's death rows. Some had been there since 1973 (that is, they were convicted under the post-*Furman* death-penalty laws). These delays infuriate death-penalty advocates. After all, deterrence theory rests on the assumption that there is a close connection between the crime and the punishment. The punishment must be swift and certain. Yet what is the alternative? To restrict the right of persons on death row to appeal their convictions would do violence to our basic standards of justice. We can't say that only some convicted persons can appeal only some aspects of their cases. Opponents of the death penalty argue that capital punishment only distorts the criminal justice process and imposes a high dollar cost on society. Of course people sentenced to death are going to explore every avenue of appeal. The appeals clog the courts for years. The cost of a trial that could result in the death penalty has been estimated at between $750,000 and $1,828,000—and that is just for the trial, which might not result in a guilty verdict or a death sentence! Then there are the costs of the appeal process (costs to the defense, the prosecution, and the courts). David Gottlieb of the University of Kansas Law School advised the

Kansas legislature that enactment of the death penalty would cost over $50 million before a single execution took place.[14]

Paradoxically, some death-penalty supporters are unhappy when executions do occur. Jim Mattox, attorney general of Texas, complained in 1987 that the death penalty was losing its deterrent effect because executions were becoming so routine! He proposed that executions be televised to increase their deterrent effect.[15]

The burden of proof lies with the advocates of capital punishment. They must show, as a matter of fact and not of faith, that executions reduce the level of serious crime. To date they have not done so.

Public debate can continue along two independent lines of inquiry. One involves a search for alternative strategies that might reduce crime. The other concerns the morality and constitutionality of capital punishment. That debate can and should continue.

Crackdown on Drunk Drivers

One of the major criminal justice efforts of the 1980s was a national campaign against drunk driving. Spurred by a wave of public outrage, virtually every state passed new laws, often several, to limit drinking and driving. Leading the crusade was a group called MADD (Mothers Against Drunk Driving), organized by Candi Lightner, whose thirteen-year-old daughter died in an automobile crash. The circumstances of that death go far toward explaining the public outcry against both the "killer drunk" and the apparent weakness of the criminal justice system in dealing with dangerously drunk drivers. The car that killed Cari Lightner was driven by a young man out on bail after a drunk-driving arrest; he had had two previous drunk-driving convictions. For Cari Lightner's death he went to prison, but he was paroled after nineteen months.

Drunk driving is outside the primary scope of our discussion of robbery and burglary, but it offers a useful illustration of the problems related to deterrence. The new laws fall into several categories. Every state except Wyoming raised the drinking age to twenty-one. Most states increased the severity of the penalties, in the form of longer jail or prison sentences. Many of the laws sought to close loopholes that permitted leniency by providing for mandatory sentences.

Approaches to Deterrence

The crackdown on drunk drivers is a classic exercise in deterrence. Virtually all of the new laws involve tougher penalties: mandatory jail or prison terms, mandatory license suspension, mandatory fines, and so on—often for first offenders. The highly publicized California law, for example, requires a minimum forty-eight-hour jail sentence along with a $375 fine and suspen-

"The good news: I gave the performance of my
life acting sober while driving past the highway patrol. The bad news: I don't think I'll win
an Academy Award for it."

sion of the driver's license for ninety days. The underlying assumption of all
the new laws is that people will be deterred from driving drunk by the threat
of mandatory and severe penalties. A further assumption is that the real
problem is pervasive leniency: drunk drivers get off too easily because
officials simply do not care about protecting the public. The new drunk-
driving laws represent an attempt to solve the problem by curbing discretion, mainly through mandatory penalties. In this respect the crackdown
closely resembles the efforts to get tough with career robbers and burglars.

Presumably it should be easier to deter the drunk driver than to deter the
robber or burglar. The threat of punishment should have more effect on
drunk drivers, many of whom are respectable middle- and upper-middle-
class people who have more to lose than the desperate lower-class robber.
Given the nature of the offense, moreover, the probability of detection and
arrest should be higher. Drunk driving is the least surreptitious of all crimes,
occurring on public thoroughfares over an extended period of time. Robbers
and burglars, on the other hand, make every effort to evade detection during
and after the commission of a crime.

Alas, deterring the drunk driver is no easier than deterring the chronic
robber. My position can be stated in three related propositions:

PROPOSITION 11a

Increasing the severity of punishment will have, by itself, no effect on drunk driving.

──────────────────────── **PROPOSITION 11b** ────────────────────────
Increasing the certainty of punishment will have little effect on drunk driving.

──────────────────────── **PROPOSITION 11c** ────────────────────────
Increasing the certainty of apprehension will have a short-term effect on drunk driving,
but that effect will disappear over the long term.

Crackdowns in Operation

Crackdowns on drunk driving are nothing new. There have been many highly publicized campaigns demanding tough treatment of drunk drivers. Most of the earlier efforts, however, were local. The remarkable aspect of the 1980s crusade was its national scope. Also, the earlier campaigns were usually short-lived and unsystematic. Only a few were carefully evaluated. In some respects it is easier to measure the extent of drunk driving than of other forms of criminal behavior because we have a reliable measure. Virtually all automobile accidents and accident-related deaths are reported. The data on these two events provide a reasonably solid baseline by which to measure the impact of new policies. Measuring the impact of an antirobbery or antiburglary program, by contrast, is difficult because so many crimes are unreported and because criminals may shift their activities to a neighboring area.

The most persuasive evidence in regard to the limits of the deterrent effect on drunk drivers comes from England. The 1967 Road Safety Act empowered the police to require a breath test of any driver and specified that refusal to submit to the test was punishable as an actual failure. The law focused on the certainty of apprehension alone; it did not increase the severity of punishment.[16]

As figure 6.2 indicates, the 1967 Road Safety Act had an immediate and dramatic effect. Weekend traffic fatalities and serious injuries dropped to one-third of their previous levels. These results were hailed as evidence that the law was an effective solution to the problem of drunk driving. But as figure 6.2 also reveals, the effect gradually wore off. Within three years fatalities had returned to their previous level.

The British experience illustrates several phenomena common to crackdowns on drunk drivers. No matter what strategy is adopted, virtually all appear to have an *initial* effect, which eventually disappears. For a variety of reasons, drunk driving seems to be particularly susceptible to short-term changes. The initial effect is genuine (and not the result of manipulated statistics) and can be attributed to real changes in people's behavior. This has been called the "announcement effect." The publicity surrounding a crackdown causes people to alter their behavior: a certain number of people at the bar or the party ask friends for a ride; they don't take that final extra drink; friends insist on driving them home. The deterrent effect is real: people respond to a perceived threat of punishment. At the

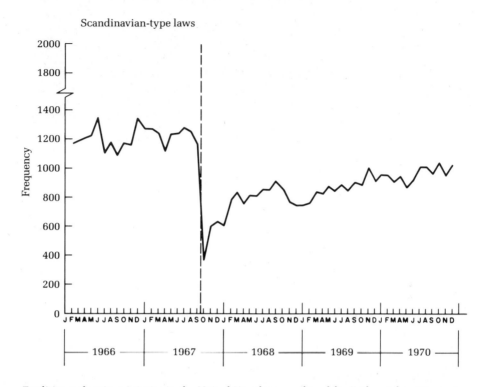

Fatalities and serious injuries in the United Kingdom: combined for Friday nights, 10 p.m. to midnight; Saturday mornings, midnight to 4 a.m.; Saturday nights, 10 p.m. to midnight; and Sunday mornings, midnight to 4 a.m. Corrected for weekend days per month and with seasonal variations removed.

Figure 6.2 The effect on traffic fatalities and serious injuries of a crackdown on drunk driving, United Kingdom, 1966–1970. (Reprinted by permission of the publisher, from *Deterring the Drinking Driver: Legal Policy and Social Control,* by H. Laurence Ross. [Lexington, Mass.: Lexington Books, D. C. Heath and Company]. Originally appeared in Ross, 1973, *Journal of Legal Studies,* University of Chicago Press.)

same time, police officers change their behavior. Even without any formal change in department policy, officers respond to the publicity by being more vigilant in their efforts to spot drunk drivers. They stop more drivers for tests and arrest more of them for drunk driving.

By its very nature, however, publicity has only a short-term effect. After a while the new policy is no longer news, gets less attention, and therefore is no longer impressed on people's consciousness. A policy has to be sustained over the long term by the fact of apprehension. The risk of apprehension for drunk driving is extremely low. In his evaluation of the English drunk-driving experiments, H. Laurence Ross estimates that the probability of being asked to submit to a breath test is one per million vehicle miles driven. The risk would be higher for many drinking drivers because their behavior would more often attract the attention of the police, but it would still be "low by any reasonable criterion," according to Ross. A U.S. Department of Transportation report concluded that a drunk driver would have to commit between 200 and 2,000 separate acts in order to be apprehended, and even then would face only a 50 percent chance of being punished.[17]

The evidence on the American crackdown on drunk driving in the 1980s is still tentative and rather ambiguous. Initially, officials hailed the campaign as a great success. Alcohol-related traffic deaths declined steadily from 1982 to 1985. Then suddenly they rose dramatically in 1986. The total was still 4 percent lower than that of 1982 but the turnaround was cause for alarm. Perhaps the decline from 1982 to 1985 was simply another example of the announcement effect. One analyst with the National Highway Traffic Safety Administration suggested that some of the decline in 1982 was a result of the serious economic recession in that year. When the economy is weak, there are fewer cars and trucks on the road, hence fewer accidents and fatalities. This argument is speculative, to be sure, but it illustrates the point that many social and economic factors influence human behavior (drinking, driving, crime) and we need to be cautious about attributing change to any one factor.[18]

Cops and Drunk Drivers

To understand the low risk of apprehension, we should look at the problem from the perspective of the police officer. Two groups of officers are theoretically on the lookout for drunk drivers: regular patrol officers and traffic enforcement unit officers. Some departments have a special drunk-driving task force within the traffic unit. Regular patrol officers are responsible for general patrol and response to calls for service. Calls take about 25 to 30 percent of their time. In addition, routine patrol requires them to cover areas that are not necessarily the prime hunting grounds for drunk drivers. Traffic units average only about 10 percent of the entire sworn officer force, and while they can and do concentrate their activities in prime hunting grounds, they too have other responsibilities that keep them from spending all their time looking for drunk drivers. Finally, drunk driving is heaviest at precisely those times when the police are busiest with other assignments. In short, few cops are in a position to concentrate on drunk drivers at any one time.[19]

If the hunters are few, the hunted are many and well hidden among law-abiding drivers. Traffic experts estimate that perhaps 5 percent of drivers are intoxicated on an average night (that is, they have a blood alcohol level of 0.05 percent). Another 5 percent have some detectable level of alcohol in their blood but are not legally drunk. On a weekend night the number is much higher; perhaps as many as 10 percent have a blood alcohol level of 0.10 percent. Not all of the drivers who are legally drunk, however, will necessarily be driving in a way that will attract the attention of a police officer. Thus, while there are a lot of drunk drivers out there on a Saturday night, the chance of a successful "hit" by a police officer is quite low.

Other factors discourage police officers from aggressively hunting drunk drivers. Traffic stops are an unpleasant and sometimes dangerous task. People resent being stopped and often let the officers know it. In the absence of any strong incentives, most cops prefer to avoid the unpleasantness. Certainly they will stop any car that is clearly out of control, but a crackdown requires them to stop many more drivers, including a lot who give only slight evidence of drunk driving. Police administrators learned long ago that some incentives, usually in the form of quotas, are required to make their officers increase the number of traffic stops.

If the typical traffic stop is unpleasant, some can be positively dangerous. Occasionally an officer encounters an armed and dangerous felon. Traffic stops constitute the third most hazardous situation for police officers in terms of officers killed on duty and the fourth most hazardous in terms of officers assaulted on duty.[20] Then there is the politically sensitive traffic stop: the officer inadvertently pulls over a driver with powerful political connections. The really hapless officer may not recognize the name on the driver's license and proceed to issue a ticket. Police officers soon learn that they will never get into trouble for not stopping a car but that they can get into very serious trouble for stopping the wrong car.

Finally, we need to consider the process of a drunk-driving arrest. Like all others, such arrests are extremely time-consuming. Herman Goldstein found that in Madison, Wisconsin, a drunk-driving arrest took an average of one and a half hours and required the assistance of at least one other officer. Two arrests, in other words, would consume about 40 percent of an officer's evening. The more arrests an officer makes, the less he or she is available for routine patrol and other assignments. An increase in drunk-driving arrests also places severe burdens on the criminal justice system. A survey conducted by the National Institute of Justice found that additional judges were required to handle such cases in Seattle, and that Cincinnati had to add an additional daily traffic court. Crackdowns also place heavy burdens on local jails. In some cities such large backlogs developed that convicted drunk drivers had to wait six or seven months before serving their jail sentences. Tennessee law mandated probation for all convicted drunk drivers and the result was a dramatic increase in probation case loads (this problem is discussed further on pp. 210–211). All of these "systems" costs are powerful incentives for scaling back crackdowns on drunk drivers.[21]

The effect of crackdowns on drunk drivers wears off because the behavior of both the drinkers and the cops returns to normal. The drinkers realize, either consciously or unconsciously, that the risk of apprehension is in fact pretty low. Publicity, moreover, is no longer continuing to convince them otherwise. The cops also fall back into their normal habits, stopping the cars that are clearly out of control but otherwise not being terribly aggressive in their enforcement patterns.

Increasing the Certainty and Severity of Punishment

Not only is the risk of apprehension very low; drunk drivers who are caught face an extremely slight risk of punishment. Many of the new drunk-driving laws have attempted to plug that loophole by making the penalties mandatory. At the same time, the new laws have tried to scale the penalties upward.

Traffic enforcement experts are generally agreed that raising the penalties, by itself, is virtually useless. After reviewing all of the past experiments, H. Laurence Ross concludes that "innovations confined to manipulation of the severity of the legal punishment, without a concomitant change in its certainty, produce no effect."[22] The main reason is that prosecutors, judges, and juries simply nullify the intent of the law. Drunk driving is a special kind of offense in several respects, one of which is the public's attitudes toward social drinking. Despite the outcry against "killer drunks," people are profoundly ambivalent when it comes to enforcement. Drinking and driving while drunk are acceptable forms of behavior to many people. In the abstract everyone can deplore the killer drunk. But in particular cases, too many people recognize that "there but for the grace of God go I." The drinking driver does not suffer the same stigma as the armed robber. Too many drunk drivers are deemed "otherwise law-abiding citizens" and therefore not suitable candidates for punishment. Prosecutors and judges reflect these attitudes and use all the devices at their command to mitigate punishment. In Omaha, Nebraska, where third-offense drunken driving is a felony, 42 percent of the cases filed as third-offense charges were plea-bargained down to a second-offense charge. Another 9 percent were dismissed, and 3 percent of the defendants were acquitted.[23]

One highly publicized crackdown on drunk driving occurred in Chicago in 1970 and 1971. On December 15, 1970, the supervising judge of the Chicago traffic court ordered that every person convicted of DWI (driving while intoxicated) would receive a seven-day jail term. The policy went into effect three days later. Although originally intended to end on January 2, 1971, it was extended for another six months. As is so often the case, this get-tough policy was accompanied by great publicity proclaiming it a success. An evaluation by Ross and his colleagues suggests otherwise.[24]

Motor vehicle fatalities in Chicago did decline during the crackdown, but they also declined in Milwaukee, where there was no change in enforcement. Data from other cities indicated a general decline in fatalities beginning in 1969. The "success" of the Chicago crackdown, according to Ross, reflected "only a chance variation from the fatality rate over the preceding five years." Moreover, the data indicated no significant change in the number of drivers tested for intoxication. This point is important because there was a significant decrease in the number of convictions of drivers who were not tested. In short, arrested drivers were often not tested, and in the absence of compelling evidence of intoxication, judges and juries were reluctant to convict. The crackdown did have some effect on drivers who were tested and convicted. The number of people sentenced to seven-day jail terms rose from 317 in 1969 to 357 in 1970 and then to 557 in 1971.

The 64 percent increase in jail terms between 1970 and 1971 is indeed significant, but its full impact on the drunk-driving problem was mitigated by three related factors: (1) the absence of a concerted arrest policy, (2) the apparent decision to test fewer drivers, and (3) the reluctance to convict in the absence of test results. Covertly, criminal justice officials undermined the intent of the traffic court judge's crackdown. Ross cites this effect as "an example of the legal system's accommodating where possible to pressures to shield offenders from sanctions considered unusually severe."[25] The informal norms of the system maintain that drunk drivers are too much like you and me to deserve harsh punishment. In precisely this veiled fashion, criminal justice officials can subvert the intent of new "mandatory" legislation.

Increasing the severity of punishment may have certain unforeseen consequences, however. The new Wisconsin law mandated a suspension of the driver's license for three to six months for a first offense, revocation of the license for six months to a year for a second offense, and revocation for one to two years for the third offense. The number of Wisconsin drivers' licenses suspended or revoked doubled between 1980 and 1983, rising from 15,049 to 30,687. Herman Goldstein's evaluation of the law, however, suggests that more people may simply have been driving without licenses. The severe penalty of losing a driver's license does not necessarily deter people from actually driving. Even worse, when these people are stopped by the police, Goldstein's evidence suggests, they are allowed to evade the consequences of their actions. The charges against many of the people who are caught are dismissed or reduced to a lesser offense (operating without a valid license, as opposed to driving without any license). Total convictions for operating without a valid license declined by 35 percent in the same period during which the number of revocations and suspensions increased by 65 percent. Once again, it appears, criminal justice officials found a way to undermine the effect of a new and punitive law.[26]

Other Approaches

One of the major activities of MADD and other anti-drunk-driving crusades has been court watching. The groups mobilize teams of volunteers to monitor the courts' handling of drunk-driving cases, on the assumption that public pressure will prevent judges from handing out lenient sentences (that is, probation) to drunk drivers. There has been no systematic study of court-watching projects, but in all likelihood they suffer from two serious defects. First, like other crackdown strategies, they may produce a temporary effect. Second, their effects may disappear sooner than most. All citizen-volunteer projects face the problem of sustaining the effort. The initial energy of the campaign quickly wears off; volunteers find that they have other priorities in their lives and fail to show up. Coordination of volunteer effort generally requires the dedication of a person who will work at the job full-time, something that most such programs do not have.

H. Laurence Ross recommends two completely different alternatives to the drunk-driver problem. His review of the evidence leads him to the conclusion that manipulating the criminal justice system is not going to produce the desired result. Instead he suggests raising the drinking age and developing crashproof cars. The former strategy, he argues, would control some teenage drinking and thereby eliminate the most reckless of the drunk drivers (although the apparent increase in traffic fatalities in the late 1980s, after most states had raised their drinking ages, suggests that he may be overly optimistic). Perhaps. Teenage drinkers are indeed a problem and they are undoubtedly the worst of the drunk drivers. Whether or not raising the drinking age a year or two would in fact keep alcohol out of their hands is another matter. After all, teenagers below even the current drinking age have little difficulty getting drunk. The efficacy of this proposal is open to serious question.[27]

Ross's idea of crashproof cars basically concedes the point that people will drink and drive. His aim is simply to minimize the damage done by accidents. Whether or not this is a feasible option, given the politics of automobile-industry regulation, is also a subject for further discussion and research.

The Myth of the Killer Drunk

Drunk driving is indeed a serious problem in this country and I do not wish to suggest otherwise. Our understanding of the problem, however, has been distorted by the image of the "killer drunk." Anti-drunk-driving crusaders try to rouse public opinion with horror stories of innocent people killed by drunk drivers. The founder of MADD joined the crusade after her daughter had been killed by someone with a history of drunk driving. When a national magazine such as Newsweek does a feature story on drunk driving, it has no trouble coming up with a long list of horror stories.[28] A closer look, however, reveals that these are classic examples of the "celebrated case." The death of a sober and law-abiding person at the hands of a drunk driver is not typical.

Herman Goldstein found that in Madison, Wisconsin, drunk drivers most often kill themselves and/or their passengers. Between 1975 and 1980 only 6 percent of the people killed by drunk drivers were pedestrians or passengers in other cars, while 62 percent of the people killed were the drunk drivers themselves and 31 percent were passengers in cars driven by drunks. Curiously, sober drivers were much more likely to kill nondrinking drivers or pedestrians.[29] I have no wish to diminish the importance of the drunk-driving problem. But the fact is that innocent bystanders are not so threatened by drunk drivers as much of the rhetoric suggests.

Postscript on Deterrence

Most of the available studies indicate that tougher penalties do not diminish crime. One recent study, completed just as this book was being finished, does suggest the efficacy of deterrence efforts.

Public policy is undergoing a rapid change in the area of spouse abuse and other domestic violence. In the 1960s, police experts emphasized the advisability of nonarrest alternatives, urging police departments to train their officers in techniques of counseling, mediation, and referral to other agencies. Morton Bard's Family Crisis Intervention project in New York City was one of the most highly publicized (though rarely imitated) police "reforms" of the late 1960s. By the early 1970s, the women's movement had shifted public opinion nearly 180 degrees. Arrest was increasingly viewed as the desirable response, primarily as a means of protecting the victimized woman. Women's groups sued the police departments of New York City and Oakland and obtained consent decrees requiring department policies that mandated arrest in serious domestic-violence cases.[30]

The Police Foundation studied the effect of arrest in situations of domestic violence in Minneapolis. It found that persons arrested for domestic violence were less likely to be involved in a repeat domestic-violence situation in the following six months (or at least to be reported to the police for one) than were the persons whom the police either counseled or ordered out of the house to cool off.[31]

Two things need to be said about these findings. First, they are still tentative and need to be analyzed carefully. Second, it is entirely possible that the study has found a genuine deterrent effect. After all, it focuses on the effect of *arrest*. As we have noted before, arrest is the weakest point in the criminal justice process. Increasing the certainty of arrest may well have the kind of effect that is lacking in attempts to increase the nominal penalty. We should also note that domestic violence is a special kind of situation. Once the victim has called the police, it is virtually 100 percent certain that the police can identify and locate the offender. This is not the case in the vast majority of robberies and burglaries and in about half of the rapes. The same certainty of apprehension (and thus the deterrent effect) therefore does not hold for these other crimes. Nonetheless, we should look forward to more detailed analyses of the effect of arrest in domestic-violence situations.

Notes

1. Franklin E. Zimring and Gordon J. Hawkins, *Deterrence: The Legal Threat in Crime Control* (Chicago: University of Chicago Press, 1973).
2. "American Attitudes toward the Death Penalty," in *The Death Penalty in America*, ed. Hugo Adam Bedau, 3d ed. (New York: Oxford University Press, 1982), chap. 3.

3. Samuel Walker, *Popular Justice: A History of American Criminal Justice* (New York: Oxford University Press, 1980), pp. 221–232.

4. Isaac Ehrlich, "The Deterrent Effect of Capital Punishment: A Question of Life and Death," *American Economic Review* 65 (1975): 397–417.

5. Ehrlich, "Participation in Illegitimate Activities: A Theoretical and Empirical Investigation," *Journal of Political Economy* 81 (1973): 521–565.

6. James Q. Wilson and Richard J. Herrnstein, *Crime and Human Nature* (New York: Touchstone Books, 1985).

7. Ehrlich, "Participation in Illegitimate Activities," 521.

8. William J. Bowers and Glenn L. Pierce, "The Illusion of Deterrence in Isaac Ehrlich's Research on Capital Punishment," *Yale Law Journal* 85 (1975): 187–208; Brian Forst, "Capital Punishment and Deterrence: Conflicting Evidence?" *Journal of Criminal Law and Criminology* 74 (Fall 1983): 927–942; Peter Passell, "The Deterrent Effect of the Death Penalty: A Statistical Test," *Stanford Law Review*, 28 (No. 1): 61–80.

9. The point is made most strongly in Forst, "Capital Punishment and Deterrence." The most complete review of the subject is in Lawrence R. Klein, Brian Forst, and Victor Filatov, "The Deterrent Effect of Capital Punishment: An Assessment of the Estimates," in *Deterrence and Incapacitation: Estimating the Effects of Criminal Sanctions on Crime Rates*, eds. Alfred Blumstein, Jacqueline Cohen, and Daniel Nagin (Washington, D. C.: National Academy of Sciences, 1978), pp. 336–360.

10. Jonathan D. Casper, David Brereton, and David Neal, *The Implementation of the California Determinate Sentencing Law: Executive Summary* (Washington, D. C.: U. S. Government Printing Office, 1982).

11. Alfred Blumstein and Jacqueline Cohen, "A Theory of the Stability of Punishment," *Journal of Criminal Law and Criminology* 64 (1976): 198–207.

12. Thorsten Sellin, *The Penalty of Death* (Beverly Hills, Calif.: Sage, 1980), p. 152.

13. William J. Bowers and Glenn L. Pierce, "Deterrence or Brutalization: What Is the Effect of Executions?" *Crime and Delinquency* 26 (October 1980): 453–484; Forst, "Capital Punishment and Deterrence"; Klein et al., "Deterrent Effect."

14. Richard Moran and Joseph Ellis, "Price of Executions Is Just Too High," *Wall Street Journal*, October 15, 1986; David J. Gottlieb, testimony, "The Cost of the Death Penalty," February 21, 1987, unpublished.

15. "Texas Official and Prisoners Fear Banality of Executions," *New York Times*, July 2, 1987.

16. H. Laurence Ross, *Deterring the Drinking Driver* (Lexington, Mass.: Lexington Books, 1982).

17. Ibid., p. 33; Department of Transportation study cited in ibid., p. 105.

18. *Law Enforcement News*, January 21, 1985; *New York Times*, March 23, 1987; *Newsweek*, December 21, 1987.

19. Herman Goldstein, "The Drinking Driver in Madison," vol. 2, "Report on a Project on Development of a Problem-Oriented Approach to Improving Police Service," unpublished manuscript (Madison, Wis., 1982), p. 48.

20. Federal Bureau of Investigation, *Uniform Crime Reports*, annual.

21. Goldstein, "Drinking Driver in Madison"; National Institute of Justice, *Jailing Drunk Drivers: Impact on the Criminal Justice System*, Research in Brief (Washington, D. C., November 1984).

22. Ross, *Deterring the Drinking Driver*, p. 103.

23. *Omaha World/Herald,* February 8, 1982, p. 1.
24. L. S. Robertson, R. F. Rich, and H. L. Ross, "Jail Sentences for Driving while Intoxicated in Chicago: A Judicial Policy That Failed," *Law and Society Review* 8 (1973): 55–67.
25. Ross, *Deterring the Drinking Driver,* p. 95.
26. Herman Goldstein, "Early Impressions of the Impact of Increased Sanctions and the Arrest, Prosecution, Adjudication, and Sentencing of Drinking Drivers in Madison, Wisconsin" (Madison: University of Wisconsin Law School, 1985), pp. 90–91.
27. Ross, *Deterring the Drinking Driver,* pp. 111–115.
28. See *Newsweek,* September 13, 1982.
29. Goldstein, "Drinking Driver in Madison," pp. 11–19.
30. Morton Bard, *Training Police as Specialists in Family Crisis Intervention* (Washington, D. C.: U. S. Government Printing Office, 1970); Nancy Loving, *Responding to Spouse Abuse and Wife Beating: A Guide for Police* (Washington, D. C.: Police Foundation, 1980).
31. Lawrence W. Sherman and Richard A. Berk, "The Specific Deterrent Effects of Arrest for Domestic Assault," *American Sociological Review* 49 (April 1984): 261–272.

Chapter 7

Unleash the Cops

T he belief that the courts have "handcuffed" the police is a central tenet of conservative crime control theology. The courts have spun a web of procedural rules—what critics call "technicalities"—that make it difficult, if not impossible, for the police to fight crime. Street-wise criminals and crafty defense attorneys manipulate the rules to beat the system. Warren Burger, former chief justice of the Supreme Court, once claimed that "thousands" of criminals are set free because of minor technicalities.[1]

Burger and other conservatives direct most of their fire at Burger's predecessor, Earl Warren. Under Warren the Supreme Court issued a long series of decisions aimed at protecting the rights of suspects. The Los Angeles Police Department once produced a chart (Figure 7.1) purporting to show how "judicial handcuffs" had contributed to the rise in crime since the late 1950s. Conservatives argue that crime has increased because court rulings prevent the police from getting the necessary evidence and/or confessions. They offer several proposals to shift the balance back in favor of the police, crime victims, and the general public.

We will now examine four conservative strategies to strengthen the police in their fight against crime: removing procedural restraints, adding more cops, improving detective work, and targeting career criminals. We begin with the two most controversial procedural restraints, the exclusionary rule and the *Miranda* warning.

Removing Procedural Restraints

Repeal the Exclusionary Rule

The exclusionary rule appears to be relatively simple. The 1961 *Mapp* v. *Ohio* decision holds that "all evidence obtained by searches and seizures in violation of the Constitution is, by that same authority, inadmissible in a

Crime Rates and Court Decisions:
Percent Increase since 1957

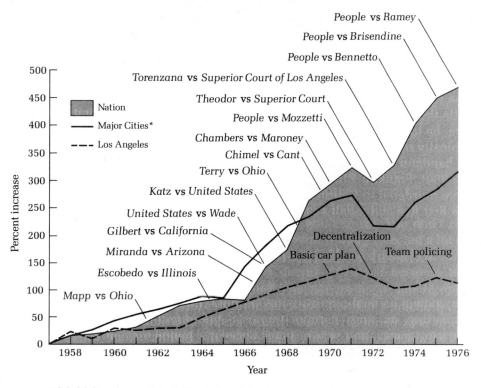

Figure 7.1 An attempt to link crime rate to Supreme Court decisions

state court." In other words, prosecutors cannot use evidence that is obtained in violation of the Fourth Amendment's guarantee that "the right of the people to be secure in their persons, houses, papers, and effects, against unreasonable searches and seizures, shall not be violated." Evidence so obtained is "excluded" from use in a criminal proceeding.

Controversy over the exclusionary rule focuses on several points; we are concerned here with the argument that the rule contributes to crime by handcuffing the police and allowing criminals to go unpunished. In general, conservatives attack the judicial activism represented by *Mapp* as an unwarranted intrusion of the federal judiciary into state and local affairs. The rule itself was not new in 1961. The Supreme Court had applied it to federal proceedings in 1914 (*Weeks v. United States*) and by 1961 it was in effect in more than half of the states. Its extension to all state proceedings was part of the broader "due-process revolution" effected by the activist Warren Court in the 1950s and 1960s.[2]

"Harold, I think this is the first time I've ever heard someone describe my beauty as 'complex and mysterious as the exclusionary rule.' "

The exclusionary rule has three basic rationales. The first is that it protects the rights of individuals against police misconduct. The history of the American police reveals a long tradition of abuse of police authority—of physical brutality, coerced confessions, and illegal searches. These abuses flourished in the absence of any institutionalized controls over police activity. The Supreme Court simply stepped into this void. The second rationale is that the rule maintains what is referred to as "judicial integrity." To maintain the integrity of its own proceedings, according to this argument, a court should not admit evidence that is tainted by the activities of other criminal justice officials. Third, the rule is designed to deter the police from misconduct. It "punishes" the police by denying them the fruits of their work: conviction of the defendant.

Most of the debate over the exclusionary rule focuses on the deterrence issue. Chief Justice Burger, James Q. Wilson, and other conservatives argue that there are more effective remedies for police misconduct, remedies that do not allow convicted offenders to go free. Judge Macklin Fleming offers the even stronger argument that the rule (along with other procedural regulations) distorts the criminal process, changing it from a search for truth to a "game," or what Roscoe Pound called a "sporting contest."[3] The exclusionary rule evokes in its critics an outrage quite different from that aroused by *Miranda.* The difference lies in the nature of the evidence being excluded. Even many prosecution-oriented critics of the Supreme Court concede that a confession may be tainted if there is any hint of coercion, however subtle. The exclusionary rule, however, deals with physical evidence, and there can be little question about the probative weight of such mute objects. Valid evidence, say the critics, should be admitted.

My position is that the rule does not contribute to crime.

PROPOSITION 12

Repeal or modification of the exclusionary rule will not reduce serious crime.

I go one step further. Modification of the rule would actually hinder effective law enforcement. The Supreme Court's due-process rulings have been a major stimulus to police professionalization; over the past twenty-five years they have encouraged tremendous improvements in police recruitment standards, training, and supervision. In short, police are more effective than they were because the Supreme Court goaded them into improving. Myron Orfield's study of Chicago narcotics officers reveals that the police— even those most heavily affected by the *Mapp* ruling—support the exclusionary rule. The officers he interviewed recognized its effectiveness in deterring many police officers from misconduct. Orfield also documented the many reforms instituted in the wake of *Mapp* which helped professionalize police work.[4]

Liberals also tend to misunderstand the effect of the exclusionary rule on the police. It does not automatically eliminate all police misconduct. For one thing, the rule comes into effect only when a suspect is formally prosecuted. It does not prevent the police from gathering evidence by questionable means when they do not intend to arrest and prosecute. (Thus police can seek to control drug users or pimps by simply harassing them with periodic shakedowns.) More troubling is the fact that rules invite evasion, even outright lying. In the immediate aftermath of the *Mapp* ruling, some observers noted an increase in the "dropsy" phenomenon: police officers claimed that they had obtained their evidence when the suspect dropped it on the ground. In some of those instances, the police officers may have been lying as a way of evading the exclusionary rule on illegal searches.

The Impact of the Exclusionary Rule on Crime

Several studies indicate that the exclusionary rule has virtually no impact on crime. James J. Fyfe concludes that the overall impact of the rule is "minuscule" and "infinitesimal." Very few people accused of robbery and burglary succeed in having their charges dismissed or their convictions overturned because of the rule. The impact of the rule appears to be confined largely to drug-related cases.[5]

A criminal case can run afoul of the exclusionary rule at several points: at the initial screening by the police, at the initial screening by the prosecutor, at the preliminary hearing or arraignment, and at trial. A lot depends on how vigorously the defense attorney challenges the evidence and the extent to which the prosecutor or judge enforces the rule.

The INSLAW study *What Happens after Arrest?* found that "due-process problems" accounted for only 5 percent of the dismissals at the initial screening and 1 percent of dismissals after charges had been filed (see tables 3.1 and 3.2). Moreover, not all of these problems involved questions of search and seizure. Virtually all of the due-process problems that arose were in the "victimless crime" category. There was no impact on robberies and very little on nonviolent property crimes. Peter F. Nardulli's study of the "societal cost" of the rule found that motions to suppress physical evidence were made in fewer than 5 percent of all cases and that most were denied. Evidence was successfully suppressed in only 0.69 percent of all cases. A General Accounting Office study of the exclusionary rule in federal courts found that motions to suppress evidence were filed in only 11 percent of the cases and that between 80 and 90 percent were denied. Thus evidence was excluded in only 1.3 percent of the cases.[6]

Considerable controversy surrounds a study of the exclusionary rule reported by the National Institute of Justice (NIJ) in 1982. The report concluded that California prosecutors rejected 4.8 percent of all cases because of the exclusionary rule. Defenders of the rule would not be displeased by this low figure. Critics, however, have charged that the NIJ report manipulated the figures in a highly irresponsible way and that the impact of the exclusionary rule is actually much smaller. The report was based on a total of 520,993 felony arrests in California between 1976 and 1979. Prosecutors rejected 86,033 of these cases for one reason or another. Illegally obtained evidence accounted for 4,130 of these rejections. The NIJ report arrived at the figure of 4.8 percent by taking the 4,130 exclusionary-rule rejections as a percentage of the 86,033 rejections.[7] In a pair of stinging critiques, Thomas Y. Davies and James J. Fyfe argue that the real impact of the exclusionary rule is seen when those rejections are considered as a percentage of all cases (4,130/520,993). Thus the exclusionary rule was responsible for rejections in only 0.8 percent of all cases. Davies also raises serious questions about another aspect of the NIJ report. For unexplained reasons, it focused on drug cases in two selected and highly unrepresentative prosecutors' offices, those in San Diego and Los Angeles. No NIJ official has yet responded to the serious charges raised by Davies and Fyfe. The controversy is an excellent example of the extent to which research on criminal justice issues can be influenced by highly partisan political considerations.[8]

All of the studies have found that the exclusionary rule is applied largely to cases involving possession of drugs or weapons. This should come as no surprise, as such cases turn on possession of the physical evidence and the related question of how the police obtained it. Eyewitness identification of the suspect is usually the crucial element in a robbery case; physical evidence is seldom the key to solving burglaries, either. In his study of the exclusionary rule in Boston, Sheldon Krantz had to focus on drug and gambling cases because the rule was cited so rarely in cases of other kinds. Krantz found that defendants were not terribly successful in invoking the rule even in drug and gambling cases. Motions to suppress evidence were raised in 13 percent of the drug and gambling cases (67 out of 512), and only 16.4 percent of those motions succeeded (11 out of 67). Thus the rule was successfully invoked in only 2 percent of the original drug and gambling cases. Krantz also found considerable variation among judges. One judge accepted 45.4 percent of the motions to suppress, while another accepted only 22.2 percent and three judges accepted none. With some creative "judge shopping" a sharp prosecutor could minimize the risk posed by the exclusionary rule even further.[9]

Nor does successful exclusion of evidence mean that defendants will go free. They may still be convicted on other evidence that was not excluded. Even when a conviction is overturned on appeal, the prosecutor can refile charges on the basis of the remaining evidence.

The exclusionary rule does not let "thousands" of dangerous criminals loose on the streets. When former chief justice Burger made this allegation, he was overreacting to a few celebrated cases. It is indeed true that some convictions are overturned and that some (perhaps even most) of the defendants involved are actually guilty. But in the context of the total amount of crime in the United States, the small number of such cases is insignificant.

As I argued in the first part of this book, we should not base our policies on the top layer of the criminal justice wedding cake. With but a handful of exceptions, robbery and burglary cases are consigned to the second and third layers. There, as we have seen, cases are processed in a routine manner and with a high degree of predictability. Most of those cases are disposed of administratively and end with either a dismissal or a guilty plea. Defense attorneys raise all the standard motions but they do so with few expectations and little actual success. They go through the motions, if you will pardon the expression, because to do otherwise would raise questions about their competence.

The routine processing of cases in the second and third layers contrasts sharply with the popular image of the "crafty" defense attorney and the "street-wise" criminal. Both images are stereotypes with little basis in reality. Most felony cases are handled by public defenders, who, while generally conscientious, are extremely overworked. Most have little time to devote to any one case, and in some jurisdictions they meet their clients only moments before entering the courtroom. Unlike the F. Lee Baileys of the legal profession, public defenders have no time to investigate each case exhaustively in order to find some weak spot in the prosecution's case.

Criminals are not necessarily as street-wise as many people think, or even as they imagine themselves to be. The tough, knowing pose they adopt in the police stationhouse is often nothing more than that—a pose, part of the act. Most felony defendants are as unsuccessful in their criminal endeavors as they were in school and on the job. Most are born with one or two strikes against them, in impoverished homes with one parent, no successful role models, and bad peer-group influences. The wonder is that more of these kids don't go on to lives of continued criminality. Most robbers and burglars are so disorganized and impulsive that they do not even plan their crimes very well. A Rand Corporation study found that 40 percent of the juvenile robbers and 25 percent of the adults had not even intended to rob anyone when they left home. As one kid put it, "It was just a sudden thing. I didn't really mean to do it. I didn't plan nothing; it just happened." Among the adult "career criminals," only 40 percent bothered to visit the sites of their crimes in advance and as few as 22 percent made an effort to check on police patrol in the area. Despite the knowing pose they may affect, these people are ill equipped to manipulate the rules of criminal procedure once they are in the hands of the law. Also, the fact that their lives are very disorganized undermines the central assumption on which conservatives base their theories about criminal activity—that criminals weigh the relative "costs" and "benefits" and then make a rational choice.[10]

Modifying the Exclusionary Rule

Alternatives to the exclusionary rule have been proposed. One suggestion is the development of alternative remedies for police misconduct. The right of citizens to sue for civil damages could be strengthened, for example. Stephen R. Schlesinger proposes that judges be empowered to hold a separate hearing to examine possible police misconduct. An independent board could be empowered to discipline officers who violate the rights of citizens. These alternatives would probably be as complex and costly as the exclusionary rule itself, and in any event they would have no effect on crime.[11]

The other alternative is the so-called good-faith search. Wilson argues that the rule "began as a court correction of a manifestly improper search [but] has come in time to be a complex, bewildering, and constantly shifting array of rules that tax the understanding of appellate judges, to say nothing of the police officer on the beat." (Yet in the next breath he concedes that "it would be a mistake . . . to argue that the rule has contributed materially to the increase in crime.")[12] In 1984 the Supreme Court accepted this idea in *United States* v. *Leon*, ruling that evidence could be admitted if it were obtained under a valid search warrant even though it was later found that there wasn't probable cause to issue the warrant. With *Leon*, conservatives achieved a major part of one of their long-sought goals. The California Supreme Court, meanwhile, in a decision involving part of the controversial Proposition 8, abolished independent state grounds for the exclusionary rule in 1985.[13]

The good-faith standard is no alternative at all. Distinctions between good-faith and bad-faith searches would be no less Byzantine than the current distinction between reasonable and unreasonable searches. John Kaplan, Yale Kamisar, and James Fyfe argue persuasively that the good-faith rule would reward police incompetence: officers could always claim that they thought it was proper to search. The current rule encourages officers to be as thorough as possible. Moreover, Fyfe maintains, the good-faith approach makes the job of judges even harder, for they have to determine whether the officer's in-court claim of good faith is an honest one.[14]

The Positive Effects of the Exclusionary Rule

There is now persuasive evidence that the exclusionary rule, far from hindering law enforcement, has been a powerful stimulus to police reform. When Myron Orfield interviewed Chicago narcotics detectives, he found that they not only supported the rule but were very concerned that its repeal or weakening would open the door to police abuse. Most of the officers who had had evidence excluded and/or lost cases because of the rule learned from the experience. They regarded the courtroom experience as valuable on-the-job training (superior to preservice classroom training) that taught them how to do it right. Finally, Orfield documented the significant reforms that were made as a result of the exclusionary rule: the Chicago police and the Illinois attorney's office developed a closer working relationship, the state attorney scrutinized applications for warrants more closely, and the police department improved its own training and supervision. As a result, Chicago detectives were doing better police work. So much for the "handcuffs" argument.[15]

Over the years the exclusionary rule has had a positive effect in helping to regulate police conduct. Many thoughtful law enforcement executives now accept and even welcome the rule. The director of the FBI, William Sessions, stated at the time of his confirmation that "the protections that are afforded by the exclusionary rule are extremely important to fair play and the proper carrying out of the law enforcement responsibility." Because of the rule, law-abiding citizens do not have to fear overzealous and intrusive action by a cop, and so the police enjoy greater public respect.[16]

Abolish the *Miranda* Warning

The *Miranda* warning is the second technicality that conservatives believe "handcuffs" the police. Criminals go free because the cops can't get them to confess. In his dissent in the original 1966 *Miranda* decision, Supreme Court Justice Byron White sounded the conservative alarm: the decision "return[s] a killer, a rapist or other criminal to the streets and to the environment which produced him, to repeat his crime whenever it pleases him."[17] The streets are not safe and the courts are to blame.

The *Miranda* decision provoked alarmist rhetoric among law enforcement officials. O. W. Wilson, the highly respected superintendent of the Chicago police, said the police "cannot live with" this and other Supreme Court decisions. The sheriff of Reno, Nevada, complained that it was "getting to the point where we can't even use a confession if a person wants to confess." The *Miranda* doctrine also inspired one of the more intemperate outbursts from Chief Justice Warren Burger. When a majority of the Court overturned a conviction in *Brewer* v. *Williams* (1977), Burger declared that "the result of this case ought to be intolerable in any society which purports to call itself an organized society."[18]

The source of all this outrage is the Supreme Court's decision in *Miranda* v. *Arizona* (1966). To guarantee the Fifth Amendment's protection against self-incrimination, the police must advise a criminal suspect of certain rights. Chief Justice Earl Warren spelled out those rights in his majority opinion, thereby creating the famous "*Miranda* warning":

> Prior to any questioning, the person must be warned that he has a right to remain silent, that any statement he does make may be used against him, and that he has a right to the presence of an attorney, either retained or appointed.

More than twenty years later, the *Miranda* warning is the most widely known and possibly most misunderstood element of police procedure. Hollywood and television writers love it. The warning adds an extra bit of drama to a story, and often dramatic complication. One movie scene shows a narcotics detective wrestling the suspect to the ground with one arm while reading from the *Miranda* warning card he holds in the other hand. This is one of the more graphic dramatizations of the idea that the police have one hand tied behind their backs. Because the warning figures in virtually every cop show on film and TV, most kids on the street know about the "*Miranda* rights." A 1976 survey found that 91 percent of all American thirteen-year-olds knew they had a right to remain silent.[19]

In 1984 the Supreme Court finally accepted the conservative argument and created a "public safety" exception to the *Miranda* warning. In *New York* v. *Quarles* the Court held that when the safety of an officer or of a citizen is threatened, as by the presence of a gun, the officer may ask questions before advising a suspect of his or her rights.[20] Like the exclusionary rule, this ruling represents a major victory in the conservatives' twenty-year campaign to reverse the rules laid down by the Warren Court. From our standpoint the question is whether this or any other modification of the *Miranda* doctrine would help the police secure more convictions. My position is:

PROPOSITION 13

Repeal or modification of the **Miranda** *warning will not reduce serious crime.*

Miranda *in operation*   A number of empirical studies have shown that the *Miranda* warning has no effect on the ability of the police to obtain confessions. Even when the warning is faithfully applied, it does not stop many suspects from confessing. Additionally, detectives can easily comply with the letter of the *Miranda* requirement while undermining its spirit. To understand the *Miranda* warning in operation, we have to leave the rarefied atmosphere of constitutional doctrine and look into a grubby police station-house where, say, a nineteen-year-old robbery suspect is in custody.

The startling fact is that many suspects voluntarily confess. Between 40 percent and 50 percent of all felony suspects give a voluntary confession. David Neubauer found 114 confessions in a sample of 248 cases in the midwestern town he studied.[21]

It is not hard to understand why so many suspects confess. The police, after all, do not arrest very many suspects. They clear only 13 percent of all robberies and 6 percent of all burglaries. They usually have reasonably good evidence against those few they manage to arrest. The suspects, knowing that they did in fact commit the crime and realizing that the police have some fairly good evidence against them, choose to confess. Their confessions are motivated in part by the hope of getting a better deal. Moreover, most criminals do have a conscience. They know they did something wrong and, when caught, feel guilty about it. Veteran detectives know this and manipulate suspects' guilt to get confessions. The so-called hardened, street-wise, and completely amoral criminal is the exception, not the rule. Some suspects do invoke the privilege of withholding confession, but they are not typical of the thousands arrested every year.

Many suspects neglect to take advantage of their "rights" under *Miranda* even when the police faithfully implement the rule. A study in the District of Columbia found that one-third of the suspects who were advised of their right to counsel did not bother to avail themselves of it. Many of those suspects simply didn't understand what was going on. The same study found that 15 percent of the suspects failed to understand the meaning of their right to remain silent, 18 percent did not understand their right to have counsel present, and 24 percent did not understand their right to have a lawyer appointed for them.[22] (In fairness, we should note that this study was conducted in the immediate aftermath of the *Miranda* decision. It is likely that suspects are more knowledgeable today, but no more recent studies have been done.) This inability to comprehend their rights is not difficult to explain. Most felony suspects have little education. Of those who end up in prison, 58 percent never finished high school (and we should remember that many who do finish are still functionally illiterate these days). These people failed to learn how to manipulate the public school bureaucracy to their advantage and they aren't much more successful with the criminal justice bureaucracy.

The *Miranda* warning, then, has limited impact even when the police faithfully implement it, as they may not always do. It is a legal truism that the Supreme Court can issue its rulings but has little power to enforce them. The history of school desegregation since *Brown* v. *Board of Education* (1954) is a classic example. Outside of the South, public schools are more

"To truth, justice, and whatever means it takes
to achieve those ends."

segregated today than they were thirty-five years ago. In the secluded world of the police stationhouse, the opportunities for evading fine legal points are even greater. As the exclusionary rule has demonstrated, externally imposed rules do not necessarily produce the intended changes in police behavior.

Police departments comply with Supreme Court decisions in varying degrees. In a study of four Wisconsin departments, Neal Milner found a high rate of compliance among those that were already somewhat professional. The less professional departments were slower to comply and had more difficulties adjusting to the new rules.[23] Because American law enforcement is fragmented among 19,691 separate agencies in a politically decentralized federal system, there is no administrative mechanism to ensure compliance. Stephen Wasby examined small-town police departments and found that many hadn't even heard about some important court decisions, while others had only vague or incorrect information. Only the largest and most professional police departments provide regular in-service training for their officers concerning recent legal developments.[24]

The Washington, D. C., study found that a significant number of suspects were never advised of either their right to remain silent or their right to an attorney.[25] We have no research on current rates of compliance by police departments. Even when the police do comply with the letter of the law, they can undermine its spirit. One technique is to ask the suspect no questions. Contrary to the popular impression, the *Miranda* decision does not oblige the police to advise suspects of their rights at the moment of arrest (some police do, but they are not required to). The warning is obligatory only before any questions are asked. If a suspect makes a confession or other incriminating remark before either arrest or interrogation, that evidence is admissible. One little game is to drive the arrested suspect to the station-house without asking any questions in the hope that he or she will volunteer some information.

The formal reading of the *Miranda* warning can be undercut in subtle ways. The police officer can diminish its apparent significance by treating it in a casual and indifferent manner, conveying the message "Let's get through with these unimportant formalities as quickly as possible so we can get on with the important business of talking about your crime." Many suspects do not understand the implications of their option to waive their rights. Once the right to silence is waived, the officer can induce a confession with the old "Let's get it off your chest" ploy.

Here again we see the potential emptiness of various constitutional guarantees. The critical points in the criminal justice process are largely hidden from view and require voluntary compliance with constitutional principles on the part of police officers. It is difficult, if not impossible, to enforce those principles when police officers make a willful attempt to undermine them. Both conservatives and liberals, in other words, exaggerate the impact of the *Miranda* decision. It does not handcuff the police, as conservatives have charged, nor did it usher in full compliance with constitutional principles, as liberals have liked to believe.

The Impact on Crime   So far we have considered the degree of compliance with *Miranda* procedures. What about the impact on the outcome of criminal cases? Does *Miranda* turn criminals loose? Does it contribute to the crime rate?

As we discovered in our discussion of the exclusionary rule, due-process problems have virtually no effect on robbery and burglary cases. David Neubauer found that only 7 of the 114 confessions in his midwestern city were challenged on appeal and but one of those appeals was sustained. (Meanwhile, out of the original 248 cases, two searches were challenged on appeal and only one of those appeals was successful.) In his study of four Wisconsin police departments, Neal Milner found that the clearance rate did drop in the unprofessional departments. It went down an incredible 51 percent in Green Bay. In the professionalized Madison police department, however, the clearance rate went up 5 percent after *Miranda*. In other words, police officers who were accustomed to operating in a professional manner (which includes respect for legal principles) had no trouble adapting to the new rule. Officers less accustomed to operating in a professional manner did have some difficulty, at least in the short run. Many law enforcement experts, in fact, argue that *Miranda* and other cases have made an important indirect contribution to police reform by forcing departments to improve their personnel and procedures.[26]

Adding More Cops

Removing procedural restraints is only one way to unleash the cops; another is to put more of them on the street. The police are there to prevent crime and arrest criminals, after all, so more police ought to help reduce crime.

The idea of putting more cops on the street enjoys two major sources of support. First, all of the experts agree that arrest is the weakest point in the entire criminal justice system. I have argued that the system is fairly effective in prosecuting, convicting, and punishing dangerous criminals once they are caught. While this point is debatable, everyone agrees that the probability of arrest is extremely low. The true clearance rate (according to NCS crime figures rather than UCR data) is only 13 percent for robbery and 6 percent for burglary. Anything that would significantly increase those figures might have some effect on the crime rate.

The second source of support is public opinion. People want more police protection. When asked to suggest improvements in their local police, they give an unequivocal answer: more police and more effective policing. Their views are expressed in various ways, but the responses listed in table 7.1—"hire more policemen" and "need more policemen . . . in certain areas or at certain times"—add up to the same thing. The National Crime Survey uncovered little concern about police corruption or misconduct. Black Americans are just as much concerned about police protection as are whites. This should hardly be surprising, given that blacks are victimized by crime far more often than whites. The rate of victimization by robbery is 150 percent higher for blacks than for whites; for victimization by burglary it's 42 percent higher.[27]

The New Police Corps

The idea of putting more cops on the street is undergoing a sudden and surprising revival. It is really yesterday's solution to the crime problem. In the crisis-ridden 1960s, many city police departments doubled in size. The Washington, D. C., police force grew from 2,500 officers in 1960 to 5,000 in 1973. The already enormous New York City police department grew from 20,000 to 30,000 officers in the same period. Hiring more cops was the primary political response to the growing fear of crime in the streets in the 1960s.[28]

A new way to add more police consists of the so-called Police Corps. Initially proposed by Adam Walinsky, former aide to Robert F. Kennedy, it is similar to the ROTC program. Under the program adopted by New York in 1986, college students receive up to $3,000 in tuition aid during their junior and senior years if they agree to serve as police officers for two years after graduating (they must pay back the financial aid if they fail the entrance exam or quit before serving two years). While in college, meanwhile, they

Table 7.1 White and black attitudes about police improvement, 1975 (percent)

	White	Black
No improvement needed	17%	9%
Improvement needed	65	75
Don't know	16	14
No answer	2	2
Most important suggested improvement:		
Hire more policemen	27	18
Concentrate on more important duties, serious crime, etc.	11	11
Be more prompt, responsive, alert	12	20
Improve training, raise qualifications or pay; recruitment policies	4	4
Be more courteous, improve attitude, community relations	7	12
Don't discriminate	1	4
Need more traffic control	1	0
Need more policemen of certain type (foot, car) in certain areas or at certain times	28	25
Other	8	5

SOURCE: U. S. Department of Justice, *The Police and Public Opinion* (Washington, D. C.: U. S. Government Printing Office, 1977), pp. 14–15.

work part-time as police cadets, earning as much as $6,000 and gaining valuable experience.[29]

The concept is a curious amalgam of conservative and liberal thinking. Walinsky argues that increases in police strength have not kept pace with the spectacular rise in violent crime: "We are allocating to each violent crime one-sixth of the police power that we allocated thirty years ago." The program is designed to provide additional street cops. Walinsky's over-heated rhetoric about diminishing police resources in the face of a tidal wave of crime is pure conservative crime control theology.[30] His solution to the problem, with its emphasis on expanded educational opportunity, is straight out of Lyndon Johnson's Great Society. The Police Corps seems to offer the best of both worlds: effective crime control and social justice all in the same package. And since the members of the Police Corps are paid less than regular officers, it also promises to get the job done more cheaply, a big point in today's economic world.

Like most other programs that seem to be too good to be true, the Police Corps is exactly that. My position is:

─────────────────── **PROPOSITION 14** ───────────────────
Adding more police will not reduce crime.

This is not to say that we should dismiss the Police Corps concept completely. In a more refined and modest version it would be a reasonable proposal. There may be ways of effectively using additional police resources. Herman Goldstein's concept of "problem-oriented policing" is currently attracting national attention as a way to use police resources in a more creative fashion. This approach needs to be carefully developed and tested. The current Police Corps idea, however, is a very immodest proposal that amounts to little more than throwing police at the problem of crime.[31]

The Police and Crime

The recent Police Corps proposal raises a larger question: Do the police prevent crime? To a certain extent, yes. But not in a way that can be reduced to a precise formula whereby x number of additional police yield y amount of crime reduction. Most of us do not commit serious crimes and most of those who do commit a robbery or burglary eventually stop. The police, however, play only a very small role in deterring people from committing crime. It is not even clear how large a role the entire criminal justice system plays. Most people are socialized to respect the law through the combined influence of family, religion, education, and peer-group pressure. These influences fail with some people and they commit crimes. For a few the socialization process collapses altogether. They become the hard core, the career criminals.

In this larger context of social control, the police are a last-resort, reactive mechanism. They intervene only after all else has failed. Since the time of Robert Peel, police patrol has been designed to prevent crime. The visible presence of police patrols is supposed to deter the person contemplating a criminal act. An arrest, meanwhile, incapacitates a criminal and sends a message that presumably deters other potential criminals. From a policy standpoint, the relevant question is: How much *more* crime will be prevented by *additional* police resources?

After more than 150 years of modern policing, police experts still cannot answer the basic question: How many police are enough? Even the most superficial evidence suggests no relationship between the number of cops and the crime rate. As table 7.2 indicates, Detroit and Philadelphia have almost the same ratio of police to population, yet Detroit has more than twice as much reported crime. Detroit and San Diego, meanwhile, have comparable crime rates despite the fact that Detroit has twice as many police in proportion to population. A large number of studies on this subject have failed to establish a clear relationship between police resources and the crime rate. If anything, the causal relationship appears to work in the opposite direction: high crime rates (especially for robbery) produce an increase in police resources. Crime generates political pressure, which leads to the hiring of more cops. The addition of cops, however, does not lead to lower crime rates.

The traditional measure of police resources consists of the FBI data on police in proportion to population. Large cities (250,000 or more people) have an average of 3.4 police employees per 1,000 citizens. This figure

Table 7.2 Crime rates and police/population ratio in ten major cities, 1978

City	Number of police officers	1978 Crimes per 10,000 population	1978 Police per 10,000 population
New York	29,443	762.3	39.3
Chicago	14,324	618.2	46.4
Los Angeles	9,649	837.7	34.6
Philadelphia	9,255	384.4	48.8
Houston	3,873	818.2	24.0
Detroit	6,371	839.5	48.4
Dallas	2,574	990.8	29.5
San Diego	1,557	847.6	19.7
Baltimore	3,912	839.4	47.3
San Antonio	1,386	687.3	18.1

SOURCE: Adapted from Herbert Jacob and Robert L. Lineberry, *Governmental Responses to Crime* (Washington, D. C.: U. S. Government Printing Office, 1982).

embraces a high of 6.9 per 1,000 and a low of 1.7 per 1,000. The national average for all cities is 2.5 per 1,000.

The FBI statistics are virtually worthless. They fail to tell us even the most rudimentary things we need to know about the relationship between police resources and crime. To explain why more police will not reduce the crime rate, we need to delve into issues of police management, which the FBI data blithely ignore. Aggregate data on the number of personnel tell us nothing. The important questions include: Who are these people? How are they assigned? What do patrol officers actually do?[32]

The FBI figures do not distinguish between sworn and nonsworn personnel. A department with a low percentage of civilian employees, for example, may be inefficiently using highly paid officers for mundane clerical tasks. Traditionally, "unprofessional" police departments have reserved a large number of "soft" assignments for favored officers. Given a certain number of sworn officers, the relevant question becomes how they are assigned. The Police Executive Research Forum has found that among police departments in big cities (500,000 or more people), the percentage of sworn officers assigned to patrol duty ranges from 32 to 64. Clearly, some departments do a far more efficient job of getting their cops out on the street than others. The way those officers patrol is equally important. New York City and Cleveland continue to rely heavily on two-officer patrols, and many of those New York City cops are on foot. San Jose and Los Angeles deploy virtually all of their patrol officers in single-officer cars. Obviously, two one-officer patrol cars can cover twice as much territory as one two-officer car.[33]

We are not quite done. So far we have discussed the issue simply in terms of numbers. While it is true that some departments are more efficient than others in placing patrol officers on the street, an equally vital question is what those officers do. Some officers are very active. They initiate a lot of activity by getting out of their cars and talking to people (both law-abiding citizens and suspects). Other officers are more passive, responding to calls when dispatched but rarely taking the initiative. Some departments encourage a high rate of activity, usually through formal or informal quotas on arrests or traffic citations. The Los Angeles police, for example, have long had a reputation for a department-wide policy of "aggressive preventive patrol." A Police Foundation experiment with the San Diego police department did suggest that aggressive patrol made some impact on crime without damaging police–community relations.[34]

Simply adding more police to an already inefficient department is throwing money (or cops, in this case) at the problem. Conservatives are fond of attacking this approach to other social programs: their point applies to policing as well. The principal fault with the Police Corps proposal is that it says nothing about how the additional officers will be used.

Let us assume for the moment that additional police officers were added to a relatively well-managed and efficient department. Would greater police presence help lower the crime rate? This question is the subject of a small but important body of police research. The most thorough study of this sort is the famous Kansas City Preventive Patrol Experiment of 1972–1973. While it was not without its flaws, the experiment was a great leap forward in police research and has exerted an enormous influence on professional thinking.[35]

The Kansas City Experiment

The Kansas City experiment was designed to reveal whether different levels of patrol activity affected the crime rate. Unlike previous experiments, it attempted to control for most of the relevant variables. Police research is extremely difficult because one cannot create laboratory conditions in a real-world setting. Earlier experiments failed to control for temporary or random changes in criminal activity, unreported crime, the possible displacement of crime into neighboring areas, and the reactions of both police officers and citizens to changes in police activity. In short, it was not possible to conclude that any changes in criminal activity were the products of different levels of police patrol.

The design of the Kansas City experiment divided the South Patrol District into three groups of patrol beats. One group kept the normal level of patrol. Another received saturation patrol, with two or three times the normal number of patrol cars. A third received no routine patrol; police cars entered those beats only in response to a citizen's request, handled the call, and then left the beat area. The absence of normal patrol in those "reactive" beats and the heavier patrol in the saturation beats was intended to test whether or not patrol had a deterrent effect on crime.

The twelve-month experiment found that the level of patrol activity had no effect on crime. Crime neither increased in the reactive beats nor decreased in the saturation patrol areas. Perhaps even more surprising, the public did not seem to notice the differences in patrol activity.

When the findings first leaked out (coverage on the evening television news and the front page of the *New York Times*), they sparked intense controversy. Many people got the impression that the experiment "proved" that patrol had no effect on crime. Most police chiefs, faced with a direct challenge to their basic operating principles, reacted negatively. The police establishment feared that budget-conscious politicians would use the experiment's findings to cut the size of police departments.

The Kansas City experiment did not conclusively prove that police patrol has no effect on crime. No beats experienced a complete lack of police presence for any extended period of time. Moreover, the secrecy of the experiment maintained the fiction that police patrol was normal in all areas; the fiction was reinforced by the periodic entry of a police car into one of the reactive beats. Thus, as far as most people—including potential criminals— were aware, patrol had not changed. Police patrol experts use the term "phantom effect" to refer to the continued belief that the police are present even when they are not. The experiment did, however, confirm the idea that *additional* police patrol would not lower the crime rate. It also suggested that police departments could be more flexible in patrol assignments. They did not have to adhere to a rigid formula of maintaining continuous patrol coverage in all areas, twenty-four hours a day.

The closest parallel to the Kansas City experiment is one carried out in England in the late 1960s. The results of that experiment, which varied the level of patrol from no officers to as many as five, are highly suggestive. A difference was found between the presence of one officer and a total lack of officers. The presence of that one officer did seem to lower the crime rate. But the addition of more officers yielded no further reductions.[36] In the 1970s a number of American cities experienced "natural" experiments in the effect of police resources. Because of budget crises, the size of the New York City and Cleveland police departments declined by 30 percent. Yet in both cities the crime rate stabilized or declined. Unfortunately, no one evaluated the way these two departments responded to these significant reductions in the number of officers.

The Mayonnaise Theory of Police Patrol

A little bit of police patrol goes a long way. Just as a modest amount of mayonnaise enhances the taste of a sandwich, so a limited amount of police patrol holds the line against crime. In both situations the point of diminishing returns is quickly reached. Just as too much mayo ruins the sandwich and wastes mayonnaise, so saturation patrol is a gross waste of resources. It costs a huge amount of money and produces no reduction in crime. (It also appears to increase public anxiety about crime. After all, why are all those cops out there?) The cost of police patrol is frightful. The addition of one police patrol to your neighborhood actually requires five new officers on the payroll (4.8, to be precise). Because of days off, vacations, sick leave, and other contingencies, it takes 1.6 officers to cover one eight-hour shift. Staffing that position around the clock, then, takes 4.8 officers.[37] A police officer with a few years' seniority in a medium-sized city earns at least $25,000. Add about 30 percent to cover fringe benefits and another $20,000 for the patrol car, and the total cost of providing that additional patrol car for your neighborhood comes to at least $250,000 a year. In big cities the cost is even higher.

No one can say with any precision how thick the layer of police patrol should be. As the figures in table 7.2 indicate, however, some cities are surviving with much thinner layers than others.

At this point the skeptic may challenge my argument by suggesting that if more cops were on duty, more of them would be available for specific crime-fighting activities. After all, aren't the police overworked? Wouldn't additional officers permit police departments to focus on productive crime-fighting tactics? Many police departments do not use their currently available personnel efficiently, nor do they manage their work loads in a rational and efficient manner. Some departments have made improvements in those areas, and their efforts merit careful evaluation.

Even if some police departments did succeed in making more efficient use of their personnel, the basic question would still remain unanswered: Would those officers be able to arrest more criminals?

Shorter Response Time

The idea that shorter response time leads to more arrests is one of the great myths of American police management. For fifty years, reducing the amount of time it took for the police to get to the scene of a call was one of the paramount police objectives. O. W. Wilson built his reputation as the leading authority on policing from the late 1930s through the 1960s on his ideas of efficient use of police resources. His four basic principles were: substituting car patrol for foot patrol; using one-officer rather than two-officer patrols; assigning patrol officers to areas on the basis of work-load demand; and reducing response time.

Common sense would seem to argue for rapid response time. Wouldn't the police catch more criminals if they got to the scene more quickly? Evidence provided by the President's Crime Commission in 1967 supported this idea. The police made an arrest in 62 percent of the cases in which the response time was one minute or four minutes or longer. More recent research has challenged these data and suggested that *police* response time is not the real problem.[38]

As far as most crimes are concerned, the police response time is irrelevant. About two-thirds are "cold" crimes: the criminal is long gone before the crime is even discovered. Most burglaries are cold crimes: you come home and find that your house or apartment has been burgled. Most street robberies are similar—by the time you are able to summon the police, the robber has fled. The speed of police response in such instances is largely irrelevant. Even when the perpetrator is present or nearby, police response time is inconsequential. In these cases the victim usually knows or can readily identify the offender.

When time counts, most often the critical delay is in the time it takes for the victim to call the police in the first place. A Kansas City study found that victims took about six minutes to call the police. About half of the victims talked to someone else first. Traumatized and disoriented by the crime, they called friends or family or simply took time to compose themselves. Given the low rate of crime reporting, we may infer that many are trying to decide whether or not even to call the police. When an average of six minutes is lost in the first critical stage, it makes little difference if the police can reduce their subsequent response time by a minute or two.[39]

In the end there are few crime situations in which response time might matter. Commercial robberies are a good example. If the storekeeper or a witness is able to notify the police while the crime is in progress, the ability of the police to arrive on the scene a minute or two more quickly might improve the chances of an arrest. But such cases represent only a very small proportion of all crimes. Improved response time potentially affects but a small fraction of the total crime problem.

Improving Detective Work

Common sense and most of our data tell us that arresting more criminals might help reduce crime. Arrest is the weakest point in the entire criminal justice process. If you commit only one burglary or robbery, your chances of arrest are extremely low (one in thirteen for burglary, one in seven for robbery). If you commit a lot of burglaries and robberies, however, your chances of being arrested escalate rapidly. Most career criminals are eventually caught.

How, then, can we improve our capacity to arrest criminals? We have already considered and rejected two suggestions. Loosening the procedural restraints on obtaining evidence and confessions will not improve police performance. Nor will simply increasing the numbers of police officers. We now turn our attention to a more common-sense approach that calls for more and better-trained detectives and more efficient use of information. Detectives are as swamped by the large volume of criminal activity as other officials in the criminal justice system. Actually, they may be more overburdened, since officials "downstream" act only after an arrest is made. Common sense dictates that if detectives only had more time, they would be able to solve more crimes. And if the department provided better training and had better procedures for handling relevant information, they might catch more criminals also.

Unfortunately, common sense is a poor guide here. My position is:

PROPOSITION 15

Improvements in detective work will neither significantly raise clearance rates nor lower the crime rate.

The Myth of the Detective

To understand why improvements in detective work will not increase the number of arrests, we must penetrate the myth of the detective. Forget every detective you have seen on TV or in the movies and every detective novel you have read. *Dragnet*, Clint Eastwood, and Sherlock Holmes have nothing to do with criminal investigation. The myth of the detective comes in several different but equally misleading varieties. In the *Kojak*/Clint Eastwood version, detective work is fast-paced, exciting, and dangerous. It also has an important moral quotient, because the detective is up against truly dangerous people. The effort to bring them to justice serves moral ends. In the *Dragnet* version, the detective succeeds through tireless, unglamorous, but thoroughly professional hard work. He is also always successful in apprehending the criminal. In the late 1960s, as the entertainment industry changed its standards in regard to what was permissible, we got the phenomenon of the "rogue cop." It was no longer necessary to portray cops as saints. It became permissible to present them as flawed, even lawbreaking people. Nor did Hollywood have to teach the lesson that crime did not pay—a lesson required by the Production Code imposed in the 1930s. The rogue cops in today's movies and TV shows probably are more lawless than real cops. In the Sherlock Holmes version, detective work is a battle of wits between a devilishly clever criminal and an equally ingenious detective.

The myth of the detective reinforces official police propaganda. The police present themselves as "crime fighters" whose primary mission is to battle crime. Individual cops have internalized the message, elevating detective work to the status of glamorous, "real" police work and devaluing the peacekeeping tasks as "garbage" and "bullshit."

The Reality of Criminal Investigation

The reality of criminal investigation is very different. For the most part it is a boring, unglamorous, and highly unproductive job. Instead of kicking in doors, ducking bullets, and wrestling with dangerous sociopaths, detectives spend most of their time writing reports. The typical case gets only superficial attention—an average of about four hours of work, including

"Eat your heart out, Kojak. Let's see you type
your reports at 105 words per minute."

report writing. And, as the clearance rates indicate, all this work is
remarkably unproductive.[40]

Most "successes" are not the result of dogged detective work. Cleared
crimes tend to solve themselves. The perpetrator either is known (and in
some cases present when the first police officer arrives) or can be identified
through information supplied by the victim. The importance of having
specific information about a particular suspect is illustrated in figure 7.2.
The President's Crime Commission examined 1,905 cases handled by the
Los Angeles police during a typical period. In 349 of the cases a suspect was
identified to the first police officer to arrive at the scene of the crime. The
police cleared 86 percent of those crimes. In the remaining 1,556 cases, no
suspect was immediately identified, and police were able to clear only 12
percent.[41]

The basic division of criminal cases according to named and unnamed
suspects is easy to understand when we recognize the circumstances of
different crimes. The four interpersonal crimes (murder, assault, rape, and
robbery) have relatively high clearance rates because the victim at least sees
the offender. In cases of murder, assault, and rape the offender often is
known or was known to the victim. Solving these crimes involves little more
than getting the name of the offender. Robbery has a significantly lower
clearance rate because most (about 70 percent) are "stranger" crimes. The
victim may have a description but does not know the offender. The four
remaining property crimes (burglary, larceny-theft, auto theft, and arson)
afford almost no opportunity for the victim to identify the offender. Most of
them are "cold" crimes: the offender is long gone by the time the police

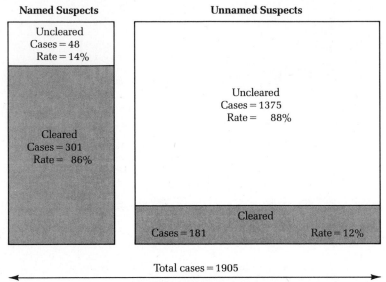

Figure 7.2   Clearance of crimes with named and unnamed suspects, Los Angeles Police Department, 1966 (President's Commission on Law Enforcement and Administration of Justice, *Task Force Report: Science and Technology* [Washington, D. C.: Government Printing Office, 1967], p. 8).

arrive. The officers have almost nothing that points to the identity of the perpetrator. The solvability of various crimes is built into the crimes themselves.[42] Some by their very nature provide police with substantial leads and others do not. Even the most determined detective work is not going to change that fact of life.

We should say something about the mystique of fingerprints. The FBI elevated fingerprints to near-mythical status. The Bureau now has nearly 200 million prints on file, and thousands of new sets arrive every day. (In the 1930s the FBI launched an abortive campaign to fingerprint the entire population.) The mystique of fingerprints was designed to project an image of the Bureau as an incredibly efficient agency—efficient precisely because it was backed by the massive weight of "science." In reality, however, fingerprints rarely solve crimes because of the difficulty of getting usable prints from a crime scene. When their own homes are burglarized, many detectives refuse to allow the fingerprint technicians in. They know from experience that the process rarely produces a usable print and only leaves a big mess. At best, fingerprints are useful in confirming the identity of a suspect once that suspect is in custody, and thus in helping the prosecution to nail down the case. But fingerprints are of little use in identifying a suspect in the first place—and that is the main problem.[43]

Despite the fact that detectives are swamped with cases, adding more detectives will not improve productivity. Even with additional time for each case, the detectives still come up against the inherent solvability phenomenon. Moreover, a Rand Corporation study of criminal investigation has indicated that improved training would yield few results. Finally, while police departments generally do a poor job of handling evidence (collecting too much irrelevant evidence, ineffectively collating and sharing potentially useful information), the Rand study did not find that departments with better procedures had higher clearance rates than poorly managed departments.[44]

Use of informants and undercover detective work are a basic part of policing, but they are relevant primarily to conspiratorial crimes, notably narcotics trafficking, white-collar crime, and organized crime. Covert tactics are useful in penetrating a criminal syndicate; they are considerably less so in solving the routine robberies and burglaries that are the focus of this inquiry.

Targeting Career Criminals

The hot new idea in criminal investigation is the targeting of career criminals. Special career-criminal units have been established in Washington, D. C., Minneapolis, and other cities.

The police career-criminal programs are based on the same logic that underlies selective incapacitation and the major-offender prosecution programs. Wolfgang's birth cohort study suggests that a very small group of offenders are responsible for a huge proportion of all crimes, and violent crimes in particular. Theoretically, even a relatively small improvement in the arrest, conviction, and incarceration of these offenders would yield a significant reduction in crime.

Police programs vary in the way they are organized within the department. Some employ patrol strategies in a modification of traditional patrol work, while in others a special group of detectives is assigned to investigate crimes. The Washington, D. C., Repeat Offender Project (ROP, pronounced "rope") involved a criminal investigation strategy. A special unit of sixty officers focused on individuals they believed were committing five or more Index crimes a week. They developed their list of suspects by cross-indexing information provided by other units in the department, such as Investigation Services, the Career Criminal Unit, the Warrant Squad, the Court Liaison Division, the district commanders, and the Youth Division. A more controversial Minneapolis program targeted eight suspects at a time. All patrol officers, rather than a special detective unit, were expected to give special attention to "Target 8" suspects. Any police officer could nominate a suspect who had at least two felony convictions and one prison term in the last ten years and who he believed was currently engaged in serious criminal activity. The idea of targeting career criminals became immediately popular in the police community and a national survey found thirty-three different programs across the country.[45]

The effectiveness of police career-criminal programs remains in doubt. An evaluation of Washington's ROP program revealed mixed results. The initial idea of doing twenty-four-hour surveillance of suspects quickly proved to be "time-consuming, frustrating, and unproductive." ROP officers then began to concentrate more on suspects with arrest warrants on file and eventually gave half of their time to this group. In this respect, then, ROP became nothing more than an intensified version of the traditional warrant squad. Like many other supposed innovations, it called for officers to do what they always said they were doing. The ROP project did succeed in arresting 58 percent of the targeted group, significantly more than the 8 percent arrested among a control group of potential suspects. Nonetheless, the overall arrest productivity of ROP officers was less than that for a comparison group of officers. Given the cost of the program ($60,000) and the reduction of nonarrest activities (order maintenance, etc.) by ROP officers, serious questions remain to be answered about the efficiency of the entire program.[46]

Producing a large volume of arrests has never been a problem for police. Producing "quality" arrests in a cost-effective and legally correct manner is a more serious concern. The potential constitutional problems involved in intensive surveillance of alleged career criminals remains to be explored. Evidence on the cost-effectiveness issue is more readily at hand. The sixty-two ROP officers produced sixty-six convictions by the end of the first year. Since this is little better than an average of one per officer per year, the cost of each conviction is about $25,000, the national average for detective salaries. Whether or not this is money well spent is a serious question.

Even more disturbing is the 37.2 percent conviction rate for ROP arrests (66 out of 177). This seems to defy the basic logic of career-criminal programs. After all, they target people who are known to have past criminal records and who the best police intelligence indicates are active criminals at the moment (committing as many as five major felonies a week). These are the real hard core we hear so much about. You would expect a high conviction rate for these suspects.

An earlier experiment in Kansas City had even less satisfactory results. LOP, or "location-oriented patrol," focused on likely crime targets, while POP, or "perpetrator-oriented patrol," focused on suspected offenders. Only one-third (31 percent) of the arrests by both LOP and POP officers resulted in convictions. The results look even worse from the standpoint of targeted *suspects* and targeted *crimes*. LOP and POP officers arrested only a handful of targeted suspects for targeted (serious) crimes: a grand total of six in the entire year, to be exact. Those six arrests cost more than 40,000 officer-hours. Put another way, the time required to produce the six arrests amounts to the work of one officer for one thousand weeks, or twenty years.[47]

Some targeted suspects were arrested for other, lesser crimes. Chief

Bouza defended his Minneapolis program on the grounds that it makes no difference what you get them on as long as you get career criminals off the street, even for a short period of time. Critics of the career-criminal programs are not so sure. ROP officers in Washington almost immediately encountered a problem in regard to priorities. As they tracked targeted suspects they observed a lot of other crimes (not surprisingly, the suspects tended to live in high-crime neighborhoods), particularly drug dealing. Making an arrest would divert them from their primary goal of arresting a targeted suspect for one of the targeted crimes. Theirs is a dilemma common in police work: whether to accumulate large numbers of gross arrests or deliberately ignore lesser crimes and concentrate on the serious offenses.

The undistinguished results of the police career-criminal programs resemble the results of programs developed to prosecute major offenders. Prosecution programs yield discouraging results because it turns out that the system is already tough on serious crime. Police programs are particularly disappointing because arrest is known to be the weakest point in the criminal justice process. LOP, POP, and ROP seem to suggest that the targeting of suspected career criminals for intensive surveillance does little to improve the situation.

Notes

1. Dissenting in Bivens v. Six Unknown Agents, 403 U. S. 424.
2. Archibald Cox, *The Warren Court* (Cambridge: Harvard University Press, 1968).
3. Sheldon Glueck, ed., *Roscoe Pound and Criminal Justice* (Dobbs Ferry, N. Y.: Oceana, 1965), p. 73; Macklin Fleming, *The Price of Perfect Justice* (New York: Basic Books, 1974).
4. Myron W. Orfield, Jr., "The Exclusionary Rule and Deterrence: An Empirical Study of Chicago Narcotics Officers," *University of Chicago Law Review* 54 (Summer 1987): 1016–1055. See also Dallin Oaks, "Studying the Exclusionary Rule in Search and Seizure," *University of Chicago Law Review* 37 (1970): 665–757.
5. National Institute of Justice, *The Effects of the Exclusionary Rule: A Study in California* (Washington, D. C.: U. S. Government Printing Office, 1982); James J. Fyfe, "The NIJ Study of the Exclusionary Rule," *Criminal Law Bulletin* 19 (May–June 1983): 253–260.
6. Peter F. Nardulli, "The Societal Costs of the Exclusionary Rule: An Empirical Assessment," *American Bar Foundation Research Journal* 1983 (Summer 1983): 585–690.
7. Controller General of the United States, *Impact of the Exclusionary Rule on Federal Criminal Prosecutions*, Report no. GGD-79-45, April 19, 1979.
8. Thomas Y. Davies, "A Hard Look at What We Know (and Still Need to Learn) about the 'Costs' of the Exclusionary Rule: The NIJ Study and Other Studies of 'Lost' Arrests," *American Bar Foundation Research Journal* 1983 (Summer 1983): 611–690; Nardulli, "Societal Costs of the Exclusionary Rule."
9. Sheldon Krantz, Bernard Gilman, Charles G. Benda, Carol Rogoff Hallstrom, and

Gail J. Nadworny, *Police Policymaking* (Lexington, Mass.: Lexington Books, 1979), pp. 189–192. See also Brian Forst, Judith Lucianovic, and Sarah J. Cox, *What Happens after Arrest?* (Washington, D. C.: INSLAW, 1977), p. 69.

10. Joan Petersilia, Peter W. Greenwood, and Martin Lavin, *Criminal Careers of Habitual Felons* (Washington, D. C.: U. S. Government Printing Office, 1978), p. 63.

11. Stephen R. Schlesinger, *Exclusionary Injustice* (New York: Marcel Dekker, 1977).

12. James Q. Wilson, quoted in *Crime Control Digest* 15 (November 16, 1981). See the rebuttal by William E. Geller in ibid.

13. United States v. Leon (1984), 468 U. S. 897.

14. John Kaplan, "The Limits of the Exclusionary Rule," *Stanford Law Review* 26 (1974): 1027–1055; Yale Kamisar, "A Defense of the Exclusionary Rule," *Criminal Law Bulletin* 15 (January–February 1979): 5–39; James J. Fyfe, "In Search of the 'Bad Faith' Search," *Criminal Law Bulletin* 18 (May–June 1982): 260–264.

15. Orfield, "Exclusionary Rule and Deterrence."

16. Sessions quoted in *New York Times,* November 5, 1987.

17. Miranda v. Arizona, 384 U. S. 436 (1966), quoted in Yale Kamisar, *Police Interrogation and Confessions: Essays in Law and Policy* (Ann Arbor: University of Michigan Press, 1980).

18. Brewer v. Williams, 430 U. S. 415 (1977).

19. U. S. Department of Justice, *Sourcebook of Criminal Justice Statistics—1978* (Washington, D. C.: U. S. Government Printing Office, 1979), p. 300.

20. New York v. Quarles, 467 U. S. 649 (1984).

21. David W. Neubauer, *Criminal Justice in Middle America* (Morristown, N. J.: General Learning Press, 1974).

22. R. J. Medalie, L. Zeitz, and P. Alexander, "Custodial Police Interrogations in Our Nation's Capital: The Attempt to Implement *Miranda,*" *Michigan Law Review* 66 (May 1968): 1347–1422.

23. Neal Milner, *The Court and Local Law Enforcement: The Impact of "Miranda"* (Beverly Hills, Calif.: Sage, 1971).

24. Stephen Wasby, *Small-Town Police and the Supreme Court: Hearing the Word* (Lexington, Mass.: Lexington Books, 1976).

25. Medalie et al., "Custodial Police Interrogations."

26. Neubauer, *Criminal Justice in Middle America;* Milner, *Court and Local Law Enforcement.*

27. U. S. Department of Justice, *Criminal Victimization in the United States, 1979* (Washington, D. C.: U. S. Government Printing Office, 1981).

28. "Crime and Punishment," *New Republic,* December 6, 1982, pp. 7–9; *Criminal Justice Newsletter,* June 2, 1986.

29. *Criminal Justice Newsletter,* June 2, 1986.

30. We should note that in at least two well-publicized instances the New York City police were found to be deliberately undercounting reported crimes. Thus much of the increase cited by Walinsky is the product of improved record keeping. See Robert Hood and Richard Sparks, *Key Issues in Criminology* (New York: McGraw-Hill, 1970), pp. 40–41; Franklin E. Zimring and Gordon J. Hawkins, *Deterrence: The Legal Threat in Crime Control* (Chicago: University of Chicago Press, 1973), pp. 333–335.

31. Herman Goldstein, "Improving Policing: A Problem-Oriented Approach," *Crime and Delinquency* 25 (April 1979): 236–258.

32. James Q. Wilson and Barbara Boland, *The Effect of the Police on Crime* (Washington, D. C.: U. S. Government Printing Office, 1979).

33. Police Executive Research Forum, *Survey of Operational and Administrative Practices—1981* (Washington, D. C., 1981).

34. John E. Boydstun, *San Diego Field Interrogation: Final Report* (Washington, D. C.: Police Foundation, 1975).

35. George L. Kelling, Tony Pate, Duane Dickman, and Charles E. Brown, *The Kansas City Preventive Patrol Experiment* (Washington, D. C.: Police Foundation, 1974).

36. All of the patrol experiments are reviewed in James Q. Wilson, *Thinking about Crime*, rev. ed. (New York: Basic Books, 1983), chap. 4.

37. O. W. Wilson and Roy C. McLaren, *Police Administration*, 4th ed. (New York: McGraw-Hill, 1977), pp. 656–671.

38. U. S. Department of Justice, *Improving Patrol Productivity*, vol. 1, *Routine Patrol* (Washington, D. C.: U. S. Government Printing Office, 1977).

39. President's Commission on Law Enforcement and Administration of Justice, *Task Force Report: Science and Technology* (Washington, D. C.: U. S. Government Printing Office, 1967), p. 9; U. S. Department of Justice, *Response Time Analysis: Executive Summary* (Washington, D. C.: U. S. Government Printing Office, 1978).

40. Peter W. Greenwood, *The Criminal Investigation Process* (Santa Monica, Calif.: Rand Corporation, 1975).

41. President's Commission on Law Enforcement and Administration of Justice, *Task Force Report: Science and Technology*, p. 8.

42. Wesley Skogan and George Antunes, "Information, Apprehension, and Deterrence: Exploring the Limits of Police Productivity," *Journal of Criminal Justice* 7 (Fall 1979): 217–241.

43. Greenwood, *Criminal Investigation Process* (Santa Monica, Ca.: Rand Corporation, 1975).

44. Ibid.

45. *Crime Control Digest*, January 17, 1983; William G. Gay, *Targeting Law Enforcement Resources: The Career Criminal Focus* (Washington, D. C.: U. S. Department of Justice, 1985).

46. Susan E. Martin and Lawrence W. Sherman, "Selective Apprehension: A Police Strategy for Repeat Offenders," *Criminology* 24 (February 1986): 155–173; Susan E. Martin, "Policing Career Criminals: An Examination of an Innovative Crime Control Program," *Journal of Criminal Law and Criminology* 77 (Winter 1986): 1159–1182.

47. Tony Pate and Robert A. Bowers, *Three Approaches to Criminal Apprehension in Kansas City: An Evaluation Report* (Washington, D. C.: Police Foundation, 1976).

Chapter 8

Close the Loopholes

Prosecute the Career Criminal

Career-criminal programs became the hottest fad in criminal justice in the 1980s. Selective incapacitation and special police surveillance programs are designed to get the few hard-core career criminals off the streets and behind bars. The prosecutorial counterpart to these programs is known as the "major offender" or "major violator" unit. The idea is essentially the same: concentrate resources on the few career criminals and make sure they are prosecuted, convicted, and incarcerated. The underlying assumption is that the system is soft on crime and that many dangerous criminals get off too easily because they either are not prosecuted at all or are allowed to plead guilty to lesser offenses.

Several jurisdictions have experimented with career-criminal prosecutorial programs. Basically, the prosecutor's office designates two categories of criminal cases. One includes defendants labeled "major offenders"; the second includes all others. Major offenders are those charged with a violent crime who also have a substantial prior criminal record (usually defined as a conviction and incarceration for at least one prior violent crime). The San Diego Major Violator Unit, for example, targets robbery and robbery-related homicide cases in which the defendant is charged with three or more separate robbery-related offenses or has been convicted of one or more serious offenses in the preceding ten years.[1]

A prosecutor who is assigned a major-violator case follows it through to completion. This approach is intended to correct what many people believe to be one of the major weaknesses of normal prosecution. In San Diego, for instance, a case would ordinarily pass through the hands of as many as seven prosecutors as it proceeded through the system. Continuity of prosecutorial attention is designed to avoid the little mistakes that can occur when someone unfamiliar with a case is assigned to it and, at the same time, to heighten the commitment of individual prosecutors to particular cases. Presumably each Major Violator Unit prosecutor will identify more closely with each case and pursue it more vigorously than might any of a series of prosecutors. In San Diego, prosecutors maintain close personal contact with witnesses. The failure of witnesses to cooperate fully and effectively is one of the main reasons that cases are "lost" (usually through dismissal). Prosecutors are also involved in the preparation of the presentence investigation (PSI) report and submit an independent "sentence statement" to the judge. In other words, they actively lobby for a severe sentence.

Career-criminal programs also typically involve limitations on plea bargaining. In San Diego, prosecutors will accept a plea only to the top felony court. Thus the defendant cannot escape the possibility of prison by pleading to a misdemeanor or a lesser felony that typically receives a sentence of probation.

In sum, career-criminal prosecution programs are designed to ensure prosecution to the top felony charge, close off the loophole of plea bargaining, avoid loss of the case through mistakes or witness problems, ensure conviction, and, upon conviction, ensure a severe sentence (presumably a long prison term).

Alas, the concept does not live up to its promises. My position is:

PROPOSITION 16

Career-criminal prosecution programs do not appreciably increase the number of convictions, lengthen sentences, or lower crime rates.

The reason for this failure is simple: we are already tough on so-called career criminals. They do not slip through unprosecuted and unpunished. Consequently, there is little to be gained by "getting tough."

Data from the San Diego Major Violator Unit program confirms the point that prosecutors were already tough on career criminals in that jurisdiction. The unit produced conviction rates of 91.5 percent, a figure that seems impressive until we discover that 89.5 percent of the so-called career criminals were being convicted under the normal operations of the San Diego prosecutor's officer. The rate of incarceration also showed a slight increase, from 95.3 percent to 100 percent. Proponents of the program can perhaps take some satisfaction in the 100 percent incarceration rate, but the normal rate of 95.3 percent hardly represents a system soft on crime.[2]

The Major Violator Unit increased the rate of prison commitments from 77.1 percent to 92.5 percent and doubled the average length of incarceration. Possibly some judges handed out longer prison terms to people they would have sentenced to prison anyway, but most of the increase comes from sending more offenders to prison rather than to jail. This effect is a result of the California practice of "split sentences": many felons are sentenced to a term in the county jail followed by probation. The practice produces some confusion in efforts to interpret California statistics because even though certain offenders do not go to prison, they are incarcerated, at least for a short term. The major-offender program apparently resulted in fewer split sentences and more direct commitments to prison. In this respect, then, the program did produce a "tougher" approach.

Did the San Diego Major Violator Unit work? Its impact was felt in two of four areas—rate of prison commitments and length of incarceration. But this accomplishment represented only marginal gains, since most of the career criminals were already being incarcerated for at least a short period of time. The evaluation of the program did not address the question of whether or not the higher rate of prison commitments and consequent increase in time served had any impact on the crime rate or on the subsequent behavior of the individual offenders.

San Diego is not atypical. The National Institute of Justice evaluated three other career-criminal programs and found a similar pattern of marginal effects. Conviction rates went from 66.6 percent to 73.4 percent in Kalamazoo, from 81.8 percent to 88.7 percent in New Orleans, and from 73.9 percent to 76.4 percent in Columbus, Ohio. Incarceration rates rose slightly in two of the cities but actually declined in New Orleans. Similarly, sentence lengths went up in two cities but went down in Kalamazoo.[3]

To understand the limited impact of career-criminal programs we need to return to our criminal justice wedding cake. The point of our distinction between the second and third layers is that prosecutors routinely divide felony cases into two categories. Their criteria include a common-sense notion of dangerousness which relies primarily on the offense charged and the defendant's prior record; these are also the two main criteria used by career-criminal programs. As I argued earlier, the toughness of the system is largely hidden because analysts typically lump all felonies or even all robberies together. The figures for the less serious crimes, and in particular the nonstranger crimes, depress the aggregate figures, masking the figures for the so-called career criminals. The Vera Institute study, which separates the stranger from the nonstranger crimes (recall figure 2.3), provides a much clearer picture of how the system routinely handles dangerous criminals.

Abolish the Insanity Defense

John W. Hinckley never succeeded at much in life, but he is probably responsible for a significant change in American criminal justice. When he was acquitted for the attempted assassination of President Reagan, he set off a national outcry against the insanity defense. Two states immediately abolished it, and similar bills were introduced in at least twenty other states and in the U.S. Congress.

Hinckley's acquittal touched one of the most sensitive of conservatives' nerves: they were outraged by the sight of a guilty person "beating the rap" and "getting off" because of a "technicality" of criminal procedure. There is little doubt that John Hinckley did in fact shoot and wound the president; we all saw the event replayed endlessly on television. It is small comfort to the outraged that Hinckley is incarcerated—the fact that he is in a room in a hospital rather than a cell in a prison is largely a matter of semantics. Nor is it any comfort that his wealth and notoriety will probably keep him there longer than he would have had to stay if he had shot some ordinary person. These practical details pale beside the symbolic impact of the "not guilty" verdict.

To conservatives and many other Americans the insanity defense is the classic loophole. Not only does it permit the guilty to get off, in their view, but it allows truly dangerous people to go free: The insanity defense conjures up images of criminally insane persons roaming the streets in search of another innocent victim. The spectacle of insanity-defense proceedings touches another sensitive nerve as well. The parade of psychiatrists and expert witnesses fuels the belief that the experts play games while ordinary people suffer. The Hinckley case also buttresses the notion that the wealthy can buy the experts who will win them acquittal.

The conservative response is to abolish the insanity defense on the grounds that it is a loophole that lets dangerous criminals escape punishment. Abolition legislation takes several forms. One bill before Congress provides that "mental illness shall not be a defense to any charge of criminal conduct." Illinois added a new "guilty but mentally ill" verdict in 1981. These subtle distinctions are important, as we shall discover when we examine the effect of abolishing the insanity defense.

Our concern here is with the impact of the insanity defense on crime. We can state unequivocally:

PROPOSITION 17

Abolition of the insanity defense or restriction of its use will have absolutely no effect on serious crime.

The proposal to abolish the insanity defense raises four separate issues. The first concerns the extent of its use. How many criminal defendants successfully win verdicts of "not guilty by reason of insanity"? If there is a loophole, how big is it? A second issue involves the fate of those who do win acquittal. Do they return to the streets? How soon? Do they endanger the public? This concern relates to the third issue: dangerousness. If some are dangerous, how can we identify them? How can we tell when it is safe to release them? The fourth issue is the effect of abolishing the insanity defense. What difference would it make? What would be the impact on crime and criminal justice?

Frequency of Acquittal

The first issue is the easiest to deal with. The insanity defense is a rare and isolated phenomenon in American criminal justice. It is seldom invoked, and very few of the defendants who attempt to use it are successful. Norval

Morris estimates that the plea is entered in only 2 percent of those cases that come to trial. Since so few cases actually go to trial, Morris estimates that the plea is raised in *one-tenth of 1 percent* of all felony complaints. The degree of public misunderstanding on this point is extraordinary. In Illinois a poll revealed that people thought that nearly 40 percent of all criminal defendants used the insanity defense. This misunderstanding explains the fact that nearly half (48.9 percent) thought it should be abolished and an incredible 94.7 percent thought it should be reformed.[4]

Pleading not guilty is one thing; winning is something else. Very few of the defendants who plead not guilty by reason of insanity succeed in gaining such a verdict. The deputy attorney general of Idaho (which abolished the defense in 1982) reported that 245 defendants introduced the plea in 1981 and only 12 were successful: a success rate of 4.8 percent. In the other 95 percent of the cases, the defense attorneys were grasping at straws, doing the best they could for their clients. Such efforts may clutter up the courts a little, but they are so sparse that they are hardly responsible for the congestion of which the courts complain.[5]

In short, the insanity defense represents a tiny and insignificant part of the criminal justice process. If this alleged loophole were closed, the effect would hardly be noticed. The attention given to the insanity defense is a classic example of the celebrated-case phenomenon. All of the well-known insanity defense cases of recent years—those of John W. Hinckley, Mark David Chapman, and David Berkowitz and them—come from the top layer of the criminal justice wedding cake. They are completely unrepresentative of the criminal justice process, but they raise potent *symbolic* issues. For many people they symbolize the apparent weakness of the criminal justice system in the face of dangerous criminals.

Defendants found not guilty by reason of insanity fall into two categories. In one group are the celebrated cases—the John W. Hinckleys—who win acquittal through elaborate and highly publicized trials. Another, very different group includes defendants who are quietly judged to be insane through informal proceedings. In Ohio, for example, about a hundred defendants are committed to mental institutions every year. Most of those commitments are the result of stipulated findings: prosecution and defense agree that the defendant is crazy. In other words, few of the total commitments follow a contested trial in which the defense successfully "beats" the prosecution.

Moreover, not all of the defendants committed to mental health institutions are dangerous in the sense of having committed a violent offense. Of the 500 men in the Bridgewater [Massachusetts] State Hospital for the Criminally Insane, more than 100 had been charged with vagrancy.[6] These people are not dangerous sociopaths. They are pathetic individuals who have serious mental health problems and cannot cope with their lives. They sank through the various safety nets and ended up on skid row, where they finally were arrested.

Aftermath of Acquittal

The fate of defendants who are committed to mental institutions after winning verdicts of not guilty by reason of insanity is a complex and controversial issue. Liberals generally contend that criminal defendants committed to a mental institution are likely to spend more time in confinement than they would if they were found guilty of the crime and sent to prison. Conservatives, on the other hand, maintain that they get out too soon. The evidence is mixed and complicated by the fact that practices have been changing. In earlier years there was considerable truth to the liberal argument. Recent court decisions and legislation have led to greater protection of the rights of the confined. One of the most important rights, in the present context, is the right to periodic review of a mental patient's condition to determine whether continued confinement is justified. The landmark case of *Baxtrom* v. *Herold* forced the release of persons held for long periods of time in the New York State Hospital for the Criminally Insane and necessitated the development of new procedures for continued confinement.

Consequently, criminal defendants now spend less time in mental institutions than they used to. But this is not to say that they necessarily get out very early. Henry Steadman studied a group of defendants found incompetent to stand trial. A defendant who is too crazy to comprehend the nature of a criminal trial is committed to an institution until he or she is able to understand the proceedings, at which point the criminal process resumes. Steadman found that those defendants deemed "nondangerous" spent less than two years in mental institutions, while the "dangerous" were confined an average of two years and two months. If convicted at trial, they faced the possibility of additional prison time. Do you "beat the rap" by taking the mental health route? asks Steadman. No. "Mental hospitals are simply an alternative place to do time." In short, the system is not turning hordes of dangerous psychotics loose on society.[7]

Danger to the Community

How dangerous are the criminally insane? Several court decisions that forced the release of criminal defendants provide some "natural experiments" that help answer the question. The 1971 *Dixon* case forced the reassessment of 586 inmates of Pennsylvania's Fairview State Hospital for the Criminally Insane. Over two-thirds of them were eventually released into the community. During the entire four-year follow-up period, 27 percent were rearrested. Only 11 percent, however, were rearrested for a violent crime. Meanwhile, some others were rehospitalized for a violent act. Altogether, then, 14.5 percent proved to be "dangerous."[8]

Once again we encounter the prediction problem. A decision to release or confine persons alleged to be criminally insane is really a prediction about their future behavior. Will they or will they not go out and commit a violent act? The success rate in predicting the dangerousness of the criminally insane is no better than in other areas of criminal justice. In another study of 160 persons found incompetent to stand trial and eventually released to the community, 96 had originally been predicted to be dangerous; yet only 13 actually proved to be so. Thus there were 83 "false positives," which is to say that the prediction of dangerousness was wrong 86 percent of the time.[9]

Effects of Abolition

Like most meat-ax approaches to criminal justice reform, "abolishing" the insanity defense is a futile effort. Even if it could be abolished or substantially changed, there would be no impact on crime for the simple reason that it is used so rarely. The insanity defense is virtually a nonexistent factor in the prosecution of robbery and burglary cases.

Substantial revision of the insanity defense also introduces serious theoretical and practical problems. "Abolition" is actually too broad a term to describe all the current proposals for change. One approach would revise the law to read, "Mental condition shall not be a defense to any charge of criminal conduct." A bill introduced in Congress in 1982 (H. R. 6653) contains this language, which, as we shall discover, does not completely eliminate consideration of mental condition. A second approach substitutes a verdict of "guilty but mentally ill" for the insanity defense. Illinois adopted this approach in 1981.

Consideration of any proposal to modify the insanity defense requires a discussion of the most fundamental principles of the Anglo-American criminal law. Our system rests on the principle that the accused is innocent until proven guilty and that the prosecution must prove guilt beyond a reasonable doubt. To prove guilt the prosecution must establish three things. First, it must prove that the accused committed the act. In legal jargon this is referred to as the *actus reus*. Then the prosecution must prove that the accused had criminal intent. This is known as the *mens rea* requirement. Finally, the prosecution must establish a connection between the two: the accused did it and intended to do it.

The heart of the matter is the *mens rea* requirement. The criminal law has long reflected the common-sense idea that there are various degrees of intent. The differences are most clearly seen in relation to murder. The law acknowledges the great difference between a murder that we planned (usually first-degree murder) and one committed in the heat of passion (second-degree). It further recognizes that some homicides occur without any criminal intent (manslaughter). The law expresses consideration of these differences in mental state by differentiating the penalties. First-degree murder, being the most heinous crime, is virtually the only crime today that carries the death penalty.

The law has historically recognized the principle that some people lack full criminal intent because they do not understand what they are doing. Two examples are commonly cited. The three-year-old who picks up the loaded handgun and accidentally shoots and kills his father does not have criminal intent. The child simply does not appreciate the nature and consequences of firing the gun. Another example involves the truly deranged person who is acting under the direction of voices from another planet. This person is so psychotic that he or she too fails to appreciate the criminal nature of the act.[10]

Unfortunately, not all cases are as simple as these examples; many are ambiguous. The legal system has struggled for nearly 150 years to develop a formula that would resolve the question of the accused's mental state. The principle of insanity first entered English law in 1843 in the famous *M' Naughton* case. This is often referred to as the "right–wrong test": did the accused understand the difference between right and wrong? Because this test is somewhat crude, legal scholars have attempted to develop alternatives. Lay persons are often mystified by the arcane distinctions among those alternatives, none of which resolves the basic problem created by the intersection of medical diagnoses, with their inevitable shades of gray, and the legal system, with its requirement of an absolute verdict of guilt or innocence.

Abolishing the insanity defense is easier said then done for the simple reason that the *men rea* requirement remains a fundamental legal principle. Let us consider what would happen under the first of the two proposed changes. The idea that "mental condition shall not be a defense to any charge of criminal conduct" could be interpreted in one of two ways. The broader interpretation would mean that absolutely no aspect of mental condition could be taken into account. In effect, this interpretation would abolish the *men rea* requirement altogether. The prosecution would not have to prove anything about the accused's mental state. Clearly, this approach strikes at the heart of American criminal jurisprudence. For one thing, it would wipe out the distinctions that separate first-degree murder, second-degree murder, and manslaughter. It is doubtful that even the most ardent opponents of the insanity defense seriously want to take this approach. So sweeping is its effect, moreover, that it would probably be found unconstitutional. We might note, for the record, that Wisconsin abolished the insanity defense in 1909, as did Mississippi in 1928. In both instances the respective state supreme courts found the new laws unconstitutional under the due-process clauses of their state constitutions.[11]

A more limited reading of the wording "mental condition shall not be a defense to any charge of criminal conduct" would mean that an affirmative plea of "not guilty by reason of insanity" could not be raised. The crucial distinction here is drawn between affirmative and ordinary defenses. An *ordinary* defense is simply an attempt to show that the prosecution has failed to connect the accused with the crime (the *actus reus* in combination with the *mens rea*). An *affirmative* defense is raised when the prosecution has connected the accused with the crime. Self-defense is a good example. The defense argues that, yes, the accused did shoot and kill the person and did so intentionally, but because the act was committed in self-defense the accused does not bear criminal responsibility for it. The same is true in the case of a criminal act committed under duress. The insanity defense, in this respect, is an affirmative defense.[12]

What would happen if insanity as an affirmative defense were abolished? Put yourself in the shoes of a defense attorney and the answer is obvious. You would attack the prosecution's case head on, on the basic *mens rea* requirement. You would argue that your client lacked the necessary criminal intent. You would not win every time, of course, but you might win some of the time, with the net result that your client would walk out of the courtroom completely free. This outcome would be even more outrageous than our current situation in the eyes of the people who oppose the insanity defense. Even when you didn't win, you would still have forced consideration of your client's mental condition in the trial. In short, eradication of the insanity defense per se would not suspend consideration of the same issues under another name. The *mens rea* requirement is a bedrock principle of our legal system and there is no getting around it.

The "guilty but mentally ill" (or GBMI) approach has three serious flaws. First, it strikes indirectly at the *mens rea* requirement, introducing the slippery notion that the accused had partial, but not complete, criminal intent. Second, it simply creates a lesser and included offense. There is considerable evidence to suggest that judges and juries are flexible and very willing to compromise in order to reach what appears to be a common-sense verdict. In some cases they believe that the accused probably did something wrong but are unwilling to bring in a verdict of guilty on the top charge. Because the accused deserves some punishment, the jury compromises by finding him or her guilty of a lesser offense, allowing some punishment but not too much. The proposed option would invite juries in doubt about the prosecution's case and the accused's mental state to resolve their dilemma with a verdict of "guilty but mentally ill." Finally, the GBMI verdict is a fraud. As proposed, it makes no provision for treatment of the person who has been declared mentally ill. In the words of one American Civil Liberties Union (ACLU) official, such a verdict is as meaningful as a declaration of "guilty but appendicitis."[13]

Prisons cannot handle the inmates with mental problems they currently have in custody. They are in no position to accept more inmates with even worse problems. We can imagine the sequence of events. The convicted offender, let's say a man, is sentenced to prison, where his behavior becomes a problem. He is then transferred to the state mental hospital for treatment. Once his behavior stabilizes, he is tranferred back to prison. Because prisons are such brutalizing institutions, his behavior is likely to deteriorate again and the cycle will repeat itself. This is not to suggest that our public mental hospitals are models of effective treatment and humane custody. They are not, and much of the "treatment" is meaningless. But sending an allegedly mentally ill person to prison is an even worse solution.

The "guilty but mentally ill" approach has already proven to be a bogus reform. The 1981 Illinois law, instead of abolishing the insanity defense, only succeeded in adding GBMI as a new alternative. In Cook County (Chicago), verdicts of not guilty by reason of insanity (NGRI) actually increased from 34 to 103 between 1981 and 1984. At the same time, GBMI verdicts went from 16 in 1982, the first year the option was available, to 87 in 1984. The law also failed to provide medical treatment for GBMI defendants. Although it had been intended to require treatment, an evaluation found that "not a single GBMI offender has been transferred from the Department of Corrections to the Department of Mental Health" for treatment. The law only "complicated rather than resolved [the] fundamental issues surrounding the insanity defense."[14]

The real function of the "guilty but mentally ill" option is to appease public sentiment. The public has little concern for the messy details of what actually happens to a mentally ill criminal defendant. It does know that some people who in fact committed crimes are found not guilty. Although the practical difference would be negligible, the public would be much happier knowing that these people were found guilty.

In sum, the various proposals to abolish or modify the insanity defense fail on two counts. Not only will they fail to reduce crime, as I asserted earlier, but they would probably do mischief to the criminal justice process.

Abolish Plea Bargaining

Plea bargaining has been attacked by both conservatives and liberals. Conservatives hold that it is another loophole that allows criminals to beat the system, either by having charges dropped altogether or by having a serious felony charge reduced to a lesser felony or misdemeanor. Liberals, for their part, believe that plea bargaining is a fundamentally irrational practice by which decisions are made on the basis of expediency rather than according to any factor related to the merits of the case. More troubling to liberals is the belief that bargaining puts a premium on pleading guilty and thereby subtly coerces defendants into waiving their constitutional protection against self-incrimination. Some argue that the practice encourages prosecutors deliberately to "overcharge," to add on more charges to be used as bargaining chips, while the defense attorney becomes more interested in maintaining good relations with other members of the courtroom work group than in vigorously defending his or her client. Thus the rights of the defendant are sacrificed in the name of efficiency.[15] Finally, plea bargains are almost completely unregulated, and their very secrecy is a source of much public suspicion about the criminal justice system.

The standard defense of plea bargaining is based on the argument that it

is absolutely essential to the operations of the American criminal courts. It is the only way to dispose of the enormous volume of criminal cases that pour into the system daily. If plea bargaining were abolished, according to this view, the system would collapse immediately. I call this argument the "nightmare defense" of plea bargaining.

For a brief period in the early 1970s there was a lot of talk about abolishing plea bargaining. The National Advisory Commission on Criminal Justice Standards and Goals recommended in 1973 that plea bargaining be abolished within five years.[16] Alaska abolished plea bargaining in 1975. Meanwhile, new sentencing laws restricted plea bargaining for certain offenses in a few states, and some local prosecutors limited bargaining for particular offenses in their jurisdictions. The opponents of plea bargaining, although numerous throughout the country, have never coalesced into an organized movement, as the well-organized opponents of the death penalty have done. Interest in abolition gradually faded.

The Phantom Loophole

Plea bargaining proved to be an extremely elusive target. As an informal process rather than a concrete event, it is simply hard to get hold of. The exclusionary rule, by way of contrast, is a manageable target. Plea bargaining is also a phantom loophole. Hard-core criminals do not routinely use it to beat the system. Abolishing plea bargaining produces results quite irrelevant to our basic goal of reducing serious crime. Public awareness of plea bargaining and outrage against it reached their peak in 1973, when Vice President Spiro Agnew, in perhaps the most famous plea bargain of all time, avoided going to prison on extortion charges by agreeing not to contest a lesser charge. The Agnew case, of course, represents the classic celebrated case. We should be careful not to overreact to such unique events. Rather, we should direct our attention to routine felony cases. As I argued in Part One of this book, the majority of felonies are handled with a profound sense of bureaucratic regularity. Most bargains are made in open-and-shut cases and little actual bargaining takes place at all.[17]

As far as the control of serious crime is concerned, we can state with confidence:

PROPOSITION 18

The abolition of plea bargaining will not reduce serious crime.

To understand plea bargaining and its effect on the crime rate, we should now look at those jurisdictions that have tried to abolish it.

Alaska Bans Plea Bargaining!

In 1975 the attorney general of Alaska banned plea bargaining throughout the state. This action constitutes the single most important experiment in plea-bargaining reform. Alaska is unique in that local prosecutors are appointed by and work under the supervision of the state attorney general. In the continental United States local prosecutors are elected and enjoy almost complete political and administrative independence. Yet none of them have the authority to abolish plea bargaining, or to make any other reforms in prosecutorial operations.

On July 3, 1975, Avrum Gross, Alaska's attorney general, issued a memorandum that read, in part:

I wish to have the following policy implemented with respect to all adult criminal offenses in which charges have been filed on or after August 15, 1975:

(1) . . . District Attorneys and Assistant District Attorneys will refrain from engaging in plea negotiations with defendants designed to arrive at an agreement for entry of a plea of guilty in return for a particular sentence. . . .

(4) . . . While there continues to be nothing wrong with reducing a charge, reductions should not occur simply to obtain a plea of guilty.

(5) Like any general rule, there are going to be some exceptions to this policy [which must be approved by the attorney general's office].

The new policy thus attacked plea bargaining in three ways. Paragraph 1 abolished the traditional practice of "sentence bargaining"; paragraph 4 abolished "charge bargaining"; and paragraph 5 established a procedure for formal supervision and allowed possible exceptions to the general policy.[18]

Contrary to popular expectations, Alaska's criminal justice system did not collapse with the end of plea bargaining. The criminal courts in Alaska continued to function much as they had been doing. Surprisingly, defendants pleaded guilty about as often as they had done before. The number of trials increased about 50 percent but the total remained quite small. The percentage of cases that went to trial increased from 6.7 percent to 9.6 percent.

The ban also failed to confirm another common prediction. Norval Morris and others argue that discretion is a fixed quantity in the administration of justice: we can't eliminate it; we succeed only in moving it around.[19] This argument holds that reducing the discretion of the prosecutor will serve only to increase the discretion of police officers. Discretion will be pushed backward in the system. Knowing that prosecutors have less flexibility, cops will be more careful about whom they bring into the system and on what charges. Evidence drawn from evaluations of other reforms indicates that this phenomenon does exist. But it did not appear to be a factor in Alaska's ban on plea bargaining.

One measure of the movement of discretion within the system is the rate of dismissals, either by the prosecutor (in what is called "postarrest screening") or by a judge at some point before trial. In theory, more cases will be dismissed because prosecutors are unable to settle them by bargaining down to a lesser offense. In Alaska, the rate of dismissals remained consistently high (about 52 percent before and after the ban). There was some increase in the rate of dismissals of drug and morals cases, but it did not seem to relate to problems of weak evidence. It appeared to be more a function of the fact that prosecutors accorded those cases low priority.

The Alaska courts not only did not collapse but actually disposed of cases at a faster rate than before the ban. In Anchorage, the mean disposition time for felony cases dropped from 192.1 to 89.5 months. Slightly less drastic reductions occurred in Fairbanks and Juneau.

With respect to sentencing, some surprising results were found. Sentences were more severe, but only for offenses not considered serious and for offenders whose records showed only minor infractions, if any. This is the trickle-up phenomenon that has been observed elsewhere. New policies designed to get tough with serious crime exert their primary effect on lesser offenses. Under normal circumstances, persons charged with lesser felonies—the lowest grade of felonious assault or burglary—or with no prior criminal record receive relatively light punishment, usually through plea bargaining. A get-tough policy, such as a ban on plea bargaining, closes off this avenue of mitigation and produces harsher penalties.

The ban did not have the same effect on defendants who were charged with serious crimes or who had substantial criminal records. The researchers who evaluated the Alaska experiment concluded that "the conviction and sentencing of persons charged with serious crimes of violence such as murder, rape, robbery, and felonious assault appeared completely unaffected by the change in policy."[20] These people were not beating the system before plea bargaining was banned. There was no loophole to close.

From the standpoint of our inquiry, the relevant question is whether or not the ban on plea bargaining affected the crime rate. Unfortunately, the evaluation of the Alaska experiment did not examine this issue. But the mere fact that the ban had no effect on the disposition of cases involving serious crimes suggests that there was no impact on crime itself.

Other Experiments

Other attempts to ban plea bargaining focus on specific offenses, such as the use of handguns and possession of narcotics. When Michigan enacted a new gun-control law providing mandatory prison terms in 1976–1977 ("One with a gun gets you two"), the Wayne County (Detroit) prosecutor supplemented it with a ban on plea bargaining. Prosecutors would not drop gun-related charges in return for a guilty plea. This was a seemingly important step. A common plea-bargaining tactic is to drop a gun-related charge to a nongun charge: from armed robbery to simple robbery, for example. In the context of the new Michigan law, that would mean evasion of the mandatory provisions of the Felony Firearms Law (no probation, no parole). There is considerable evidence that this charge-reduction element of the plea-bargaining process has historically been a way of evading mandatory or especially severe sentencing requirements.[21]

An evaluation of the Michigan law found no significant change in minimum sentences for homicide and armed robbery cases. The going rate for armed robbery continued to be about six years in prison. Nor was there any evidence that Wayne County prosecutors had previously been exceptionally lenient in bargaining with defendants charged with those crimes. There was a noticeable change in sentences for defendants charged with felonious assault. In another illustration of the trickle-up effect, the law resulted in greater minimum sentences. In general, prosecutors view assaults as less serious than other crimes, such as robbery, rape, and murder, and therefore assault cases are more often subject to bargaining in regard to both charge and sentence. The new law did close off some avenues for such defendants. But the same degree of leniency was not traditional for the more serious cases of murder and armed robbery. Here leniency was not the problem, and getting tough by ending plea bargaining was no solution.

The 1973 New York drug law, widely advertised as "the nation's toughest drug law," also restricted plea bargaining. Persons charged with a Class A-I drug felony (which carried a mandatory penalty of fifteen or twenty-five years to life imprisonment) could not plead to a lesser felony. Persons charged with a lesser drug charge could not plead to a misdemeanor. An extensive evaluation of the New York law found that it was ineffective in reducing either drug use or violent crime.[22] We examined the New York law in detail earlier in our discussion of mandatory sentencing.

Meanwhile, in Hampton County, Iowa, a local prosecutor ran for office successfully on a platform of "no deals with dope pushers." The policy only served to push discretion further back in the system. In 1972, before the new policy went into effect, guilty pleas were accepted in 107 out of the 109 drug-sale cases disposed of. Eighty-eight of those 107 defendants pleaded guilty to a reduced charge. By 1974, a year after the policy went into effect, all of the guilty pleas were to the original charge. Yet only 41 drug-sale cases were disposed of (37 by plea and 4 by trial). The number of drug cases disposed of had dropped by more than 60 percent. Only part of this decline can be attributed to outright dismissals. The dismissal rate increased slightly, from 31 percent to 36 percent. More significant was the decline in cases filed in the first place: from 157 in 1972 to 63 in 1974. Getting tough in this instance meant getting tough with far fewer cases, a message that hardly represents getting tough with the original crime problem.[23]

In Search of Bargains

Plea bargaining resists abolition for many reasons. First, as we have seen, the courtroom work group can easily evade the intent of any major change imposed by outsiders. Second, and perhaps more important, plea bargaining simply may not be the problem many people think it is. Peter Nardulli's study of plea bargaining in three states (Illinois, Pennsylvania, Michigan) confirms our analysis of the "going rate." He found a "rather high level of order" in the 7,500 cases he analyzed. The charges were changed significantly in only 15 percent of the cases in which defendants pleaded guilty. In 60 percent of those 5,600 cases, the original charge was not changed at all. Nardulli found some reduction in 26.7 percent of those cases and some enhancement of the charges in 13.3 percent. In other words, prosecutors were not wheeling and dealing with charges as if the courts were some kind of Middle Eastern bazaar.[24]

Regulation, Not Abolition

The evidence yielded by attempts to abolish plea bargaining confirms our general theory of the criminal justice wedding cake. Prosecutors routinely make moral judgments about criminal cases. Cases that fit a common-sense label of "serious," because of either the nature of the crime or the defendant's prior record, fall into the second layer. Those deemed "not serious" fall into the third layer. The relationship between the offender and the victim is a crucial element in this judgment. Robberies and rapes between people who know each other quickly find themselves in the third layer, where most bargains are to be found. But armed robberies and rapes by strangers are grouped in the second layer, where prosecutors are routinely fairly tough. See Chapters 2 and 3.

Much can and should be done about plea bargaining short of abolishing it. The most reasonable proposals call for regulation.[25] Bargaining should be brought out of the closet, so to speak, through the requirement of a written record. Formal policy guidelines could also establish criteria for reduction of charges and sentence recommendations. Implementation of these proposals would bolster public confidence in the administration of justice. It is the appearance of injustice and arbitrary decision making, as distinct from substantive injustice, that generates so much public cynicism and distrust of the administration of justice. Building public confidence and trust is a worthy goal, but we should recognize that it is something very different from reducing crime.

Restrict Appeals

Speaking for many conservatives, Judge Macklin Fleming argues that the criminal justice system is undermined by a quixotic search for "perfect justice," which not only permits but encourages multiple postconviction appeals. The number and variety of postconviction appeals theoretically available to a convicted offender is truly impressive. Judge Fleming lists twenty-six potential challenges to a criminal charge available to a convicted offender in California (from arrest through postconviction appeals) on search-and-seizure grounds only:

1. At the preliminary examination. If, disregarding improperly seized evidence, there is insufficient cause to hold the defendant, he must be discharged.

2. At a motion to set aside the accusation as having been brought without reasonable or probable cause. If on hearing the motion the court determines that evidence has been improperly seized and concludes that without this illegally seized evidence insufficient cause to charge the defendant is present, defendant must be discharged.

3. If the motion to set aside the accusation in step 2 is denied, defendant can apply for a writ of prohibition to the court of appeal.

4. If unsuccessful in step 3, defendant can apply to the California Supreme Court for the same writ.

5. Defendant can move for an evidentiary hearing to suppress the evidence he claims was unlawfully seized.

6. If his motion to suppress evidence is denied, he can apply for a writ of mandate or prohibition to the court of appeal. Ordinarily, prosecution of the cause will be stayed pending such review.

7. If unsuccessful in step 6, defendant can apply for the same writ in the California Supreme Court.

8. Defendant can seek to remove the cause to the federal district court on the claim that he has been denied his federal civil rights.

9. If removal is denied by the federal district court, he can appeal the order of denial to the federal court of appeals.

10. If the federal court of appeals rules against him, he can petition the United States Supreme Court for certiorari.

11. Defendant can initiate a new action in federal court charging violation of his civil rights and seeking injunctive relief, suppression of evidence, etc.

12. If preliminary relief is denied him in step 11, he can appeal the denial to the federal court of appeals.

13. Thereafter he can petition the United States Supreme Court for certiorari.

14. At his trial defendant can object to the admissibility of evidence on the ground it is the product of unlawful search and seizure. While California appellate courts have been firm in their rulings that a defendant who has previously been granted an evidentiary hearing is not entitled to a further evidentiary hearing at the trial nor entitled to renew an earlier motion, nevertheless he is entitled to object to admission of the material into evidence and is entitled to make a new motion based on new grounds, as for example that the law has been changed by a later appellate ruling or that new evidence to support a motion to suppress has been discovered.

15. If defendant is convicted, he can renew his claims on a motion for a new trial. This motion is subject to the limitations mentioned in step 14. But again the possibility exists that some new mandatory retroactive interpretation of the law of search and seizure by some appellate court will require reconsideration of a former ruling.

16. Defendant can appeal his judgment of conviction to the court of appeal and obtain a further review of the lawfulness of the challenged search and seizure.

17. If the appeal in step 16 is lost, he can petition for a hearing in the California Supreme Court.

18. If the petition for hearing in the California Supreme Court is denied, or if that court affirms the judgment against him, he can petition for certiorari to the United States Supreme Court.

19. Thereafter, defendant can apply for postconviction relief in the California superior court on the ground that his conviction was obtained by means of unconstitutionally seized evidence.

20. If relief is denied, he is entitled to a free transcript of the hearing in the superior court to enable him to apply for the same relief to the court of appeal.

21. If relief is denied by the court of appeal, he can petition the California Supreme Court for the same relief.

22. Thereafter he can petition for certiorari to the United States Supreme Court.

23. Defendant can also pursue postconviction remedies in federal district court by seeking a writ of habeas corpus on the ground that his conviction was obtained through use of unconstitutionally seized evidence.

24. If the federal district court denies relief, he can appeal to the federal court of appeals.

25. Thereafter he can again petition for certiorari to the United States Supreme Court.

26. At any time he can petition the California appellate courts for an extraordinary writ to vacate the original judgment. These writs are variously entitled Petition to Recall Remittitur or Petition for Writ of Error Coram Nobis, and are principally used when there has been a retrospective change in applicable law.

SOURCE: From *The Price of Perfect Justice*, by Macklin Fleming, pp. 50–51. Copyright 1974 by Basic Books, Inc. Reprinted by permission.

Nor is this the end of the story. Fleming points out that "in almost every one of the foregoing steps the losing defendant can petition for a rehearing or reconsideration by the particular court that ruled against him." Thus potential appeals just on a search-and-seizure question number more than fifty. And should that method fail, the offender may be able to start over again on some other issue, such as incompetent counsel. For the imaginative and determined offender the possibilities are seemingly endless.[26]

The use of all possible appeals is most evident in death-penalty cases. Obviously, with the stakes so high, the defense attorney has a powerful incentive to explore every possible avenue. Appeals in death-penalty cases can take as long as ten years. The average appears to be about seven years. The sudden increase in executions in late 1983 and early 1984 represents the exhaustion of appeals for offenders convicted under post-1976 statutes.

Conservatives argue that multiple appeals undermine the administration of justice in six ways. The first problem is the work load they impose on the courts. Former chief justice Burger made this one of his major issues during his tenure on the Court. He has spoken out repeatedly on the problem of the Court's increasing work load and has proposed several solutions. Restricting criminal appeals is one of them.[27]

From a crime control perspective, the most serious problem is the lack of finality. Finality is an extremely important issue for conservatives. If the criminal justice system is to deter people from criminal acts, it must send a clear message to potential criminals. "Swift and certain" punishment is designed to impress upon them the wrongfulness of criminality. If the punishment is to be certain, the judgment must be final. Protracted appeals leave the final judgment in limbo. The continued possibility that the conviction will be reversed undermines the deterrent effect. Conservatives believe that this uncertainty encourages criminality.[28]

Liberals see the absence of finality as a virtue. Protection of individual rights requires recognition of the possibility of error in the criminal justice process. Do errors occur? Hugo Bedeau and Michael Radelet estimated that for every twenty persons executed in this country since 1900, at least one innocent person was convicted of a capital crime. They identified a total of 343 miscarriages of justice; 25 of these victims were executed and many others served prison terms of up to 25 years.[29] To make sure that no innocent person is convicted, or convicted through an improper procedure, the door to a rehearing should be kept open. In the early 1960s the U.S. Supreme Court opened that door a little wider. *Fay v. Noia* (1963) expanded the right of an offender convicted in a state court proceeding to obtain a rehearing in federal court through habeas corpus. Restricting that right of habeas corpus is the primary focus of the conservative attack on multiple appeals.

Somewhat related to the finality question is the argument that appeals undermine the moral condemnation of criminal behavior. The criminal law is a statement of the values of society, and particular sentences express those values.[30] If we are to maintain the moral order and preserve the basic standards of society, it is important to make such statements. Protracted appeals that delay or even overturn the final judgment inhibit the process.

A fourth problem is that excessive appeals transform the criminal justice process from a search for truth into a "sporting contest." Judge Fleming is the most notable proponent of this view. Our excessive concern with procedural regularity, what he labels the pursuit of "perfect justice," has caused us to lose sight of the original purpose of the criminal justice process, the search for truth. The result is that we all become cynics, viewing the process as a mere game. Public respect and confidence in the criminal justice system are thereby undermined.

A fifth problem is that appeals inhibit the rehabilitation process. If we assume that rehabilitation is a legitimate purpose of imprisonment, we must recognize that it can work only if the offender acknowledges guilt and begins the process of rehabilitation. The offender who pursues an appeal has obviously not acknowledged his or her guilt.

Finally, conservatives see appeals on the grounds of habeas corpus as creating a serious federalism problem.[31] They argue that the federal courts have intruded themselves into too many state and local issues (for instance, school integration and the drawing of voting districts). Justices Burger, Rehnquist, and O'Connor consistently rule in favor of limiting the scope of the federal judiciary in state and local issues. Restricting the right of habeas corpus is one means to that end.

The Proposed Remedy

To remedy the alleged ills of multiple appeals, conservatives propose that the right of habeas corpus be restricted. The Attorney General's Task Force on Violent Crime recommended a three-year statute of limitations on habeas corpus petitions and a prohibition on federal courts' holding evidentiary hearings "on facts which were fully expounded and found in the state court proceeding."[32] Legislation embodying this proposal is before Congress.

To understand the nature of this proposal we need to review briefly the habeas corpus right. Habeas corpus is a venerable part of Anglo-American law. The British Parliament formalized it with the Habeas Corpus Act of 1679 and Americans wrote it into the U.S. Constitution. Article III, Section 9, of the Constitution reads, "The privilege of the writ of habeas corpus shall not be suspended, unless when in case of rebellion or invasion the public safety may require it."

The writ of habeas corpus is a device to challenge the detention of a person taken into custody. Someone in custody (under arrest, perhaps, or imprisoned as a convicted felon) may demand an evidentiary hearing before a judge to examine the legality of the detention. The writ is purely procedural: it guarantees only a right to a hearing. It says nothing about the substance of the issue at hand. At the hearing the person in custody must argue that the detention is illegal because of an illegal arrest or, in the case of most postconviction hearings, that the conviction was improper because of some constitutional violation. The right of habeas corpus has been around for centuries; the present controversy stems from two U.S. Supreme Court decisions, *Brown* v. *Allen* (1953) and *Fay* v. *Noia* (1963). Both rulings expanded the right of a prisoner convicted in a state proceeding to appeal the conviction in federal court.

The door opened by *Brown* and *Fay* would be partially closed in two ways if the conservatives' proposal were implemented. First, it would prohibit federal courts from reviewing cases under habeas corpus if the facts had already been considered by a state court. The general conservative view is that federal courts, and the U.S. Supreme Court in particular, should defer to state authorities. The second change would impose a three-year statute of limitations on the filing of habeas corpus petitions. The three-year period would begin with the date of the final court judgment or the discovery of new evidence bearing on the case.

Any proposal to limit the historic privilege of habeas corpus raises serious constitutional questions. Civil libertarians oppose any limitation.[33] There is also some question as to whether a statutory limitation would be constitutional. Our primary concern here is crime control. Conservatives propose the restriction of habeas corpus as a remedy for serious crime. My position is:

─────────────────────────── **PROPOSITION 19** ───────────────────────────
*Limiting the right to petition for a writ of habeas corpus in the federal courts
would have no effect on serious crime.*

As in respect to the exclusionary rule, conservatives grossly exaggerate the impact of appeals on the criminal justice process. In fact, there aren't many habeas corpus petitions. The Administrative Office of the U.S. Courts found a total of 7,031 habeas corpus petitions from state prisoners among 196,757 criminal and civil filings in U.S. district courts in 1979–1980. This figure represented a total of 3.5 percent of all filings and 4.16 percent of civil filings.[34] In short, the federal judiciary is not being overwhelmed by habeas corpus petitions from state prisoners. If the courts are facing a steadily rising work load, it is because of the general increase in civil litigation, not because of habeas corpus.

If few habeas corpus petitions are filed by state prisoners, fewer still are successful. The Administrative Office of the Courts found that following summary review (probably by the judge's clerk) 96.5 percent of those 7,031 petitions were dismissed before trial. Only 2 percent were disposed of by trial—that is, the prisoner obtained a full evidentiary hearing. To put this in some perspective, we note that 6.5 percent of all civil cases went to trial. Unfortunately, the Office of the Courts did not determine how many of those evidentiary hearings resulted in the release of the prisoner.

These data indicate that habeas corpus petitions have only a marginal impact on the work load of the federal courts. The main conservative argument, however, is that these appeals contribute to crime. There is no evidence to support that claim and, given the limited number of appeals and the even more limited success rate, it is doubtful that such an effect exists.

The real importance of appeals based on habeas corpus lies in their *symbolic* role. As in the case of the exclusionary rule, conservatives are reacting to the spectacle of an occasional prisoner who gets off. And it is true that such cases do occur from time to time. But those are the truly celebrated cases, which do not reflect the general pattern of business in the criminal courts. Judge Fleming's list of twenty-six motions available to the convicted offender (or fifty-two, if the defendant petitions for a rehearing at each step) is purely theoretical. In practice, few of those motions are ever made. We need to recall that very few cases in the second and third layers of the wedding cake go to a contested trial. The overwhelming majority are either dismissed or settled through a negotiated plea. In other words, there is no contested point to be appealed.

The second part of the conservative proposal, calling for a three-year statute of limitations on habeas corpus petitions, would eliminate some but by no means all of the appeals. Moreover, even the drafters of the bill introduced in the Senate (S. 653) saw the need to include an exception allowing federal habeas corpus petitions when there had been "cause and prejudice" in the state court hearing. Errors are indeed possible, as the exception acknowledges, and few thoughtful conservatives are willing to close the door completely on relief in such instances. Thus the conservative proposal is hedged by exceptions that negate its intended effect.

Postconviction appeals are not a significant aspect of the criminal justice process in the overwhelming majority of felony cases. They *appear* to be significant because of the occasional celebrated case and the many death-penalty cases (about 1,300 by the end of 1983). Indeed, each death-penalty case could be regarded as a celebrated case, or at least an exceptional one. Appeals of death-penalty cases do drag on for years. They do pose an enormous burden on the courts (and on the prosecution and the defense). But we should not confuse that small group of cases with the vast number of robbery and burglary cases. Those defendants file few appeals and win even fewer. In fact, it could be argued that abolition of the death penalty and the substitution of an appropriate but less final penalty would immediately eliminate the huge burden imposed by these appeals.

Notes

1. U. S. Department of Justice, *An Exemplary Project: Major Violator Unit—San Diego, California* (Washington, D. C.: U. S. Government Printing Office, 1980).
2. Ibid.
3. Eleanor Chelimsky and Judith S. Dahmann, *National Evaluation of the Career Criminal Program: Final Report* (McLean, Va.: MITRE Corp., 1979).
4. Norval Morris, *Madness and the Criminal Law* (Chicago: University of Chicago Press, 1982); Valerie Hans, "An Analysis of Public Attitudes toward the Insanity Defense," *Criminology* 24 (May 1986): 393–414.
5. *Criminal Justice Newsletter*, July 22, 1982.
6. *Newsweek*, May 24, 1982.
7. Henry J. Steadman, *Beating a Rap? Defendants Found Incompetent to Stand Trial* (Chicago: University of Chicago Press, 1979), p. 104.
8. Terence P. Thornberry and Joseph E. Jacoby, *The Criminally Insane: A Community Follow-Up of Mentally Ill Offenders* (Chicago: University of Chicago Press, 1979).
9. Henry J. Steadman and James J. Cocozza, *Careers of the Criminally Insane* (Lexington, Mass.: Lexington Books, 1974).
10. Morris, *Madness and the Criminal Law.*
11. Grant H. Morris, *The Insanity Defense: A Blueprint for Legislative Change* (Lexington, Mass.: Lexington Books, 1975), p. 4.
12. Bruce Ennis, "Straight Talk about the Insanity Defense," *The Nation*, July 24–31, 1982, pp. 70–72.
13. Testimony of Benson Wolman, Executive Director, Ohio ACLU, before Senate Judiciary Committee, July 22, 1982.
14. John Klofus and Ralph Weisheit, "Guilty but Mentally Ill: Reform of the Insanity Defense in Illinois," *Justice Quarterly* 4 (March 1987): 39–50.
15. Abraham Blumberg, *Criminal Justice* (Chicago: Quadrangle, 1970).
16. U.S. National Advisory Commission on Criminal Justice Standards and Goals, *Courts* (Washington, D.C.: U. S. Government Printing Office, 1973), p. 46.
17. Lynn Mather, "Some Determinants of the Method of Case Disposition: Decision-Making by Public Defenders in Los Angeles," *Law and Society Review* 8 (Winter 1974): 187–216; David Sudnow, "Normal Crimes: Sociological Features of the Penal Code in a Public Defender Office," *Social Problems* 12 (Winter 1965): 255–276.
18. Michael L. Rubinstein, Stevens H. Clarke, and Teresa J. White, *Alaska Bans Plea Bargaining* (Washington, D.C.: U. S. Government Printing Office, 1980).
19. Norval Morris and Gordon J. Hawkins, *Letter to the President on Crime Control* (Chicago: University of Chicago Press, 1977), p. 61.
20. Ibid.
21. Colin Loftin and David McDowall, " 'One with a Gun Gets You Two': Mandatory Sentencing and Firearms Violence in Detroit," *The Annals* 455 (May 1981): 150–167.
22. U.S. Department of Justice, *The Nation's Toughest Drug Law: Evaluating the New York Experience* (Washington, D. C.: U. S. Government Printing Office, 1978).
23. Thomas W. Church, "Plea Bargains, Concessions, and the Courts: Analysis of a Quasi–Experiment," *Law and Society Review* 10 (Spring 1976): 377–401.
24. Peter F. Nardulli, Roy B. Flemming, and James Eisenstein, "Criminal Courts and

Bureaucratic Justice: Concessions and Consensus in the Guilty Plea Process," *Journal of Criminal Law and Criminology* 76 (Winter 1985): 1103–1131.

25. Milton Heumann, *Plea Bargaining* (Chicago: University of Chicago Press, 1978).
26. Macklin Fleming, *The Price of Perfect Justice* (New York: Basic Books, 1974), pp. 50–51.
27. See Warren E. Burger, "Annual Report to the American Bar Association," *Criminal Justice Newsletter*, February 16, 1981, pp. 2–4.
28. Herbert Packer, *The Limits of the Criminal Sanction* (Stanford: Stanford University Press, 1968), chap. 8.
29. Hugo Adam Bedeau and Michael L. Radelet, "Miscarriages of Justice in Potentially Capital Cases," *Stanford Law Review* 40 (November 1987): 21–179.
30. James Q. Wilson, *Thinking about Crime* (New York: Basic Books, 1975).
31. U.S. Department of Justice, *Attorney General's Task Force on Violent Crime: Final Report* (Washington, D. C.: U. S. Government Printing Office, 1981), p. 59.
32. Ibid, p. 58.
33. Testimony of Stephen Gillers on behalf of ACLU before Senate Judiciary Committee, Subcommittee on Courts, November 13, 1981.
34. Administrative Office of the United States Courts, *Annual Report* (Washington, D. C.: U. S. Government Printing Office, 1981).

Chapter 9

Protect the Victims

Traditionally the forgotten person in American criminal justice, the crime victim has received enormous attention over the past decade. For many people, the treatment accorded the crime victim symbolizes everything that is wrong with the criminal justice system. In 1982 the President's Task Force on Victims of Crime submitted sixty-eight separate recommendations for reform. Earlier that year, the voters of California passed Proposition 8 by a 2-to-1 margin. This so-called Victim's Bill of Rights added twelve controversial items to the state constitution and the criminal code.

The victims' rights movement draws much of its energy from the horror-story syndrome. Everyone has a story about an atrocious crime that can be blamed on some failing of the criminal justice system. Mark Mosely, former place kicker with the Washington Redskins, told a Senate subcommittee about his sister, raped and beaten to death by a man who had been paroled only two months before. Such stories can be repeated endlessly. The anger they arouse points increasingly in one direction: Do something for crime victims!

Conservatives have seized the victims' rights issue and made it their own. In California, for example, the backers of Proposition 8 were the traditional prosecution-oriented advocates of law and order, while civil libertarians were the principal opponents. The President's Task Force on the Victims of Crime was also dominated by traditional conservative spokespersons. Thus the movement for victims' rights can be considered part of the conservative crime control package.

The victim's rights movement embraces one of the basic conservative assumptions: the "system" protects the guilty rather than the innocent; guilty people "beat the system" and "get off easy." The most controversial victim's rights proposals attack constitutional protections for criminal defendants. They are designed to "redress the balance" and build in some protections or rights for victims.

A wide variety of proposals march under the banner of victims' rights. The sixty-eight recommendations for federal and state actions of the President's Task Force on victims of crime, and the twelve items in Proposition 8 vary widely in their scope and potential impact.

1. Legislation should be proposed and enacted to ensure that addresses of victims and witnesses are not made public or available to the defense, absent a clear need as determined by the court.
2. Legislation should be proposed and enacted to ensure that designated victim counseling is legally privileged and not subject to defense discovery or subpoena.
3. Legislation should be proposed and enacted to ensure that hearsay is admissible and sufficient in preliminary hearings, so that victims need not testify in person.
4. Legislation should be proposed and enacted to amend the bail laws to accomplish the following:
   a. Allow courts to deny bail to persons found by clear and convincing evidence to present a danger to the community;
   b. Give the prosecution the right to expedited appeal of adverse bail determinations, analogous to the right presently held by the defendant;
   c. Codify existing case law defining the authority of the court to detain defendants as to whom no conditions of release are adequate to ensure appearance at trial;
   d. Reverse, in the case of serious crimes, any standard that presumptively favors release of convicted persons awaiting sentence or appealing their convictions;
   e. Require defendants to refrain from criminal activity as a mandatory condition of release; and
   f. Provide penalties for failing to appear while released on bond or personal recongizance that are more closely proportionate to the penalties for the offense with which the defendant was originally charged.
5. Legislation should be proposed and enacted to abolish the exclusionary rule as it applies to Fourth Amendment issues.
6. Legislation should be proposed and enacted to open parole release hearings to the public.
7. Legislation should be proposed and enacted to abolish parole and limit judicial discretion in sentencing.
8. Legislation should be proposed and enacted to require that school officials report violent offenses against students or teachers, or the possession of weapons or narcotics on school grounds. The knowing failure to make such a report to the police, or deterring others from doing so, should be designated a misdemeanor.

9. Legislation should be proposed and enacted to make available to businesses and organizations the sexual assault, child molestation, and pornography arrest records of prospective and present employees whose work will bring them in regular contact with children.

10. Legislation should be proposed and enacted to accomplish the following;

    a. Require victim impact statements at sentencing;
    b. Provide for the protection of victims and witnesses from intimidation;
    c. Require restitution in all cases, unless the court provides specific reasons for failing to require it;
    d. Develop and implement guidelines for the fair treatment of crime victims and witnesses; and
    e. Prohibit a criminal from making any profit from the sale of the story of his crime. Any proceeds should be used to provide full restitution to his victims, pay the expenses of his prosecution, and finally, assist the crime victim compensation fund.

11. Legislation should be proposed and enacted to establish or expand employee assistance programs for victims of crime employed by government.

12. Legislation should be proposed and enacted to ensure that sexual assault victims are not required to assume the cost of physical examinations and materials used to obtain evidence.

    SOURCE: President's Task Force on Victims of Crime, *Final Report* (Washington, D.C.: U.S. Government Printing Office, 1982), pp. 17–18.

We can divide the various proposals into three categories. Some of the proposals are sound, humane, constitutional, and long overdue. Others are positively harmful, either because they subvert constitutional guarantees or because they produce adverse practical effects. Finally, many are simply irrelevant to the basic issue of helping crime victims. My position, therefore, is stated as three separate propositions:

──────────────────── **PROPOSITION 20a** ────────────────────
Some victims' rights proposals are sound social policy but will have no effect on crime.

──────────────────── **PROPOSITION 20b** ────────────────────
Some victims' rights proposals are harmful to the criminal justice system and to victims.

──────────────────── **PROPOSITION 20c** ────────────────────
Most victims' rights proposals are irrelevant to the effort to reduce crime.

Let us consider these proposals with the same single-minded focus we have maintained throughout this inquiry: the relevant test is whether or not a specific proposal will reduce serious crime. A number of victim-related proposals have considerable merit but not for reasons related to crime control. They should be adopted because they are sound social policy even though they will have no effect on crime.

Sound, Humane, Constitutional, and Overdue

Crime victims have been said to be "forgotten" because in fact the criminal justice system does forget about them. Typically, the crime victim never hears from the police once the initial report is taken. To learn the status of the investigation (I'm assuming now that no one has yet been arrested), the victim must take the initiative and call the police—who often return a disinterested or even rude response. Nor do prosecutors keep victims posted on the status of a case, unless, of course, the victim is a key witness. Even when victims are witnesses, however, little accommodation is made to their needs. Finally, and most important, prosecutors never inform victims about the nature of plea bargains. This failing is the source of some of the bitterest complaints voiced by victims, particularly when the bargain involves a substantial reduction in the charge and/or a sentence of probation rather than imprisonment. Typically, the victim learns about the disposition of the case by reading about it in the newspaper.

To correct this situation, the President's Task Force on Victims of Crime recommends that police departments should establish procedures to ensure that victims of violent crime are periodically informed of the status and closing of investigations. Furthermore, prosecutors should assume ultimate responsibility for informing victims of the status of a case from the time of the initial charging decision to determinations of parole.

This proposal is sound, humane, constitutional, and overdue. Simply from the standpoint of building and maintaining public confidence, police and prosecutors should make every effort to keep crime victims informed. Victims, after all, are the most direct clients of the system. If they are displeased with the service they receive, then the agencies have failed in one of their most basic responsibilities. Although police departments have invested enormous resources in "police–community relations" programs directed at general and amorphous audiences (usually civic groups and schools),[1] they have ignored their main clients: crime victims. Whether this kind of recontact would have the desired effect of increasing public satisfaction is uncertain, however. "Victim recontact" was one of five strategies adopted in an ambitious fear-reduction experiment in Houston. Police officers contacted crime victims to express their sympathy and ask if they needed any further assistance or information. Unfortunately, the program achieved none of its goals. In fact, victims with poor English skills were actually more fearful than those who were not recontacted.[2]

This finding suggests that much of the political rhetoric about public

"Hello, your call has been transferred to me so that I may assure you that everything is being done to bring your case to a quick and satisfactory conclusion . . . Hello, your call has been transferred to me so that I may assure . . ."

alienation from the police and the criminal justice system is misdirected. Most people probably do not want more contact with the police. They want to be left alone. A call from Officer Friendly isn't going to change their attitude toward the department. Those people who do not speak English well and don't understand exactly why the officer is calling will only be alarmed. In a lengthy review of recent victims' rights proposals, Lynne Henderson suggests that prevailing assumptions about the positive psychological effect on crime victims are unverified and would not hold up under careful scrutiny.[3]

Victims' advocates also want speedy trials on the grounds that the victim should not have to wait months or even years while the criminal case remains pending. Justice delayed is justice denied for the victim as well as for the defendant. This is a worthy idea that enjoys a constitutional foundation in the Sixth Amendment. The irony, of course, is that speedy trial has traditionally been seen as a defendants' rights issue: accused persons have a right to have the cases against them resolved quickly. When the accused is innocent, the importance of speed is obvious. In this instance the rights of the victim and of the defendant are identical.

Speedy-trial laws are currently in effect in the federal system and in several states. Similar laws should be adopted in the remaining states.[4] There is one respect in which speedy trials might help reduce crime. We have already found in our discussion of bail that most crimes committed by persons out on bail occur after the sixtieth day of release. Speedy trial, particularly for robbers, might reduce the number of these crimes. But we should have no illusions about this particular reform. First, it may not actually produce speedier trials. Malcolm Feeley's review clearly indicated that members of the courtroom work group have no trouble negating the intent of such laws. Second, and more to the point here, speedier trials may not reduce crime very much. Crimes committed by persons out on bail are a small proportion of all the crimes committed. A modest gain is not to be sneered at, but we should not exaggerate its significance.

Harmful and Unconstitutional

Many of the items on the Victim's Bill of Rights agenda are positively harmful and unconstitutional. The harm has a special, cruel irony to it: proposals designed to help crime victims turn out to hurt them. Civil libertarians have traditionally defended the exclusionary rule, for example, on the grounds that it protects the rights of the accused. It turns out that the rules of evidence offer important protections for crime victims as well.

Debate over victims' rights proposals turns on several distinct issues. There is the question of whether a specific reform would intrude on the rights of the suspect and/or the victim. An entirely separate matter is whether the proposal would reduce crime. Conservatives believe we can reduce crime by getting tough with criminals. But there are many ways of getting tough. A meat-ax approach can have the dubious distinction of harming all concerned and failing to reduce crime simultaneously.

Modifying the Exclusionary Rule

We have already examined the exclusionary rule in detail, but let us now take another look at it from the perspective of victims' rights. California's Proposition 8 attacked the exclusionary rule with a "truth in evidence" section permitting introduction of "all relevant evidence." This provision was designed to close an alleged loophole and tip the balance in favor of the prosecution. Within weeks of the proposition's enactment it was clear that the "truth in evidence" clause might benefit suspects more than victims. "All relevant evidence" is a very broad category. California defense attorneys quickly found that it allowed them to introduce questions related to a rape victim's background and character and thereby cast doubt on the victim's innocence. While Proposition 8 specifically excludes the admission of evidence concerning a rape victim's past sexual activity, other evidence about the victim's habits is admissible (and allows jury members to imagine whatever they want). One defense attorney obtained an acquittal by introducing evidence concerning the victim's "colorful" background. The result has undermined years of progress toward the elimination of questioning about the past sexual conduct of rape victims. Under Proposition 8, rape victims now face often humiliating questioning by defense attorneys. Some

". . . And in spite of Proposition 8, please
protect my person, house, papers, and effects
against unreasonable searches and seizures."

defense attorneys now recommend that victims not testify at all. In one
notable case the defense attorney succeeded in introducing as evidence a
lie-detector test indicating that the defendant, accused of attempted murder,
thought the house he fired into was empty. This evidence, which was
inadmissible before Proposition 8, was now considered "relevant." It helped
produce a hung jury, and the defendant ultimately pleaded guilty to a lesser
charge of firing into an unoccupied dwelling. The "truth in evidence" idea
hardly helped the victim, in this case a woman who took a shotgun blast in
the face.[5]

The supporters of Proposition 8 did not intend these results, of course.
But you cannot be selective about the meaning of broadly worded phrases.
"All relevant evidence" means just that—*all* evidence, not just evidence that
favors the prosecution. California's attempt to repeal the exclusionary rule is
a classic example of the meat-ax approach, a reform that backfires and
produces worse results than the alleged ailment it was designed to cure. I
should add, as a cautionary note, that it is still too early to evaluate the
impact of the various portions of Proposition 8. So far, only the horror stories
have been widely reported, and it would be a mistake to base our evaluation
on a few celebrated cases.

Along the same lines is the hearsay-evidence proposal of the President's
Task Force (recommendation 3): in order to protect the victim from the
trauma of testifying in person, hearsay evidence should be admissible at
preliminary hearings. Relaxing the established rule of evidence to permit
hearsay evidence at any stage in the criminal process sets a dangerous
precedent. Allowing it only at preliminary hearings is silly and misleading.

Evidence admitted at an early stage in the process is of little help if it is inadmissible at trial. Precious time and energy will be wasted on cases that will not result in conviction. In many instances, prosecutors would be encouraged to pursue cases in the hope of obtaining a guilty plea without the need to bring the victim to the stand in a trial. In other words, it would only encourage prosecutorial bluffing—and counterbluffing by the defense attorney (who would probably have figured out that there were problems with the victim's testimony). Neither the interests of justice nor the interests of crime control are served by this result.

The Victim's Voice

The President's Task Force also recommends the addition of the following language to the Sixth Amendment: Likewise, the victim in every criminal prosecution shall have the right to be present and to be heard at all critical stages of judicial proceedings.

Several states have enacted laws to this effect. In approving Proposition 8 in 1982 California voters agreed that "the victim of any crime, or the next of kin of the victim . . . has the right to attend all sentencing proceedings . . . [and] to reasonably express his or her views concerning the crime, the person responsible, and the need for restitution."[6] The judge is required to take the views of the victim into account in imposing sentence. The intent of giving the victim a voice in criminal proceedings is to ensure that criminals do not "get off" through reduction of the charges, lenient sentences, or early parole. This proposal rests on two unverified assumptions: that a lot of criminals get off easy and that a lot of victims are interested in appearing and testifying at various stages in the criminal justice process.

The great danger is that the presence of the victim would add a note of vengeance to the process—or at least a greater one than now exists. One of the main purposes of a professional criminal justice bureaucracy is to ensure fair and impartial treatment of all persons accused of crimes. Impersonality is one of the hallmarks of professionalism. A professional police officer enforces the law without regard to his or her personal feelings toward the offender. A lawyer has a professional obligation to provide the best defense for all clients, regardless of his or her personal feelings. Reintroducing an element of personal vengeance would be a major step backward for our criminal justice system.

An important practical question is exactly when and where the victim should appear. The criminal justice process is not a single event but a series of stages at which critical decisions are made: bail setting, preliminary hearing, indictment, arraignment, and trial. Through all of these formal stages is woven the informal plea-bargaining process. The victim's appearance at *all* critical stages would create a time-consuming and costly burden. For most victims the loss of time on the job would be prohibitive. Appearance at one critical stage, moreover, does not prevent an important decision from being made at some other stage. Finally, and most important, plea bargaining is not a specific event or stage. How do we ensure the presence of the victim during plea bargaining? This question is especially critical because the belief that criminals are allowed to plead to a meaningless low charge is the major rationale for bringing the victim into the process in the first place. One possible solution would be to adopt some of the proposed reforms of plea bargaining, particularly the idea of a plea "conference" at which all participants would be present.

Early research suggests that giving victims a voice in the criminal justice process has little effect. First, most victims do not want to play an active role. Judge Lois Forer of Philadelphia routinely invites victims to participate but few bother to appear. In Connecticut, where victims have a legal right to participate, they appear at only about 3 percent of all sentencings. Exactly the same percentage of victims appeared in California under the new law. An NIJ study concluded that, overall, the victim's-voice provision of Proposition 8 had "little effect."[6]

An Ohio law requires judges to make "victim impact" statements at sentencing and victims are allowed to make their own sentencing recommendations. Victims made recommendations in 60 percent of the 417 sexual assault cases between 1980 and 1983 (and such cases, it should be noted, are always emotionally charged; participation undoubtedly would be much lower in other types of felony cases). Yet these recommendations had little effect on sentencing. There was a high level of agreement between the sentence the victim recommended and the sentence the judge considered appropriate. To give the victim a voice in sentencing, the evaluation concluded, was essentially to offer a placebo. It gave the impression that "something was being done" when in fact it made little difference.[7]

Irrelevant or Harmless

The last category of victims' rights proposals includes those that are irrelevant to the issue of crime control or are merely harmless reforms. The President's Task Force recommended the abolition of parole and limits on judicial discretion in sentencing. These are worthy ideas that enjoy considerable support among both conservatives and liberals. As we shall see farther on, parole is virtually indefensible as a rehabilitative tool. Unstructured discretion in sentencing has invited abuses. The proper solution to these problems requires careful study and planning. It would be a grievous error to abolish parole, for example, without taking into account the impact on the rest of the system.

Whatever their merits, the ideas of abolishing parole and structuring sentencing discretion are irrelevant to the issue of protecting crime victims. Conservatives promote the abolition of parole in the belief that too many dangerous people get out of prison too early. The available evidence suggests, however, that the length of prison terms has little effect on recidivism. Keeping offenders in prison longer will not serve to rehabilitate them any better. It will keep them off the streets, but, as I have shown elsewhere, the dollar cost of an increased prison population is prohibitive. With respect to sentencing reform, it is still too early to say whether any of the initial experiments with determinate sentencing make any difference.

An example of meaningless rhetoric is the declaration in California's Proposition 8 that a child has a constitutional right to attend a safe school. This statement is pure demagoguery. Of course we all want children to be safe, at school and at all other times. These particular words in Proposition 8, now a part of the California state constitution, do absolutely nothing to achieve that end.

Victims' rights advocates also promote the concept of restitution. Like the abolition of parole and the structuring of sentencing, restitution is an idea with much to recommend it. The victim receives some compensation for his or her loss and the offender must deal directly with the personal cost of the crime. Experiments with restitution have been flourishing across the country for several years now. They should be studied carefully and, if successful, adopted more widely.

Restitution sounds great but may not work in practice. Its effectiveness depends on the offender's ability to pay something back. Most white-collar criminals may be able to do so, but not most robbers and burglars. The typical robber or burglar is either unemployed at the time of the offense or has a very irregular employment history. A genuine full-employment policy not only would make restitution possible but also would go a long way toward reducing the amount of crime committed in the first place.

A Final Word

Crime inflicts terrible pain and suffering on its victims. Without question, the best thing that can be done for victims and potential victims is to reduce the astronomical level of predatory crime in the United States. Unfortunately, the proposals advanced on behalf of victims will not achieve that goal. Most of the rhetoric about victims' rights is demagoguery: a playing upon very real feelings of pain, fear, and outrage to advance dubious proposals. The so-called Victim's Bill of Rights will do nothing for victims and nothing to reduce crime. If anything, these proposals will trample on established constitutional rights, which do in fact protect victims.[8]

Notes

1. Samuel Walker, The Police in America: An Introduction (New York: McGraw-Hill, 1983), chap. 9.

2. Lee P. Brown and Mary Ann Wycoff, "Policing Houston: Reducing Fear and Improving Service," *Crime and Delinquency* 33 (January 1986).

3. Lynne N. Henderson, "The Wrongs of Victim's Rights," *Stanford Law Review* 37 (April 1985): 937–1021.

4. See Malcolm M. Feeley, *Court Reform on Trial* (New York: Basic Books, 1983), pp. 156–188.

5. *Los Angeles Times,* April 19–22, 1983; *Wall Street Journal,* November 26, 1982; Gerald F. Uelmen, "The 'Victims' Bill of Rights'—Who Are the Victims, Who Will Pay the Bill?" (paper presented at California Attorney for Criminal Justice seminar, November 1982).

6. Lois Forer, *Criminals and Victims: A Trial Judge Reflects on Crime and Punishment* (New York: Norton, 1980); *Newsweek,* March 14, 1983; National Institute of Justice, *Victim Appearances at Sentencing under California's Victims' Bill of Rights,* Research in Brief (Washington, D. C., August 1987).

7. Anthony Walsh, "Placebo Justice: Victim Recommendations and Offender Sentences in Sexual Assault Cases," *Journal of Criminal Law and Criminology* 77 (Winter 1986): 1126–1141.

8. Samuel Walker, "What Have Civil Liberties Ever Done for Crime Victims? Plenty!" *ACJS Today,* October 1982, pp. 4–5; American Civil Liberties Union, *The Rights of Crime Victims* (New York: Bantam, 1984).

PART THREE

GUNS AND GUN CRIMES: THE MIDDLE GROUND

Virtually everyone agrees that gun-related crimes are an extremely serious part of the American crime problem. Here is a point on which conservatives and liberals agree. They also agree that something needs to be done about gun crimes, but they disagree over exactly how to attack the problem. With the possible exception of one promising approach on which they do agree, the policies recommended by conservatives and by liberals reflect their fundamentally different assumptions about crime and crime policy. In this section we will examine four strategies for dealing with gun-related crimes.

Chapter 10

Controlling Handguns

No issue arouses passions more surely than gun control. You don't see bumper stickers demanding repeal of the exclusionary rule, but a lot of bumpers carry the anti-gun-control slogan: "When guns are outlawed, only outlaws will have guns." The country is deeply polarized between the advocates and the opponents of gun control. The actions of two small towns in 1982 symbolized the division. Morton Grove, Illinois, banned the possession of all handguns; Kennesaw, Georgia, retorted with an ordinance requiring a gun in every home. Five years later the *New York Times* reported that neither law was being enforced. Kennesaw had not issued a single citation for failure to possess a gun.[1]

Gun control incites passionate opposition for several obvious reasons. With the exception of crackdowns on drunk driving, no other crime control proposal affects, or potentially affects, such a broad segment of the population. Nearly one-fourth of all homes have a handgun and another 25 percent have some other kind of firearm. Ownership of firearms is deemed a "right" by most gun owners, and any attempt to infringe on that right arouses deep and often irrational fear—fear that the National Rifle Association (NRA) has skillfully manipulated over the years. About 40 percent of the people who own a handgun have it to protect their homes. Fear of crime is both deep and widespread. The people who express the greatest fear actually run the lowest risk of victimization—but don't try to tell them that.[2] As far as other crime control policies are concerned—the exclusionary rule and mandatory sentencing, for example—most of these people will not be directly affected by them. Gun regulation, however, is perceived as a direct intrusion into their private lives. The more paranoid regard gun control as a Communist plot to disarm America and set the stage for a Russian invasion.

The deep emotional attachment to guns on the one side is matched by a vigorous and growing gun-control movement on the other. The movement is strongest at the local level. Washington, D. C., banned the acquisition of new handguns after 1975. San Francisco banned the possession of all handguns (until the law was overturned by the California Supreme Court). Cleveland banned the possession of "Saturday-night specials."

The movement draws its support from the grisly facts of handgun violence. Half of all murders are committed with handguns—an average of thirty victims every day. One-third of all robberies and rapes involve a firearm. Over half of all suicides are committed with handguns—and the percentage has been increasing. Two-thirds of all police officers killed in the line of duty are slain by handguns. Pete Shields, of Handgun Control, Inc., calls this slaughter the "American Gun War." A former corporation executive, he took up the gun-control cause after his son was shot and killed in a typically senseless handgun murder. As he points out, more Americans died by handgun (52,000) between 1966 and 1972 than died in combat in Vietnam (42,300). Franklin Zimring and Gordon Hawkins observe that more people were murdered in Detroit in one year (751 in 1973) than died by violence in the first five and a half years of the civil war in Northern Ireland.[3]

Liberal Indictment/Conservative Indictment

Liberals and conservatives have their own ideas about the exact nature of the gun problem. The liberal indictment runs as follows: No other country in the world is as permissive about the ownership of handguns; no other country has as much violent crime; guns, especially handguns, are used in a large proportion of murders and robberies; the availability of handguns in the home contributes to our high level of domestic violence; handguns are also the frequent cause of accidental injury and death and are often used by suicides; the majority of Americans favor gun control, but effective legislation is blocked by a small but powerful lobby, the NRA. The liberal policy prescription, which logically follows from this indictment, reads: Reduce the possession of guns in America and we will reduce the level of crime, interpersonal violence, accidental death, and suicide.[4]

The conservative indictment points in a different direction: no other country has so much violent crime; crime flourishes because the criminal justice system fails to punish criminals, especially offenders who commit violent crimes. The conservative prescription is to reduce violent crime by arresting, convicting, and incarcerating for longer terms criminals who use guns. Mark H. Moore makes a useful distinction by defining the liberal approach as "supply reduction" and the conservative approach as "demand reduction." Supply should be reduced, liberals argue, so that potential criminals would find it less easy to get their hands on a gun. Demand—the desire to commit weapons offenses—should be reduced, conservatives argue, by the threat of swift, certain, and severe punishment.[5] Another helpful distinction is to think in terms of "availability restriction" strategies and "place and manner control" strategies. The former strategies represent attempts to keep guns out of people's hands; the latter represent attempts to control the way they use them. It is interesting to note that liberals and conservatives reverse positions when the subject turns to marijuana. Conservatives advocate supply reduction (cutting off the supply of drugs) while liberals favor demand alteration (decriminalization of possession of small amounts of marijuana and tough penalties for major dealers).

Both sides are guilty of wishful thinking on the gun-control issue. While there is no question that violent crime is a terrible plague in the United States and that guns play a major part in it, the prescriptions offered do not realistically address the problem. My position is as follows:

PROPOSITION 21a

Current gun-control proposals do not offer realistic hope for significant reductions in violent crime in the near future.

I have qualified this proposition with the words "current," "significant," and "near future." It is possible that some policy, or combination of policies, may make a worthwhile contribution in the long run. This guardedly optimistic view, of course, is a very modest offering. At the moment, the only policy that does appear to have some effect is the one embodied in Massachusetts' Bartley-Fox law, which prohibits the carrying of a handgun outside of the home without a permit. The evidence in support of this policy, while tentative, does offer some hope. Thus I can supplement my position with:

PROPOSITION 21b

Policies limiting the unauthorized carrying of handguns outside of the home may help to reduce gun violence.

My endorsement of the Bartley-Fox approach is provisional. Further research is needed to confirm the initial findings about the effect of the Massachusetts law. If it does prove to be a successful approach, ways to supplement it by other policies should be explored.

Gun-Control Issues

Considerable confusion exists concerning several important issues: the extent of gun ownership, the criminal use of guns, and public attitudes toward guns and gun control.

The Extent of Gun Ownership

There are between 30 and 50 million handguns in the United States today. No one really knows exactly how many. The existence of the guns is a central fact of life that all gun-control proposals must confront. Unfortunately, many gun-control advocates choose to evade the difficult problem posed by the fact that these guns will not vanish.[6]

A lot of confusion arises from the failure to distinguish between firearms and *handguns*. The distinction is important because handguns are the key to our crime problem. The total number of firearms in private hands is no less than 100 million. Of these, 37 percent are rifles, 33 percent are shotguns, and 30 percent are handguns. Robbers use handguns, not rifles. Of the weapons used in robberies, 96 percent were handguns and only 4 percent were long guns.[7]

About half of those handguns are small weapons, .32 caliber or less; thus some but not all fall into the category of the so-called Saturday-night special. The Bureau of Alcohol, Tobacco and Firearms defines a "special" as a gun of .32 caliber or less, with a barrel less than three inches in length, and priced at $50 or less. (Not all gun experts are happy with this definition, but it is the one generally used.) The other half of the handguns are large weapons with a caliber of .38 or more.

The supply of handguns has increased at a truly frightening rate. Through domestic production and imports we are adding about 1.5 million each year, and 2 million are added in peak years. In the 1950s, domestic production amounted to only about 400,000 per year. It increased to about a million a year in the 1960s and has continued to climb. Zimring and Hawkins explain the increase in terms of the "fear and loathing" thesis: Americans are arming themselves out of fear of crime.[8]

Who owns all these guns? A closer look reveals some surprising patterns. Despite the huge increase in the number of handguns (the total probably doubled between 1968 and 1978 alone), the percentage of *households* with handguns has not increased so rapidly. In 1959, 12.6 percent of all American homes contained a handgun. That proportion increased to 15.4 percent in 1972 and to 20.5 percent in 1977. In other words, only a fifth of all homes have a handgun. While that number is large, ownership is far from universal. The great increase in the number of handguns is the result of the purchase of additional weapons by previous gun owners. The home that once had one handgun now has two or three. The people with no taste for guns remain firm in their opposition.[9]

A glance at table 10.1 reveals some other interesting patterns. With one exception, handgun owners and nonowners differ very little. The most significant difference is regional, between southerners and northerners. Southerners own handguns at a rate 50 percent higher than the national average, while nonsoutherners own them at a rate lower than the overall national average. People who associate violent crime with the cities of the Northeast, as many do, are surprised to learn that gun ownership is lowest in that area and is generally lower in urban areas than nonurban areas. The extent of handgun ownership is directly related to the use of handguns in crime. According to Zimring and Hawkins, handguns were used in only 13

Table 10.1 Percentage of Americans who owned a handgun, 1959 and 1976, by social characteristics

Characteristic	1959	1976	Percent change
Total U. S. population	12.6	21.4	8.8
(N)	(1,538)	(1,499)	
By political party			
Democratic	13.7	21.9	8.2
Independent	10.7	·21.6	10.9
Republican	12.5	20.7	8.2
By religion			
Protestant	14.0	25.8	11.8
Catholic	10.9	13.3	2.4
Jew	1.9	14.8	12.9
By head's occupation			
White collar	13.6	21.9	8.3
Blue collar	12.8	24.7	11.9
Farm	12.3	19.5	7.2
By education			
Less than high school	10.1	21.3	11.2
High school graduate	16.1	20.0	3.9
Some college	19.9	25.8	5.9
College graduate	8.3	20.5	12.2
By age			
18–30	11.5	19.1	7.6
31–54	13.7	23.2	9.5
55+	11.6	21.3	9.7
By sex			
Men	14.6	25.6	11.0
Women	10.7	18.1	7.4
By race			
White	12.9	21.5	8.6
Nonwhite	10.2	20.3	10.1
By city size			
Open country, farm	16.3	25.8	9.5
City less than 10,000	13.5	23.8	10.3
10,000–50,000	15.1	30.0	14.9
50,000–250,000	8.1	23.0	14.9
250,000 and up	9.7	15.8	6.1
By region			
South	16.9	30.1	13.2
Non-South	10.9	17.3	6.4

SOURCES: AIPO (Gallup), no. 616 (1959); NORC GSS (1976). Reprinted by permission from James D. Wright, Peter H. Rossi, and Kathleen Daly, *Under the Gun: Weapons, Crime, and Violence in America* (New York: Aldine Publishing Co.). Copyright © 1983 by James D. Wright, Peter H. Rossi, Kathleen Daly.

percent of all robberies in New York City, compared with 72 percent in Houston and 70 percent in St. Louis.[10]

These figures certainly undercount the extent of illegal gun ownership. New York City, with its strict Sullivan Law, dating back to 1911, is estimated to harbor 2 million illegal handguns! The illegal handgun subculture is a second basic factor that all gun-control proposals must confront—but more about this later.

Why do they have those guns? It is not entirely true that Americans are arming themselves out of fear of crime. This is the reason given by slightly less than half of the people who own handguns. Forty percent own guns to protect their homes and another 5 percent have them to protect their businesses. The rest have guns for essentially recreational purposes—target practice, hunting, and gun collecting, for example—or because their jobs require them to carry a gun.

The Criminal Use of Guns

Handguns are a major element of American crime and violence. About half of all murders are committed with handguns; in 1981 more than 11,000 people were murdered with handguns. Additionally, handguns are used in one-third of all robberies and one-third of all rapes. Not all robberies are equally likely to involve a handgun. Commercial robberies involve handguns three or four times as often as do personal robberies. Handguns are not a significant factor in burglaries, since the residents are not home 90 percent of the time.[11]

International comparisons strongly suggest a link between the availability of guns and American criminal violence. European countries have very strict gun-control laws and much less violent crime. In truth, however, the connection between the prevalence of weapons and gun-control laws is just the reverse of what many people assume. Gun-control laws are strong in those countries because there are few weapons, not the other way around. People in those countries support restrictive laws because they do not value (or possess) handguns.

The liberal thesis that fewer guns would mean less criminal violence hinges in large part on the substitution hypothesis. The absence of handguns would have two effects. First, crimes would be less serious because offenders would substitute less lethal weapons. Assaults with fists, clubs, or knives are much less likely to end in death than assaults with guns. Second, there would be some substitution in type of crime. Some unarmed robberies would replace armed robberies, simple assaults would replace aggravated assaults, and so on. Some potential offenders might be altogether deterred. The terrifying power of the handgun emboldens people to commit crimes, runs this line of reasoning. Without the gun, the potential criminal might not commit a crime at all. Not all gun-crime experts accept the substitution theory completely.[12]

A related argument might be called the "gun culture" hypothesis. The prevalence of handguns creates a cultural environment in which guns not only are prized but are seen as an acceptable means of settling problems. Individuals are socialized into this culture and the American love affair with guns perpetuates itself. Reducing the sheer number of guns, so one argument runs, would begin a long process of weaning the population away from guns.

Table 10.2 Public attitudes toward various gun-control measures (percent)

	Strongly favor	Somewhat favor	Somewhat oppose	Strongly oppose	Do not know
A crackdown on illegal sales	72%	13%	5%	6%	5%
Institute a waiting period before a handgun can be purchased to allow for a criminal records check.	74	14	4	3	5
Require the registration of all handguns now owned	57	17	9	11	6
Require mandatory prison sentences for all persons using a gun in a crime	68	15	6	6	6
Require mandatory prison sentences for all persons carrying a handgun . . . without a license	38	17	17	21	8
Ban the future manufacture and sale of cheap, low-quality handguns	54	16	10	13	7
Ban the future manufacture and sale of all handguns	23	9	22	36	10

SOURCE: Adapted by permission from James D. Wright, Peter H. Rossi, and Kathleen Daly, *Under the Gun: Weapons, Crime, and Violence in America* (New York: Aldine Publishing Company). Copyright © 1983 by James D. Wright, Peter H. Rossi, Kathleen Daly.

Public Attitudes toward Handguns and Gun Control

The public is profoundly ambivalent about handguns and gun control. Unfortunately, the issue of public attitudes has been muddied by misreporting of the survey data. A majority of Americans do favor gun control, as the gun-control advocates say. They have very different ideas, however, about exactly what kind of control they support.[13]

At most, only a third of Americans favor a complete ban on the possession of handguns. Even fewer support an outright ban on the manufacture of handguns. What a majority does support is keeping guns out of the hands of the "wrong" people. As table 10.2 indicates, 72 percent "strongly favor" a crackdown on illegal gun sales and another 13 percent "somewhat favor" the idea. Similarly, a combined total of 88 percent support a waiting period to allow for a check of criminal records.

Far more controversial are the proposals to register guns and license gun owners. Despite the fact that we register automobiles and license drivers, nothing arouses the wrath (and the lobbying muscle) of the NRA more quickly than the notion of following suit with guns. As the gun-control advocates argue, however, most Americans do support these ideas. A combined total of 74 percent support the registration of all guns and the same number support the licensing of gun owners.

Getting tough with criminals who use guns is also widely favored. A combined total of 83 percent support mandatory prison sentences for people who commit crimes with guns. Significantly, a much smaller number support mandatory prison sentences for people who are merely caught carrying guns without a required license (in violation, that is, of the Massachusetts Bartley-Fox law or its equivalent). The difference between these data reflects a distinction in the public mind between "criminals" and "law-abiding" people who just happen to be caught carrying a gun.

Current Gun Laws

It is not true that the United States has no gun-control laws: we have an estimated 20,000 laws regulating guns! What we lack are *effective* laws to control the ownership and use of guns.[14] Our federal system, with its crazy quilt of federal, state, and local jurisdictions, is a major source of this problem. The laws are weakest where they could be most effective: at the federal level. Given our patchwork of fifty separate state laws relating to guns, federal laws could be most effective in maintaining any system of licensing or registration and in regulating the manufacture and sale of weapons. The NRA can be credited or blamed for the weakness of the federal effort.[15] The laws are strongest where they can be most readily undermined: at the local level. Tough controls on the sale and possession of guns in one city, or even in one state, are easily undone by the importation of illegal guns from somewhere else. The strongest political support for strict gun control is now found at the municipal level. Washington, Cleveland, San Francisco, and other cities have enacted strongly worded local ordinances. The NRA, which virtually holds Congress hostage, has been completely outflanked at the local level.

Gun-Control Proposals

Everyone wants to do something about handgun violence, but we can't agree on exactly what to do. Basically, liberal prescriptions call for limiting the availability of guns, while conservatives want to punish their illegal use. On a few specific proposals the two sides manage to agree.

The factors underlying the ineffectiveness of existing gun laws are extremely relevant to our discussion of proposed new policies. Many current recommendations are rhetorical endorsements of existing laws. Others would involve more vigorous enforcement of those laws. A third group represent new policies but come up against familiar problems. Let us take a look at the four categories of gun-control proposals, each with its own specific policies.

Ban Handguns

Gun-control hard-liners want to prohibit the ownership of handguns completely. The gun-control movement is currently divided between the abso-

"By the way, Senator, before I give you your medication, are you *for* or *against* gun control?"

lutists, who want to press for a complete ban, and the self-styled pragmatists, who will settle for a limited but more politically feasible ban.[16] "Banning" handguns actually involves three distinct alternatives. The first is a complete prohibition of the ownership of all guns. The second, which is compatible with and often accompanies the first, is to ban the manufacture and importation of handguns. The third, a political compromise, calls for a ban on Saturday-night specials only.

Ban ownership The idea of a complete ban on gun ownership is enjoying growing support. Washington, D. C., San Francisco, and Morton Grove have taken this route with varying degrees of success. Washington outlawed the purchase, sale, transfer, and—with one important exception—ownership of handguns. The exception permitted continued possession of handguns and long guns that had previously been registered under the 1968 gun-registration law. (The law was passed in 1975 but did not take effect until 1977 because of court challenges.)

The U. S. Conference of Mayors, one of the leading gun-control groups, issued a report in 1980 claiming that the Washington, D. C., law was responsible for a "significant reduction in both firearm and handgun crime." This claim was challenged by gun-control opponents. We should rely on the more cautious assessment of Edward D. Jones III, who rated the mayors' report as flawed and inconclusive. Jones found comparable cities that experienced even greater reductions in gun-related crime during the same period, without the benefit of gun control. Jones conceded that he could not prove the law to be without effect: "This is not to say that the Firearms Control Regulations Act did not have a beneficial effect in reducing handgun crime in the District of Columbia." But he could not prove a positive effect either, and he called for additional research.[17] To date no evaluations of other experiments in the complete banning of handguns have been published.

All attempts to prohibit the ownership of handguns encounter the same, possibly insurmountable obstacles. The first is the lack of political support for Congressional action. Support does exist in many cities, and some have acted to ban possession of guns. But given the nature of our federal system, residents of those cities can easily acquire a gun elsewhere. This circumstance points to an even more serious problem.

The fact is that 30 to 50 million handguns are already in private hands. It is probably too late to prohibit ownership. Many of the gun-control hardliners refuse to face this simple fact. Nor are they willing to face the implications of prohibition. We already have the lessons of two monumentally unsuccessful experiments with prohibiting a desired commodity. John Kaplan of Stanford observes, "One must be struck by the similarity between the arguments for gun control and those concerning the prohibition of drugs." He might have cited the "Great Experiment" of the 1920s as well. Crusaders focus on the dangerousness of the product, but "little time and energy are spent in computing the costs of attempting to enforce such laws and the degree of effectiveness that can be expected from any particular policy."[18]

Realistically, you would expect only the most devout law abiders to turn in their handguns. Mayor Dianne Feinstein of San Francisco surrendered hers only after she had been badgered by the media. Most gun owners would become covert law breakers, thus further eroding respect for the legal system. People with past or potential criminal intent would simply ignore the law. James Wright, Peter Rossi, and Kathleen Daly offer a sober observation on this point: "One of the NRA's favorite aphorisms is that 'if guns are outlawed, only outlaws will have guns.' There is more truth to this point than the sophisticated liberal is usually willing to admit."[19]

A number of undesirable side effects would result from any attempt to enforce a prohibition. In the face of widespread noncompliance, enforcement would necessarily have to be very intrusive. Some of the worst law enforcement abuses arise in the attempt to police "victimless" crimes. Without a complaining victim, as there would not be in the case of gun possession, police would have to engage in a lot of spying, either directly or through informants.

Prohibition would also introduce a "crime tariff." As the supply contracted, the price would rise. The gun traffic would increasingly resemble the present heroin and cocaine markets. Restricted supply and rising prices would mean higher potential profits, and entrepreneurs would move in to corner the market. The entrepreneurs in this case would be the organized crime syndicates. At the moment, the syndicates have no incentive to deal in handguns because they are so cheap and plentiful. Prohibition of guns would only create a new field of opportunity for them.

Ban manufacture and importation   Advocates of a ban on the manufacture and importation of handguns take the long view and seek to dry up the supply. Many gun-control advocates propose such a ban in conjunction with an ownership prohibition, and the two strategies logically complement each other.

Unfortunately, this approach faces two serious obstacles. First, the level of its political support is very low. With only 32 percent of citizens in favor, it is one of the least popular ideas. Moreover, since the gun industry is concentrated in a few states, a federal prohibition bill would automatically arouse a self-interested opposition. A second problem involves the entire "dry up the supply" concept. Wright, Rossi, and Daly estimate that one out of every hundred handguns is used illegally every year (1 million firearms incidents, 100 million firearms). Thus, if the manufacture and importation of firearms stopped immediately and each remaining weapon were used in a criminal incident only once, the existing supply would provide for all criminal incidents for the next hundred years.[20]

Another variation on the manufacturing ban is the idea of banning the manufacture and sale of bullets as a health hazard. In 1979 the U. S. surgeon general identified guns as a major health hazard; several years before that, the U. S. Conference of Mayors asked the Consumer Product Safety Commission to ban bullets. It was an interesting idea and it received some attention in the gun-control movement. The problem with it is obvious: bullets are quite easily made at home and many hunters already pack their own. Prohibition would stimulate a sizable cottage industry in bullet manufacturing.

Yet another variation on the "dry up the supply" approach is the policy of buying back privately held handguns. Baltimore tried this approach in 1974. With the help of federal funds, the city offered to buy back handguns at $50 apiece. Eventually it bought 8,400 guns, or about one-fourth of the estimated number in the city. The buy-back approach has serious drawbacks. When it is limited to only one jurisdiction, it simply absorbs guns from other areas. Some critics suggested that the $50 price tag was too high for inexpensive Saturday-night specials. The program may only have allowed some people to trade up to a more expensive and more deadly weapon in a perverse manifestation of the substitution hypothesis.[21]

Ban Saturday-night specials   Banning only the so-called Saturday-night special is a far more popular idea than a ban on all guns. About 70 percent of all Americans favor this move, and Senator Edward Kennedy felt confident enough about their support to make it a major campaign issue in his unsuccessful bid for the 1980 Democratic presidential nomination (Kennedy's campaign had many serious problems, but his stand on gun control was not one of them).[22] The specials account for about half of all handgun offenses, or, to be more precise, they represent 45 percent of the guns confiscated in two separate enforcement projects. Actually, there is some disagreement about the role of the specials in crime. Some analysts put the figure at only about 25 percent. The implications of this dispute are important. People who cite the lower figure argue that elimination of the specials would have only a marginal effect on criminal activity. They therefore see this approach as a flawed political compromise.[23] A ban limited to the specials is politically attractive because these guns have no use as sporting weapons and therefore have no purpose other than crime. If one focuses only on the specials, it is politically possible to be against crime without directly threatening the owners of larger handguns.

Eliminating production and importation of the specials is a worthy goal. Such a ban, however, might only stimulate an undesirable substitution effect, encouraging criminals to trade up to larger weapons. It might also impose a crime tariff on the larger guns, raising their price. We simply don't know what the effect of such a policy would be. The impact of Cleveland's ban on possession and sale of the specials has not yet been analyzed.

Regulate the Sale, Purchase, and Possession of Handguns

Regulation of the ability to purchase and possess a handgun is the traditional American approach, one that is reflected in most of the 20,000 gun laws on the books. A vast majority of Americans support the idea of keeping handguns out of the hands of the "wrong" kind of people (that is, criminal offenders). Unfortunately, our experience to date suggests that such a policy is utterly futile.

There are at least three ways to regulate the sale, purchase, and possession of handguns. The first is to regulate the gun dealers. The second is to regulate the sale of guns, usually by restrictions imposed on the persons who can buy them and also by a required waiting period to allow for a records check. The third is to require permits and/or licenses for the gun, the owner, or both.[24]

The federal Gun-Control Act of 1968 is the most important federal law in the area of handguns and, in principle at least, the most serious attempt to regulate gun dealers. (Dealers are licensed in at least a dozen states and perhaps another dozen cities.) The law not only prohibits the sale of guns to certain categories of people (minors, ex-felons, the mentally ill, and drug users) but requires dealers to keep detailed records of all sales. We do not know the potential effect of this law. Franklin Zimring's detailed study of it reveals that the federal government committed few resources to enforcement efforts. There were 160,000 licensed dealers in 1972 and relatively few Bureau of Alcohol agents to police them. Even if the commitment to enforcement were made, it is not clear what its effect would be. Tightening up enforcement of legal sales only drives unqualified purchasers into the illegal gun market.[25]

The license/permit approach is a monumental failure. Historically, the strictest law in the country was New York City's Sullivan Law, originally passed in 1911, which requires a permit to own a gun (it has since been superseded in strictness by a number of recent local laws). Yet law enforcement officials estimate that there are at least 2 million illegal handguns in the city of New York. ATF Project Identification of the U. S. Bureau of Alcohol, Tobacco and Firearms (BATF) found that 57 percent of the illegal guns seized in New York City were purchased in just four states: Florida, Georgia, South Carolina, and Virginia.[26] In our patchwork federal system, any attempt to enforce a strict local law is all but futile.

The most serious weakness of existing laws regulating the sale of guns is the simple fact that few criminals purchase their weapons through commercial outlets. James D. Wright found that only one-sixth of all gun-using felons acquired their guns through retail transactions. Half had stolen a gun at one time or another. Other guns were readily available "on the street."[27] Even if these sources did not exist, the potential criminal would evade existing laws. State and local governments make only token gestures toward enforcing the laws—and of course some states have no regulations at all. The dealer often has nothing more than the purchaser's word that he or she has no criminal record or history of mental illness. National criminal records are incomplete and often inaccurate, so it is not possible to determine if the gun purchaser has a criminal record in some other state. Determining whether or not someone has a history of mental illness is next to impossible. Some jurisdictions require a waiting period between the application for purchase and the final transaction. Designed to facilitate a records check, it works only if an adequate system of records is available.

Not all handgun sales involve commercial dealers. Mark Moore estimates that between 500,000 and 750,000 gun transactions take place between private individuals every year. A few state and local laws attempt to regulate these sales, but such efforts are even more minimal than those directed at commercial dealers. And then of course there are the estimated 100,000 handguns stolen every year—guns that, by definition, go directly into the hands of people unqualified to buy them.[28]

Franklin Zimring argues that stricter control of the sale and ownership of guns is in fact possible. "National handgun registration is only peculiar in that it has not yet been accomplished," in his view. "Since 1938, federal law has required most of the essential data for registration, but the records have been decentralized in a way that has effectively guaranteed they cannot be used." Modern data-processing techniques make a national system of handgun registration records possible. Had it not become such an important political issue, gun registration would seem to make sense.[29]

Zimring's suggestion raises questions of both a practical and a civil libertarian nature. On the practical side, maintaining an accurate data bank is more easily said than done. Law enforcement agencies have been struggling for years to develop a national data bank of criminal records. Yet the system is notoriously inaccurate: data are not entered, corrections are not made, and, most serious, records are not updated or purged when they should be. Thus we hear many horror stories of people arrested and detained because they are listed as wanted in the National Crime Information Center files when in fact those original charges have long since been disposed of.[30] The practical questions about data management are directly related to civil liberties problems. In and of itself, any national data bank is disturbing—and is one issue that unites many liberals and conservatives. Thoughtful Americans of all political persuasions are concerned about the growth of computerized data banks and their implications for individual privacy. The prospect of data banks containing inaccurate criminal history information is even more horrifying to contemplate. One final practical question remains. Even if we assume that the technical problems of data management can be resolved and that effective controls can be developed to prevent the misuse of such a file, would a national data bank of registered handguns keep guns out of the wrong hands and help to reduce handgun crime? Or would it simply enhance the importance of the illegal gun market?

Restrict the Carrying of Handguns

Most states have traditionally had laws regulating the carrying of handguns outside the home, usually by prohibiting the carrying of concealed weapons or by requiring some kind of permit. The most important new policy initiative in this area and in the entire gun-control movement is Massachusetts' 1974 Bartley-Fox law, which mandates a prison term for people who are caught carrying a handgun outside of their homes without a permit.

We have already discussed the Bartley-Fox law in connection with mandatory sentencing. Suffice it to say here that the law did appear to have some effect in reducing violent crimes. The effect was not entirely clear, however, since other cities without the benefit of such a law experienced declines in murder and armed robbery greater than the decline reported in Boston.

Bartley-Fox is a promising alternative, and similar laws need to be experimented with elsewhere. For one thing, Bartley-Fox is politically workable. Because it focuses on the misuse of handguns, it appeals to both conservatives and liberals.

Impose Mandatory Sentences for Gun Crimes

The establishment of a mandatory sentence for anyone who commits a crime with a gun is a favorite conservative crime control strategy. It is also popular with the general public: 83 percent support the idea. At least twenty-four states have revised their laws to add or enhance such a penalty in the last few years.

The mandatory sentencing approach rests on both deterrence and incapacitation theories. The threat of imprisonment will deter would-be criminals either from using a gun or from committing the crime in the first place. If they commit the crime and are convicted, the prison term will incapacitate them for the duration. Variations of this approach involve restrictions on plea bargaining over gun-related charges and/or increases in the lengths of sentences.

The experience of Detroit allows us to assess the effects of both mandatory imprisonment and controls on plea bargaining. A new state law in 1977 mandated two years' imprisonment, without the possibility of probation or parole, for persons convicted of a gun-related crime. The law was advertised as "one with a gun gets you two." At the same time, the Wayne County (Detroit) prosecutor announced a new policy prohibiting plea bargaining of gun charges under the new law.

An evaluation by Colin Loftus and David McDowall focused on two questions: did criminal penalties increase in certainty and severity, and did the new policies affect the crime rate? The key issue in regard to the severity of sentences concerned the effective minimum prison terms—that is, how much time could a convicted offender reasonably expect to do before becoming eligible for release, when reductions for both good time and parole were taken into account? The investigators found "no statistically significant change in the expected minimum sentence" for gun-related murders and armed robberies, but a significant increase in the expected minimum sentences for gun-related assaults.[31]

Two factors—the going rate and the trickle-up theory—explain this differential impact. The expected minimum sentences for murder and robbery did not increase because the going rate for these crimes was already high. Armed robbers in Detroit had been serving prison terms averaging six years before the new law, and few convicted robbers ever got probation. The system was simply not soft on crime, so getting tough had no effect.

Sentences for assaults increased because the going rate for those offenses was rather low. Probation and suspended sentences were common, and incarcerated offenders got an average of six months. Much of this seeming leniency stems from the ambiguity of the crime of assault. The nature of the act is often difficult to specify with precision, and it may be difficult to determine who initiated the altercation. Moreover, our criminal justice officials routinely treat assaults between people who know each other as essentially private disputes. Such cases are frequently dismissed or disposed of by a bargain to a lesser offense. The new law raised the sentences by eliminating these common-sense distinctions and lumping all assaults into one undifferentiated category. Assault cases that had previously been treated leniently were now subject to more stringent penalties. The trickle-up effect applies here; penalties designed to deal with serious crimes have their greatest effect on less serious offenses.

Loftus and McDowall concluded that "the gun law did not significantly alter the number or type of violent offenses committed in Detroit." Murder, robbery, and assault did decline, but the decrease in rate began five months before the law went into effect—long enough in advance to rule out the possibility of the "anticipation effect" found in the Bartley-Fox evaluation and in some crackdowns on drunk driving.

Other evidence suggests that the system is not overly soft on gun-related crimes. Wright, Rossi, and Daly analyzed the Prosecutor's Management Information System (PROMIS) data from California and found that gun-related crimes were 34 percent more likely to be accepted for prosecution at the initial screening and 24 percent more likely to be accepted at the preliminary hearing stage than nongun crimes. Gun users were less likely to plead guilty, but a guilty plea did not do them much good. Trials were 30 percent more likely for gun-related offenses. Of those gun wielders who were convicted at trial, 67 percent went to prison, compared with only 33 percent of other offenders. Moreover, the use of a gun added nearly two years (600 days) to the average sentence. The use of any other weapon added only about thirty days. Pleading guilty did not help either. Seventy-four percent of those who pleaded guilty to a gun-related crime went to prison, compared with 45 percent of all others who copped a plea. And for their plea they got 400 additional days of prison time. These figures hardly paint a picture of a system soft on gun crimes.[32]

Criminal court systems have been very successful in evading the intent of mandatory sentences for gun crimes. California enacted a mandatory sentencing "enhancement" for use of guns in 1977: an additional one year for possession, two years for actual use of the weapon in a crime, and a third year for its use in a sexual assault. A study of the law's effect between 1977 and 1979, however, found that it had no significant effect on the lengths of sentences. A Florida law (the Glisson Amendment), meanwhile, mandated a prison term of between three years and life for certain specified offenses. Yet one study of 525 cases "eligible" under the new law found that only half of the offenders were given the mandatory sentence. Officials in the criminal court work group found ways to evade the intent of the law.[33]

Summary

Gun violence is an intractable problem in American society. There is no obvious solution. "Banning" guns is an empty gesture given the number of handguns already in circulation. We have ample evidence of the futility of prohibiting alcohol and drugs, and the situation is no different with respect to handguns. Attempts to keep guns out of the wrong hands have proven hopeless. Nor does it appear that threats of severe punishment will be any more effective in deterring people from committing gun crimes than they have been in discouraging other kinds of lawbreaking. The best hope we have at present lies in the evidence of the Bartley-Fox law in Massachusetts. Perhaps the casual carrying of weapons can be reduced and gun violence cut back as a consequence. This is a slim hope, but it is the best we have, and we should make the most of it.

Notes

1. *New York Times,* October 25, 1987.
2. Frank F. Furstenburg, Jr., "Public Reaction to Crime in the Streets," *American Scholar* 40 (Autumn 1971): 601–610.
3. Pete Shields, *Guns Don't Die—People Do* (New York: Arbor House, 1981); Franklin E. Zimring and Gordon Hawkins, *The Citizen's Guide to Gun Control* (New York: Macmillan, 1987), pp. 3–4.
4. James D. Wright, Peter H. Rossi, and Kathleen Daly, *Under the Gun: Weapons, Crime, and Violence in America* (New York: Aldine, 1983), chap. 14.
5. Mark H. Moore, "Controlling Criminogenic Commodities: Drugs, Guns, and Alcohol," in *Crime and Public Policy,* ed. James Q. Wilson (San Francisco: ICS Press, 1983), chap. 8.
6. Wright et al., *Under the Gun,* chap. 2.
7. Ibid., p. 42.
8. Zimring and Hawkins, *Citizen's Guide to Gun Control,* p. 25.
9. Wright et al., *Under the Gun,* chaps. 3, 5, 6.
10. Zimring and Hawkins, *Citizen's Guide to Gun Control,* p. 53.
11. Wright et al., *Under the Gun,* chaps. 8, 9.
12. Franklin E. Zimring, "Is Gun Control Likely to Reduce Violent Killings?" *University of Chicago Law Review* 35 (1968): 721–737.
13. Wright et al., *Under the Gun,* chap. 11.
14. Ibid., chap. 12.
15. Robert Sherrill, *The Saturday Night Special* (New York: Charterhouse, 1973), pp. 183–215; Shields, *Guns Don't Die,* chap. 8.
16. Shields, *Guns Don't Die,* pp. 145–146.
17. Edward D. Jones III, "The District of Columbia's 'Firearms Control Regulations Act of 1975': The Toughest Handgun Control Law in the United States—or Is It?" *The Annals* 455 (May 1981): 138–149.
18. John Kaplan, "The Wisdom of Gun Prohibition," *The Annals* 455 (May 1981): 11–23.
19. Wright et al., *Under the Gun,* p. 320.
20. Ibid.
21. Kaplan, "Wisdom of Gun Prohibition," pp. 19–20.
22. Sherrill, *Saturday Night Special,* pp. 97–117.
23. Wright et al., *Under the Gun,* pp. 180–182.
24. Ibid., chap. 12; Philip J. Cook and James Blose, "State Programs for Screening Handgun Buyers," *The Annals* 455 (May 1981): 80–91.
25. Franklin E. Zimring, "Firearms and Federal Law: The Gun Control Act of 1968," *Journal of Legal Studies* 4 (1975): 133–198.
26. Wright et al., *Under the Gun,* pp. 177–181.
27. James D. Wright, "The Armed Criminal in America," Research in Brief (Washington, D. C.: Institute of Justice, November 1986); James D. Wright and Peter Rossi, *Armed and Considered Dangerous: A Survey of Felons and Their Firearms* (New York: Aldine, 1986).
28. Mark H. Moore, "Keeping Handguns from Criminal Offenders," *The Annals* 455 (May 1981): 92–109.
29. Franklin E. Zimring, "Handguns in the Twenty-first Century: Alternative Policy Futures," *The Annals* 455 (May 1981): 3.

30. U. S. Congress, Office of Technology Assessment, *An Assessment of Alternatives for a National Computerized Criminal History System* (Washington, D. C.: U. S. Government Printing Office, 1982).
31. Colin Loftin and David McDowall, " 'One with a Gun Gets You Two': Mandatory Sentencing and Firearms Violence in Detroit," *The Annals* 455 (May 1981): 150–167.
32. Wright et al., *Under the Gun*, pp. 302–307.
33. Ibid., p. 306; Alan Lizotte and Marjorie S. Zatz, "The Use and Abuse of Sentence Enhancement for Firearms Offenses in California," *Law and Contemporary Problems* 49 (1986): 199–221.

PART FOUR

REFORM:
THE LIBERAL
PRESCRIPTION

Liberals have traditionally taken a hopeful attitude toward the subjects of crime and criminals. We need not have crime, or at least not as much as we do. People are not inherently wicked or prone to criminality. It is possible to reduce the incidence of crime, if not to eliminate it. Reform is the prescription. In this section we will investigate four reform strategies. The first calls for rehabilitation of the individual offender. We will look at four programs designed to rehabilitate or correct criminals. Second, liberals believe, we could reduce crime by eliminating many of the laws dealing with less serious offenses. We will consider two dimensions of the decriminalization strategy. Liberals also believe that the criminal justice system itself contributes to crime through its own unjust practices. We will weigh their proposals for means to eradicate injustice as a way of reducing crime. Finally, liberals believe that criminality is largely the result of a lack of social and economic opportunity. Their fourth strategy involves expanding opportunities for disadvantaged groups. We will examine this approach to reducing crime.

Chapter 11

Rehabilitation

The concept of rehabilitation is the cornerstone of the liberal approach to crime control. The rhetoric has changed over the years but the basic idea has not: we will reduce crime by correcting the behavior of criminals, thereby causing them to stop their illegal behavior. The National Academy of Sciences defines rehabilitation as "any planned intervention that reduces an offender's further criminal activity."[1] The key words in this definition are "planned" and "intervention." Most criminals stop their criminal activity sooner or later. But they stop according to their own timetable and not necessarily as a result of some treatment program. Our problem is to make them stop sooner through a program of planned intervention.

Background

"Rehabilitation" does not have a single meaning. There are many kinds of correctional programs, some old and some new, all designed to change the behavior of criminal offenders. Many represent old ideas dressed up in new rhetoric. Among their differences is time of intervention. Some programs intervene early in the criminal process, such as before prosecution, while parole, for example, comes at the very end of the process.

We shall examine four rehabilitation programs. The first two, diversion and probation, occur early in the process and are aimed at keeping offenders out of institutions. The third, prison reform, is intended to enhance the rehabilitative effect of prison sentences. The last, parole, is designed to release prisoners early, upon evidence of their rehabilitation, and to continue the correctional treatment through parole supervision.

Some general points about rehabilitation must precede a discussion of specifics. All discussions of rehabilitation today are dominated by the so-called Martinson report, which is purported to have found that rehabilitation does not work. Before considering diversion, probation, prison reform, and parole, we need to determine just what Martinson did and did not say about the effectiveness of rehabilitation.

The "Nothing Works" Controversy

The criminologist Robert Martinson dropped a bombshell on the criminal justice community in 1974 with a report concluding that "with few and isolated exceptions, the rehabilitative efforts that have been reported so far have had no appreciable effect on rehabilitation."[2] The article was originally titled "What Works?" but the findings were immediately translated as "nothing works." The phrase "nothing works" became an instant cliché and exerted an enormous influence on both popular and professional thinking.

Martinson did not actually say that nothing works. As several critics have pointed out, he found positive outcomes from a large number of correctional programs. In fact, 48 percent of the programs reported at least some success. The popular and professional audience, however, heard the message that "nothing works" because it was an idea whose time had come. By the mid-1970s, disillusionment with the dominant ideas and programs in criminal justice was widespread. The public was fed up with a decade of soaring crime rates and the apparent failure of correctional programs to reduce crime. Conservatives led a revival of the concepts of retribution, deterrence, and incapacitation. Liberals attacked the established correctional programs because of the due-process problems connected with them. For example, if there is no scientific way of measuring the extent of a prisoner's rehabilitation, parole decisions will inevitably be arbitrary.[3] At the same time there was more general disillusionment with social reform programs. Martinson's article was published in *The Public Interest*, a neoconservative journal that specializes in exposing the ineffectiveness of liberal social programs. In this context, the idea that "nothing works" found a receptive audience.

Was Martinson right? Is it true that few, if any, correctional treatment programs work? Is rehabilitation a failure? The answer is both yes and no. A sensible review of the subject of rehabilitation provides little comfort for holders of extreme views on either side. On the one hand, it is not true that absolutely nothing works. Some programs do work, in the sense of encouraging rehabilitation in a cost-effective manner. On the other hand, Martinson was right in charging that most correctional programs had difficulty proving their effectiveness.

Martinson's singular accomplishment was to change the terms of the debate over rehabilitation. In effect he threw down the gauntlet to the correctional establishment and demanded that it prove, in a scientifically verifiable way, the effectiveness of its programs. The burden of proof now lies with the establishment, and the standards of proof have escalated considerably.

A suspicion lurks in some minds that perhaps Martinson drew the wrong conclusions from his evidence. These doubts should be laid to rest. Under contract from the New York Governor's Special Committee on Criminal Offenders, Martinson and his colleagues reviewed all existing evaluations of correctional programs. They did not evaluate programs themselves; they merely synthesized the findings of previous evaluations. The Governor's Special Committee had an obvious interest in the findings. It was beginning to receive vast amounts of money from the Law Enforcement Assistance Administration (LEAA), and wanted to know what kinds of treatment programs to invest in.

The story of Martinson's report is fascinating in itself, quite apart from its findings, and embarrassing for the American correctional community. Martinson and his staff surveyed all evaluations of correctional programs published in English between 1945 and 1967. They were able to find only 231 that were acceptable by rigorous scientific standards. They rejected most evaluations simply because they were not scientific: they used unreliable measures, or failed to describe the "treatment" adequately, or did not use proper control groups, or drew questionable conclusions from the data. These disclosures were scandalous. Martinson exposed the correctional community's failure to develop a systematic process of evaluation. Despite the fact that it was responsible for programs costing millions of dollars which processed thousands of criminal offenders week in and week out, it never seriously inquired into what worked and what didn't.[4] The academic community shared much of the responsibility, as formal evaluations were done either by researchers under contract or by in-house professionals with academic training. The net result was a case of massive professional irresponsibility.

It is not hard to understand why the correctional community avoided rigorous evaluation. As Martinson discovered, the record was not especially good, and no bureaucrat is eager to reveal such things. The correctional establishment had a vested interest in the status quo, which in this case meant maintaining both existing programs and the sanctity of the underlying rationale of rehabilitation. The role of the academic community was even less honorable, since at least in theory university-based researchers were independent truth seekers. Their independence was undermined, however, by their need to maintain comfortable relations with correctional officials. It is an old story: the researcher who asks embarrassing questions runs the risk of being denied access to the data needed to do the work.

The Martinson saga gets even worse. Apparently because Martinson's findings were so threatening, the Governor's Committee attempted to suppress the report. It did not publish the report on its own and refused Martinson permission to publish it himself. Legal action finally released a copy for publication.

The basic question is whether Martinson's analysis of his own data is valid. To answer this question the National Academy of Sciences convened a

Panel on Research on Rehabilitative Techniques. It concluded that "Martinson and his associates were essentially correct." Reviewing the same material, the panel found that the Martinson team had drawn reasonable conclusions from the evidence. Pursuing its own inquiry, the panel found "little in its review of existing studies . . . to allay the current pessimism about the effectiveness of institutional rehabilitation programs as they now exist." Furthermore, it could "make no recommendations about ways of rehabilitating offenders . . . with any warranted confidence."[5]

Other Surveys

For the record, I should point out that Robert Martinson was not the only person ever to survey evaluations of correctional programs. His report has received the most attention because of the timing and circumstances of its release.

Three other studies reached conclusions that differed little from Martinson's. They also found most of the evaluation research to be shoddy. Walter Bailey found only twenty-two scientifically acceptable studies published between 1940 and 1960. Charles Logan found that just 18 of the 100 studies he examined were acceptable, and William E. Wright and Michael Dixon found only nine acceptable studies dealing with delinquents. The three studies found a higher rate of success among the scientifically valid studies than Martinson did. Bailey found positive or at least promising outcomes in 77 percent of his studies (17 out of 22). Logan's success rate was 56 percent (10 out of 18), and Wright and Dixon's was 67 percent (6 out of 9). Martinson's reported rate was 48 percent.[6]

The meaning of "success" is a matter of some controversy, however. Ted Palmer, one of Martinson's critics, defends rehabilitation on the grounds that nearly half of the programs Martinson studied (48 percent) appeared to be successful. The question is: How successful? A finding of statistical significance in a program evaluation is one thing. Whether those figures have a practical significance in the real world is something else entirely. Offenders in one treatment program might do better than a comparable group in another kind of program, but the differences may not be great enough to justify the investment of large amounts of public funds.[7]

The Future of Rehabilitation

In a subsequent report, the National Academy of Sciences panel concluded cautiously that more research on rehabilitation was needed: "It is now time to undertake more systematic, long-term, and focused research that will have a substantial probability of improving techniques and programs that can be evaluated in ways that will produce more definitive conclusions."[8] On one level, this is the old academic copout: we don't know the answers right now and need more research. But implicit in the panel's call for more research is

"I ask you, Spock—Are the Klingons *worth* rehabilitating?"

the assumption that we are likely to discover correctional treatment programs that work. John Conrad dismisses this assumption. In his view, the panel "skipped over the most obvious question of all: Why was it that rehabilitation never worked as a system with a goal to achieve?"[9] In other words, the critics may be right. There may be some fundamental flaws in the entire concept of rehabilitation. Investment in new programs or better programs or more sophisticated research designs may not lead to the Holy Grail of effective correctional treatment.

In the current political context, more than a little bit of nonsense is circulating concerning rehabilitation. We cannot discuss it intelligently as a single enterprise. My review suggests that at least one treatment program—probation—does work and should be maintained. At the same time, however, two programs offer no evidence of success and one relatively recent innovation appears to be counterproductive.

Diversion

Diversion was one of the great reforms of 1965–1967. It received a strong endorsement from the President's Crime Commission in 1967, was supported by more than $112 million in LEAA funds, and involved an estimated 1,200 separate programs during the 1970s. By the end of the decade, however, a backlash set in. Expert opinion maintained that diversion not only had failed to achieve its stated goals but had actually worsened the problem it set out to solve.[10]

The Concept

Diversion programs take many forms, but the basic elements are constant. The primary objective is to get the individual out of the criminal justice system at the earliest possible point. The new diversion programs emphasized two exit points: before formal arrest and before prosecution. In either case, the suspect or defendant would be diverted out of the criminal justice process and into a treatment program.

Diversion was actually nothing new in the 1960s. Historically, a great many offenders are diverted from the criminal justice system at an early stage. Police officers routinely ignore misbehavior or let it go with a stern warning. Prosecutors have always dismissed cases when prosecution would "not serve the interests of justice." These traditional practices represent the "old" diversion. The distinguishing features of the "new" diversion involve a formal programmatic element: stated goals, staff, and, most important, treatment services.[11]

As a crime-reduction strategy, diversion is intended to rehabilitate offenders in three ways. First, it keeps people accused of relatively minor offenses out of the criminogenic environment of jails and prisons. Professional thinking in the 1960s had a strong anti-institutional bias. Institutions were bad; big institutions were even worse; prisons were the worst of all. Prisons were viewed as "colleges of crime" where inmates, far from being rehabilitated, developed a stronger identification with the criminal subculture and learned new criminal techniques. Diversion advocates argued that this experience was especially harmful to three groups: young offenders, first offenders, and persons charged with minor offenses. We could best rehabilitate them by keeping these people out of jail or prison and helping them maintain or rebuild a normal, "law-abiding" way of life (one with family, job, and so forth).

Diversion would also foster rehabilitation by permitting offenders to avoid the stigmatizing effect of the criminal label. Labeling theory was a popular criminological concept in the 1960s. Once a person had been labeled a "criminal" or a "delinquent," he or she would only proceed to act out the role and commit further criminal acts. Contact with the criminal justice system "amplified" antisocial behavior, especially among juveniles. Most juveniles would "mature out" of their antisocial behavior if they were left alone. Diversion at the earliest possible point would minimize the labeling effect.[12]

Finally, diversion programs would provide social services that addressed the offender's real problems. The criminological consensus in the 1960s held that society dealt with many alcohol, drug, and employment problems by processing people through the criminal justice system. Not only did this process needlessly label them as criminals and overburden the criminal justice agencies, but it failed to provide effective treatment for the original problem. Diversion would provide the proper intervention, in the

"Dear, now would be a good time to tell him
that this type of behavior may eventually lead
to a clash with the criminal justice system and
subsequent criminal labeling."

form of drug treatment, alcohol counseling, or help in finding employment.[13]

In addition to achieving these crime control goals, diversion was
expected to be much cheaper than imprisonment. Thus it would offer the
best of both worlds: greater effectiveness at lower cost.

An old adage says that if something seems too good to be true, it probably
is. Diversion qualifies. Rigorous evaluations have found that diversion
programs do not live up to their promises and may well do more harm than
good. My position is:

―――――――――――――――― **PROPOSITION 22** ――――――――――――――――
Diversion will not enhance the effectiveness of rehabilitation or reduce serious crime.

The Manhattan Court Employment Project

As one of the earliest and most highly publicized diversion programs, the
Manhattan Court Employment Project served as inspiration and model for
the entire movement. Sponsored by the Vera Institute, the project provided
employment services to persons suspected of criminal acts. Since unemployment was believed to be a major cause of crime, individuals who found
steady employment were expected to be less likely to commit further crimes.

Each day staff members of the Court Employment Project reviewed the
arrest docket and identified those defendants who met the program's criteria:
to be eligible a man or woman had to be a resident of New York City between
the ages of sixteen and forty-five, unemployed or earning less than $125 a

week, and charged with a felony other than homicide, rape, kidnapping, or arson; in addition the suspect had to have no prior jail or prison experience of one year or longer. With the consent of the prosecutor, criminal process-ing was suspended for ninety days. During that period the defendant received counseling, assistance in obtaining any short-term public assis-tance for which he or she might be eligible, and referral to a job opening with one of the four hundred cooperating employers. Charges were dropped if the defendant "succeeded" by keeping a job. If the person "failed," the prosecu-tor could prosecute the case.

An early evaluation declared the Manhattan Court Employment Project a huge success. In its first three years the project accepted 1,300 clients, about half of whom (48.2 percent) succeeded in having their charges dropped. About 70 percent of these 626 people had been unemployed when they were arrested. Fourteen months later, about 80 percent of those who could be located were still employed. Only 15.8 percent of these successful clients committed another crime in the twelve months following their release from the program. This recidivism rate was half that for both offenders who failed in the program and a control group. The program cost only $731 per client, or $1,518 per success.[14]

A subsequent evaluation, however, disclosed a very different picture. The project in fact was achieving none of its stated goals. It did not reduce recidivism and had no discernible effect on the employment record or the behavior of its clients. Moreover, it did not reduce pretrial detention time and did not lower the number of convictions. A major problem was that about half of the clients would not have been prosecuted at all if there had been no court employment project. Here we see again the expanding-net syndrome.[15]

The Expanding-Net Syndrome

Developed to get people out of the system, diversion actually brings more people in. This cruel betrayal of the project's basic purpose appears to be a problem inherent in all programs designed to offer a less punitive or less restrictive alternative to incarceration.

The net "expands" in the sense that more people are subject to some form of social control than beforehand. Instead of using the less restrictive alternatives for people they would otherwise arrest, prosecute, and incarcer-ate, officials apply them to people who would otherwise exit the system under the old diversion practice. More than half of the juveniles referred to fifteen diversion projects in California would not have entered any kind of program under traditional practice.[16]

The reason for this contradictory outcome is not hard to understand. Officials operate in a political context that imposes two constraints on them. The first is pressure to avoid responsibility for releasing to the community someone who promptly commits another crime. Judges routinely handle this problem by using high money bail to detain persons charged with violent crimes. They honor the right to bail in principle, knowing full well that they are denying it in practice. Diversion programs are under the same pressure to err on the safe side. Their administrators do not want to be accused of having diverted a person who has gone on to commit a serious crime. Caution leads them to admit into the program only low-risk offenders. Officials know very well that it takes only one highly publicized failure, such as commission of rape by a client of a diversion program, to destroy the entire program.

Pressure to demonstrate success, the second constraint, has the same effect. No official wants to admit to a low success rate (say, under 30 percent). "Keeping the numbers up" becomes a major bureaucratic goal. Officials easily achieve it by admitting only low-risk clients. Most of the people admitted into diversion programs would take care of their own problems without any formal intervention. These include the young, the first offenders, and those charged with relatively minor crimes—precisely the kind of people who are not criminals. Under the old diversion tactics, officials regularly dismissed such cases early on. Police officers did not arrest these people, or prosecutors dismissed the charges. Under the old diversion system, these offenders were genuinely diverted out of the system and were free of all formal social control. Under the new diversion programs they are brought under some form of control.

When Thomas G. Blomberg reviewed juvenile diversion programs, we found that they produced a 32 percent increase in the total number of juveniles under some form of control. Other evaluations have found varying degrees of expansion, but an expanding net nonetheless.[17]

Rehabilitation, Cost, and Due Process

Diversion programs also failed to rehabilitate. The Des Moines (Iowa) Adult Diversion Project—initially touted by LEAA as one of its "exemplary projects" and offered as a model for other communities—had "little impact in reducing recidivism among diverted, compared to nondiverted offenders." In another program diverted offenders had lower recidivism rates than juveniles sent to juvenile court but, alas, had higher recidivism rates than kids released outright without the benefit of any "treatment."[18] The expanding-net phenomenon makes evaluation of diversion programs tricky. Since many of the clients would not have been prosecuted at all in the absence of the program, there is a built-in bias toward successful outcomes. It is necessary to compare nondiverted offenders with only those comparable offenders who would otherwise have been prosecuted.

Diversion advocates also misrepresented the cost savings. When the net is expanded, there is no real reduction in the number of people under control or supervision. The true cost of a diversion program should be measured not in terms of the cost of diversion as opposed to prosecution and/or incarceration for the clients served but rather in terms of the cost of the program as opposed to the very minimal cost of early dismissal under the old diversion system. And the more highly developed the treatment program—the more professional counseling and so forth—the higher the cost.

Finally, diversion introduces serious questions of due process. A person who agrees to enter a treatment program in the expectation of having criminal charges dropped is, in effect, admitting guilt. Rather than contest the charge, the person is saying, "Yes, I have done something wrong and you have a right to force me to undergo some treatment." By offering a seemingly more attractive alternative to prosecution and possible incarceration, the program coerces this tacit admission of guilt in a subtle but powerful way. In addition, there are problems related to fairness in the selection of the program's clients and in measurement of a client's success.[19]

In the end, diversion offers a false promise. It fails to achieve its own goals, may well contradict them, and does not offer a realistic solution to the problem of serious crime. For the most part it does not involve persons charged with robbery or burglary. Nor is there persuasive evidence that it rehabilitates lesser offenders in such a way as to keep them from becoming serious offenders.

Probation

Probation is the one correctional treatment program that seems to work. It achieves its stated goals and serves broader social needs. Granted, it does not succeed all of the time. A number of probationers fail in the sense that they go on to commit more crimes. Some even become career criminals. Nonetheless, the success rate is rather high. Probation succeeds, however, for reasons that are not particularly comforting to the correctional establishment. Probation succeeds in the sense that most convicted offenders do not go on to become career criminals. The data in Marvin Wolfgang's birth cohort study persuasively documents the fact that most people who have some contact with the police desist from criminal activity.

Probation is the most common sentence given to convicted criminals. More than half of all convicted adult felons are placed on probation, and the rate is even higher for juveniles. Sentencing practices vary widely across the country. Detroit sends only 38 percent of its adult felons to prison, while Indianapolis incarcerates 75 percent. (Cross-jurisdictional comparisons are complicated by such oddities as California's "split sentences," whereby the offender spends some time in jail and then is placed on probation.) Probation is even more common in juvenile courts. As many as 80 to 90 percent of juveniles who receive a formal disposition are placed on probation.[20]

My position is:

PROPOSITION 23

Probation is an effective program that should be maintained in its present form.

Probation in Operation

Probation works because most of the offenders placed on probation do not go on to become career criminals. As Wolfgang's birth cohort data indicate, half of the juveniles who have an initial contact with the criminal justice system do not have a second. To be sure, this does not mean that they stop committing crime, only that they aren't caught. A third of those who get caught the second time do not have a third contact. In other words, the desistence rate is rather high. Most kids stop their lawbreaking, leaving only the small group of truly hard-core career criminals (6 percent of the total group and 18 percent of the delinquents, according to Wolfgang). Each of the offenders who does not commit another crime can be counted a success.

Probation also serves other desirable social goals. It is an appropriate sentence for the crimes that most offenders have committed. Larceny is certainly a felony, but few people believe it warrants a prison term. Nor is prison appropriate for most first offenders. Probation is so frequently used in juvenile court because few people really want to send juveniles to a penal institution. Probation is much cheaper than imprisonment—perhaps one-twelfth or one-fifteenth the cost.

Recent research, however, indicates a serious and growing crisis in probation. Joan Petersilia and her colleagues discovered two related problems. The first is an "explosion" in probation case loads. In California the average case load was between 150 and 300 offenders per probation officer. The situation has gotten much worse in the past decade. Petersilia found that between 1975 and 1983 the number of probationers in California increased 15 percent while the number of probation officers declined 30 percent. The situation in New York City is identical. Probation case loads rose from an average of 130 to 240 between 1978 and 1987. The number of people on probation doubled while the number of probation officers declined by 20 percent. In effect, the probation population explosion parallels the prison population explosion. Indeed, the two developments are probably related. Increased public pressure for harsher punishment has pushed more people into prison and onto probation. Most of these offenders are probably drunk drivers or persons guilty of other lesser offences who previously would have been given a suspended sentence. The prison construction boom, meanwhile, has diverted public revenues from probation and parole services.[21]

The other grim news concerns the failure rate among probationers. A forty-month follow-up study found that 65 percent of the probationers were rearrested and 51 percent were reconvicted. These are not encouraging figures. Moreover, one-third of those reconvicted (18 percent of the original sample) were reconvicted of a serious violent crime. Nor did they wait very long. The probationers reconvicted of a violent crime took an average of only eight months to recidivate. Those reconvicted of property offenses took an average of only five months.[22] Petersilia's report raises anew the basic questions about probation. Is it an appropriate sentence for many of the offenders who receive it? Can the effectiveness of probation supervision be improved?

Even when probation works, the results may have nothing to do with the "treatment." Most offenders rehabilitate themselves independently (although some do take a little longer than others). A job, marriage, or simply the aging process leads many young offenders away from crime. Probation supervision has long been a myth, amounting to little more than bureaucratic paper shuffling. The offender reports to the probation officer once a month and has a brief conversation about work, drugs, alcohol, crime, whatever. The probation officer fills out the required reports and that is that. The recent explosion in the probation case load has eroded even this minimal supervision.[23]

In all probability most offenders would do just as well without any of this alleged treatment—that is to say, would do just as well with a suspended sentence (which is simply probation without the supervision). John Conrad's blunt question about parole is relevant here: "Who needs a doorbell pusher?" His point is that the so-called treatment of probation supervision is an empty bureaucratic routine: probation officers call on their clients (push doorbells) and fill out the required reports. This process provides little substantive assistance to the client.[24]

Enhancing Probation's Effectiveness

Can probation be made more effective? Can we lower the recidivism rate and increase the success rate? There is some weak evidence that some kinds of probation supervision are slightly more effective than others. Ted Palmer's main point in his criticism of Martinson is that about 48 percent of the studies that Martinson examined, including some probation experiments, found positive results.[25]

Intensive probation is currently a hot idea in criminal justice. This strategy involves a small case load for each probation officer and more frequent contacts between the office and the offender. The Georgia Intensive Probation Supervision (IPS)—the program that has received the most attention recently—involves five face-to-face contacts per week. Probationers are also subject to unannounced alcohol and drug tests. Each two-officer team is assigned twenty-five probationers. This case load of 12.5 contrasts sharply with the case loads of up to 200 or 300 in other jurisdictions. The cost of the program in 1987 was $4.37 per day per probationer (about $1,600 per year). This was much higher than the 76 cents per day for normal probation but far less than the estimated $30.43 per day for incarceration. An evaluation declared the program a success.[26]

That evaluation, however, was conducted in midstream by in-house researchers. Although they declared the Georgia IPS program a success— and the Justice Department actively promoted this report—the data could be interpreted to indicate a 50 percent failure rate. Most (68 percent) of the offenders were still in the program at the time of the evaluation. Meanwhile, 15 percent had successfully completed the program, 1 percent had been transferred to another jurisdiction, and 16 percent had been returned to prison. This does not appear to be a great success rate. Moreover, if any of the 15 percent who completed the program were to commit a crime in the next year or two, he or she would have to be counted a "failure," bringing the overall success rate well below 50 percent.[27]

We must wait for a rigorous, independent evaluation of the Georgia IPS program before we pronounce it a success. Earlier intensive probation experiments were less successful than their adherents claimed. The most notable was the San Francisco Project, conducted by the federal probation system during the 1960s. Offenders granted probation were randomly assigned to probation officers with case loads of various sizes. Two groups received "intensive" supervision from probation officers who had only twenty clients each. For two other groups, whose officers each had forty clients, the level of supervision was deemed "ideal." Another group had only "minimum" supervision under officers who had several hundred clients. All other offenders were assigned to groups with "normal" levels of supervision, meaning that probation officers had between 70 and 130 clients.[28]

Careful evaluation revealed no significant difference in the recidivism rates of offenders in the various groups. Intensive supervision did not consistently reduce the failure rate. One significant *programmatic* effect did occur, however. Intensive supervision caused probation officers to cite their clients for a larger number of technical violations (that is, violation of one of the conditions of probation—travel restrictions, the use of alcohol, and so on—as opposed to genuine criminal conduct). The special program induced changes in the behavior of the officials running the program rather than in the clients. Bureaucratic dynamics encouraged low-ranking officials to adapt their behavior, consciously or unconsciously, to meet the expectations of the higher-ranking officials who had launched the program. This variation of the well-known "Hawthorne effect" is endemic in correctional treatment experiments. The most significant behavioral changes occur in the bureaucrats, not in the offenders.

In general, the effectiveness of special probation programs has not been proved convincingly. The fault lies with both probation officials and evaluation researchers. As the surveys by Martinson and others reveal, the quality of research in the area of corrections is truly scandalous. Walter Bailey concluded that "evidence supporting the efficacy of correctional treatment is slight, inconsistent, and of questionable reliability." James Robison and Gerald Smith concurred, finding "no evidence to support any program's claim to superior rehabilitative efficacy."[29]

Another approach to improved probation is to offer a wider range of programs in an effort to provide more "treatment" than conventional probation supervision affords. The Unified Delinquency Intervention Services (UDIS), operated by the Illinois Department of Corrections, involved five treatment services for delinquents who had very high arrest rates and who would otherwise have been incarcerated as hard-core offenders. Designed to provide more treatment than conventional probation but to be less drastic than incarceration, the five services were at-home placement, community-based group-home placement, a short-term wilderness program, an out-of-town residential camp, and an intensive-care residential therapeutic program. An evaluation indicated that the arrest rate for delinquents in the program declined by as much as 70 percent. Presumably these hard-core delinquents were either deterred or corrected as a result of the special treatment they received.[30]

As is so often the case, however, the early claims of spectacular success with the UDIS program do not withstand close scrutiny. The major program involves what is known as a "regression artifact." Whenever we find an unusually high rate of activity, we find that it has a natural tendency to return to a more normal level (regress to the mean). A baseball hitter who goes on a hitting streak for two weeks (say, bats over .400 for the period) will eventually return to his .250 lifetime average. This effect is seen in criminal justice agencies. We can see how it may be misunderstood by considering what happens when several traffic accidents occur in a short period at a busy intersection. The local police department often responds by placing traffic officers there. The incidence of accidents returns to normal very quickly. The presence of the police officer (the "intervention" or "treatment") may have had no effect at all. The level of accidents would have returned to normal in any event.

In the case of the UDIS program, the treatment may have appeared to be effective because the delinquents selected for the program had been committing offenses (or at least getting arrested) at an extremely high rate. They would probably have returned to a lower level of criminal activity (that is, a more "normal" level) sooner or later, with or without any "treatment" from the Illinois Department of Corrections. Any program can achieve an appearance of success if it enrolls only people who are currently very active. The passage of time alone will cause them to return to a lower level of activity.[31]

The Prediction Problem Again

The basic question concerning probation arises at sentencing: should the offender be incarcerated or granted probation? Liberal prison reformers argue that we send far too many people to prison, particularly low-risk offenders who represent no threat to public safety. Conservatives are outraged by the number of offenders who do not go to prison. These two points of view cannot be easily reconciled, largely because both sides are partly right. Some low-risk offenders go to prison while some high-risk offenders receive only a slap on the wrist.

Could we afford to send fewer people to prison? Martinson found a few studies indicating that, under certain circumstances, some offenders would do just as well if they got probation instead of prison. The Rand Corporation lends additional support to this view in its report *Selective Incapacitation*, which calls for the sentences of low-risk offenders to be so far reduced that many would not go to prison at all. Such a policy is intended to make room for high-risk offenders, who will be sent to prison for longer terms.[32]

The choice between prison and probation once again brings us to the prediction problem. The problem is the same for the rehabilitation-oriented liberal as for the incapacitation-minded conservative. Both are required to predict the offender's future behavior. As Norval Morris has reminded us, sentencing decisions have always been based on implicit predictions. These predictions, however, have been based on hunch and intuition rather than on scientific evidence. Rehabilitation programs are bedeviled by "false positives," in the form of people who are selected for probation and then recidivate, and "false negatives," in the form of people who are sent to prison but who in fact are not recidivists.

The Expanding Net

Many liberals propose an increased use of probation. The National Council on Crime and Delinquency, the ACLU National Prison Project, and others argue that persons convicted of nonviolent crimes should not be imprisoned. Restitution, community service, or other nonprison alternatives should be available as sentencing options.[33] Unfortunately, the creation of alternatives does not necessarily result in fewer prison inmates. In their book *Imprisonment in America*, Michael Sherman and Gordon Hawkins point out that the states that have the highest incarceration rates also have the highest rates of persons on probation. Conversely, states with low incarceration rates have low probation rates. This seeming incongruity is another manifestation of the expanding net. Probation is not an alternative to imprisonment but an additional option that allows more people to be brought under some form of social control. The people placed on probation would probably have received suspended sentences or have had their cases bargained down to misdemeanors or, in the absence of a sizable probation program, dropped altogether.[34]

Electronic Jails: Effective Probation or Police State?

The latest fad in American corrections is home detention: prisoners are sentenced to serve their time at home rather than in prison. The significant innovation is the use of electronic monitoring devices to guarantee that the offender is in fact at home and not out on the street. There is considerable debate over whether home detention—or "electronic jail," as it has been called—represents an effective form of criminal sanction or an emerging police state.[35]

Home detention emerged in response to several factors. On the one hand, it represents an effort to find a mid-range sanction, something between imprisonment and conventional probation. As Elliott Currie argues, the debate over crime and punishment is usually presented in terms of extreme alternatives (prison/no prison) without any exploration of middle-range sanctions.[36] Home detention has attracted a lot of attention because it appears to be a reasonable alternative when prison seems excessive but routine probation appears too lenient. Confinement to one's home does deprive one of liberty and therefore is a significant punishment. It is neither so brutal nor so expensive as imprisonment. In some respects it is a possible solution to the prison overcrowding problem. At the same time, home detention is an innovative form of probation. In practice, offenders are supervised by probation officers. The new technology simply facilitates intensive supervision.

The technology itself takes a variety of forms and is rapidly changing. One popular device is a tamperproof bracelet or anklet that emits an electronic code to a monitor that includes an automatic telephone dialer. If the offender goes beyond a prescribed distance, the monitor automatically dials the probation officer. If the conditions of probation include employment, the monitor can be programmed to operate only during the hours when the offender is supposed to be at home. An alternative system involves computer-generated telephone calls to the offender's home to verify his or her presence. One variation of this approach involves frequent but random calls by the probation officer. For all practical purposes, this is nothing more than intensive probation.[37]

The most serious potential problem is the expanding-net syndrome. It is entirely possible that the offenders sentenced to home detention—whatever the form of monitoring—will be those who would otherwise receive routine probation or a suspended sentence. Thus, like diversion, home detention would bring more people under some kind of social control. This strategy would not relieve the prison overcrowding problem and in fact would involve substantial additional costs. A related problem, as we have seen, is the due-process question that inevitably arises.[38]

Electronic bracelets and computer-generated calls to monitor your behavior conjure up images of 1984, with Big Brother constantly monitoring everyone's behavior. We are already a long way down that road. Modern technology has enormously expanded the ability of government and private employers to monitor behavior we used to think of as private. Drug testing of employees is only the most highly publicized new program. Employers also have the ability to monitor employees' time at their desks and to know how often and how long they talk on the telephone. "Computer matching" gives the government the ability to cross-check data in one set of files (e.g., your IRS returns) with other files (your Social Security records, your student loan, the NCIC crime records). Private investigators can use parabolic micro-phones or other high-tech devices to penetrate our private lives. In short, the erosion of basic standards of privacy, particularly the privacy of the home, is rapidly becoming a major social issue. Electronic home confinement is only one part of a larger trend.[39]

Home detention is still in the experimental stage and no rigorous evaluations have been conducted. An early report on home detention by the Rand Corporation was fairly optimistic. It concluded that home detention was indeed cost-effective (as low as $1,350 per year, whereas the cost of imprisonment can run as high as $20,000) and that, when properly run, it can successfully divert nondangerous offenders from prison. The report did urge courts to proceed cautiously with new sentencing alternatives and not to regard money as the only criterion.[40] In the end, some of the more elaborate electronic monitoring devices might be sabotaged by their own sophistication. All sorts of technological problems may arise, such as false alarms triggered by interference with the signal (by a refrigerator, for example). Then there are the mundane human problems. Workers in one federal probation office decided not to purchase an electronic monitoring system when they realized that it would involve much more work for them. It would call to their attention every little violation. In fact, they are aware of these violations today but choose to overlook them, usually because such violations are relatively minor. The lesson here is an old one in criminal justice: technology is rarely the panacea it promises to be. Consider the case of the police patrol car and the unforeseen and in some cases undesirable consequences that resulted from elimination of foot patrol.

Summary

Where does this leave us? We are left muddling through with our existing programs intact. Despite the very grim news on the recidivism rate among probationers, it is not clear what a reasonable and effective alternative would be. The prisons are already bursting at the seams. Sending even more people to prison hardly makes sense. Some of the new forms of probation may be more effective but it is still too early to tell. Probation works most of the time for most offenders. There is a general consensus that most people who currently receive probation do not deserve to go to prison anyway. Probation does not always work. There are many failures and some of those failures are egregious ones. Unfortunately, because of our inability to predict human behavior with great precision, it is unlikely that we can improve the success rate for probation.

Prison Reform and Prison Industries

Certainly one of the more curious developments of the mid-1980s was the emergence of Warren Burger as the leading advocate of prison reform. The former chief justice has made the issue a personal crusade, speaking out on numerous occasions about society's "moral obligation" to improve prisons. He suggests we turn our prisons into "factories with fences" where inmates receive both basic education and vocational training. Upon release, these inmates would be able to take their places as responsible, law-abiding citizens—they would be, in a word, rehabilitated.[41]

Given his conservative, law-and-order position on the exclusionary rule and other issues, it was surprising to find Burger an advocate of rehabilitation—especially because almost no one else these days believes prisons can rehabilitate anyone. Efforts of prison reform today are focused primarily on prisoners' rights, improving prison conditions, preventing additional prison construction, and getting nondangerous offenders out of prison. Few knowledgeable experts retain any faith in rehabilitation.

Burger's idea of "factories with fences" coincides with a revival of interest in prison industries.[42] The new movement aims to bring prison industries under private management. The idea is to give inmates *real-world* experience: pay them competitive wages to work in businesses that compete in the open market.

My position is:

─────────────── **PROPOSITION 24** ───────────────

Prison industries will not reduce crime.

The Long, Sad Story of Prison Reform

There is something a little pathetic about Burger's prison-reform crusade because it requires a remarkable degree of historical amnesia. Prison reform and prison industries have a long history. It is not a happy story. The cycle of reform and failure has been repeated at least three times.[43] Today many experts believe that there is something inherently contradictory in the juxtaposition of prison and rehabilitation and that prisons are unreformable.

As instruments of rehabilitation, American prisons are an obscene joke. Only the most hardened bureaucrats in the correctional establishment pretend that these so-called correctional facilities do anything to help prisoners. Even then, it is largely the higher-ranking officials who pay lip service to the old clichés. The guards, who run the prisons day in and day out, have no such illusions. Guard and inmate slang has always been a truer guide to the reality of prisons. A guard is a "hack" or a "screw" to the inmates, not a "correctional officer." Solitary confinement is "the hole," not an "adjustment center." Both guards and inmates refer to the "goons" in the other group.[44] The overriding goal of penal institutions is to keep the inmates in custody. Wardens know they will never lose their jobs because the recidivism rate goes up; they may well lose them if the inmates escape or riot. Rehabilitation is a distinctly minor element of the day-to-day reality of the prison.

The backlash against rehabilitation arose in the wake of the 1971 Attica prison rebellion. The riot ended in a full-fledged assault by New York State Police officers which left forty-three persons dead. The carnage was dramatic evidence of the failure of rehabilitation. Out of the ashes of Attica arose a broad-ranging philosophical debate about the nature of punishment and the purposes of sentencing. The debate spurred interest in determinate sentencing. For a very brief period liberals and conservatives joined in an odd coalition in favor of determinate sentencing.[45]

The antirehabilitation movement drew upon several criticisms that had been developing for a decade. Conservatives charged that rehabilitation was ineffective. There was, and still is, much debate about the success of the treatment represented by prison and parole. In 1964 Daniel Glaser attacked the popular myth that "two-thirds return." He argued that only one-third of all prison inmates were eventually sentenced to another prison term. Subsequent research suggests that the figure is somewhat higher. A lot depends on the length of the follow-up period. The most thorough research, with an eight-year follow-up, indicates that 56 percent of all prisoners will eventually be convicted and sentenced to prison again. In any event, Martinson contended that there was no evidence that any particular form of correctional treatment—prison, parole, or anything else—shortened criminal careers more effectively than any other.[46]

Liberals, meanwhile, attacked rehabilitation on the grounds that it involved wholesale violations of due process. Both judicial sentencing and parole release decisions were wildly arbitrary, with no rational or scientific basis. The parole release process encouraged deceit and cynicism on the part of inmates as they sought to manipulate the rules of the game to obtain early release. Furthermore, prison conditions, far from encouraging rehabilitation, violated minimum standards of human decency.[47]

As the attacks on parole from right and left converged, a number of thoughtful observers questioned the basic idea of the prison as a place of correctional treatment. Norval Morris argued in The Future of Imprisonment (1974) that rehabilitation could never take place in the punitive environment of the prison; cure cannot be coerced. David Rothman took a historical approach. His prize winning book, The Discovery of the Asylum (1971), like Martinson's study three years later, offered an argument whose time had come. Rothman examined the origins of the prison and found the institution flawed from the very beginning.[48]

The prison originated as an enlightened reform, designed to replace barbaric forms of punishment. By cutting the inmate off from bad influences and encouraging the habits of hard work, self-scrutiny, and religious study, the prison environment would transform criminals into law-abiding citizens. It didn't quite work out that way. The prison was an immediate failure. The original goal of total isolation or silence drove inmates mad and was enforced through the most brutal punishments. Prisons became more savage than the corporal punishments they were designed to replace. Prison industries degenerated into a new form of slavery as officials handed inmates over to industrialists or plantation owners who had absolutely no concern for their welfare.

The continued failure of the prison brought on a second generation of penal reformers. The response of these reformers is instructive. Rather than question the fundamental premise of the prison, they tried to make it more effective. They developed what they thought was the magic key to correctional treatment: the indeterminate sentence and parole. Zebulon Brockway, founder of the Elmira Reformatory, proclaimed the new gospel to the world at the 1870 international prison congress in Cincinnati. The prison had failed because it provided no incentive for inmates to change their behavior. An indeterminate sentence with discretionary release on parole could provide that incentive. Responsibility for an inmate's release was to be placed in his or her own hands: if the inmate gave evidence of being rehabilitated, early release would follow; if not, he or she would stay in prison.

Brockway's ideas did not gain immediate acceptance. Over the next thirty years only a few institutions experimented with the indeterminate sentence and parole. Then, in an incredible burst of reform between 1900 and 1915, these ideas swept the country and became the foundation of modern correctional treatment. Brockway's magic key worked no better than the original prison system had done. Under the indeterminate sentence, prison terms actually lengthened. Parole release decisions were completely arbitrary and prison conditions hardly improved. A public backlash against parole set in during the 1920s and reform went into eclipse.[49]

A third generation of reformers emerged in the 1930s, and their ideas eventually dominated correctional thinking. Following Brockway's lead, these reformers did not question the basic premise of the prison but looked for a magic key to make it work. Their new ideas were diagnosis and classification. It was a mistake, they argued, to treat all inmates alike. The new social and behavioral sciences would permit diagnosis of each prisoner's circumstances. Inmates could then be classified accordingly and prescribed the proper correctional treatment. Nearly fifty years of effort went into the pursuit of individualized treatment.

Suffice it to say that the search was in vain. The institutional reality of prisons did not change. Classification systems were crude at best. The standard distinction between high-, medium-, and low-security prisoners really reflected considerations of security, not prospects for rehabilitation. No more than 10 percent of institutional budgets went for rehabilitative programs, and inmates readily understood that release on parole was the prize to be won in a game. Few inmates received anything that could

honestly be described as individual attention or an opportunity to participate in a program tailored to their individual needs.

Prison Industries

Meanwhile, prison industries had a checkered history of their own. As soon
as the first prisons were built, legislators and prison officials discovered that
they could defray costs and possibly even turn a profit by leasing out their
inmates. In the North, contractors brought their tools and materials into the
prisons; in the South, inmates were generally leased out to plantation
owners. In either case, state officials abandoned all responsibility for the
inmates, and a new form of slavery emerged. Prison reformers attacked this
system on humanitarian grounds, but it was economic considerations that
eventually brought the contract/lease system to an end. In the late nineteenth century a coalition of organized labor and small business gradually
secured laws restricting prison industries. Then, in the 1930s, federal laws
prohibiting the interstate sale of prison-made goods delivered the coup de
grace[50] and prison industries became a minor part of the correctional scene.

Virtually all experts agree that in the absence of meaningful work,
idleness is the great curse of the prisons. Inmates have little to do, even in
the form of makework. Most of the jobs tend to be menial and take only a few
hours at the most. Many factors contribute to the absence of meaningful
work programs. Laws restricting the manufacture and sale of various items
are only one consideration. Effective vocational programs require what any
enterprise needs: good management and adequate funding. Neither is in
abundance in American prisons. Security considerations are also important.
Most industrial jobs require a certain amount of free movement and, even
more important in a prison setting, the use of the appropriate tools, many of
which can readily be transformed into weapons. This long history of failure
sets the context for the recent calls to transform prisons into "factories with
fences."

Free Venture: The New Prison Industry

Free Venture is the hot new idea in prison industries. The system is
currently operating in Minnesota, Kansas, and other states. Two federal
agencies, including the usually skeptical General Accounting Office, have
examined and endorsed it.[51]

The primary goal of Free Venture is to bring the real world of free
enterprises into the prisons. Inmates work in businesses managed by private
entrepreneurs, who are there to make a profit, and are paid competitive,
real-world wages. In most Free Venture industries, wages begin at the legal
minimum and rise as the inmate gains experience and seniority. Because the
enterprise is competing on the open market, pressure to maintain productivity and quality falls on the inmate-employees. If they slack off or don't

produce, they are "fired"—sent back into the general prison population. By contrast, most prison work involves the production of goods for a captive or subsidized market, usually the state itself, and there are no incentives for productivity.

Free Venture has several objectives. At a minimum, it provides work for inmates and reduces the curse of idleness. More important, it is intended to give them experience in economically viable trades and to encourage good work habits. Presumably these accomplishments will translate into employment when inmates are released from prison, and their jobs will in turn lead them into law-abiding lives. Free Venture is supposed to succeed where previous prison industries failed because it is managed by real businessmen rather than by prison officials, who typically have neither the skills nor the experience required for successful entrepreneurship.

A certain amount of high-tech glamour surrounds the Free Venture concept. The most successful Minnesota project is Stillwater Data Processing Systems, Inc., which employs sixteen inmates as computer programmers behind the walls of the Stillwater penitentiary. An LEAA-funded report on the possibilities of Free Venture in Connecticut recommended the development of microfilming services, solar energy, and data processing, among other enterprises.[52]

Does Free Venture work? It is still too early to give a definitive answer. Two early government reports gave it passing marks.[53] Success, of course, depends on your criteria. At last report, Stillwater Data Processing Systems was still in business, so by that criterion it is successful. But two other industries in Minnesota prisons had gone out of business. Business failure is a normal part of free enterprise in the real world, of course, and we should not expect prison industries to do any better.

Business success is not our primary concern, however. The real issue is the impact of the program on the inmate-employees. At this point it is not clear that Free Venture businesses make a real difference in the lives of their employees. The acid test is whether they take prisoners with few skills and checkered employment histories and turn them into employable citizens. This question can be answered only by a rigorous follow-up study of Free Venture graduates. To date, no such study has been completed.

While we wait, some cautionary observations are in order. In the midst of all the enthusiasm for Free Venture, we should not forget that it is the latest in a 150-year history of prison reform schemes, all of which were launched with great hopes and which then failed. Free Venture encounters a number of problems inherent in the attempt to operate a business behind prison walls. Security considerations remain paramount. Free Venture businesses have already been troubled by "lockdowns," during which prison officials confine all inmates to their cells for extended periods. A lockdown shuts down a Free Venture industry and threatens its ability to fulfill its contracts.

More troublesome is the matter of selecting inmates as Free Venture employees. To enter the program a prisoner must pass through a two-stage screening process: one by prison officials and a second by the Free Venture management. The question that needs further research is whether the program simply selects those few inmates who already have relatively good job skills and work habits. Most inmates don't.[54] The typical American prisoner never finished high school and probably went only as far as the ninth grade. Three-fourths of all prisoners were unemployed at the time of their arrest and most can be classified as long-term or hard-core unemployed. Moreover, most of the early Free Venture industries are high-tech businesses, such as data processing. A lot of law-abiding high school graduates are not equipped for these jobs. It would be very easy for Free Venture to succeed by selecting only the cream of the inmate population. It would leave untouched the mass of unemployable prisoners and consequently would have no rehabilitative effect on them. Finally, even if Free Venture is successful, how many inmates can it hope to enroll? In Minnesota, Stillwater Data Processing employs a grand total of sixteen inmates. There are a half-million prisoners in the United States and the number is steadily rising. How many of them could be rehabilitated by Free Venture?

Parole

Parole is the unwanted child of American criminal justice, arousing the fury of both conservatives and liberals. Conservatives argue that it allows prisoners to get out too soon. Softhearted parole boards turn dangerous criminals loose to prey on law-abiding people.[55] Parole boards (along with "good time" provisions) do in fact shorten prison terms to a considerable degree. Only a small percentage of prisoners serve their full terms. Convicted robbers serve an average of about three or four years; the going rate for second-degree murder is about five or six years.

Some liberals have had second thoughts about parole and now defend it on the grounds that the sentence-shortening function is essential. The real problem, in their view, is the indeterminate sentence. Sentencing statutes typically provide judges with a wide range to choose from (one to fifty years, ten to life, and so forth). As a result, they dish out extremely long sentences. With the exceptions of the Soviet Union and South Africa, our two rivals for penal excess, no other country in the world gives such long sentences as the United States. By shortening sentences, parole boards moderate punishment. It effect, two bad systems tend to balance each other out.[56]

The real question, of course, is how much time is enough. Conservatives assume that longer sentences have a greater deterrent and incapacitative effect. Liberals reply that the available evidence suggests that prisoners who serve short sentences do just as well (or as poorly) as those who serve long terms. Thus we can achieve the same ends at much less cost to society and less suffering to the inmate by giving shorter prison terms.[57]

"What do you mean, 'when are we eligible for parole?' Slaves don't get paroled, dummy!"

Liberals indict parole on due-process grounds. Parole boards routinely make decisions about people's liberty with no rational or scientific basis. Parole release decisions are arbitrary in general and often discriminatory against minorities. The decisions are inextricably linked with the original criminal sentences, which liberals also view as examples of uncontrolled discretion.[58] The idea of determinate sentencing initially attracted a great deal of support among liberals because they thought it would bring the discretion of both judges and parole boards under control. For the most part, their enthusiasm quickly disappeared when it became obvious that in the current political climate, legislators would prescribe very long determinate sentences.

Parole Survives

Despite the broad-based attack, parole continues to survive (except in the federal system, where it was abolished by the 1987 sentencing guidelines). This is not the first time it has weathered a major assault. David Rothman has found that parole was everyone's favorite whipping boy in the 1920s as well. It survived because it serves the practical needs of prison officials, specifically their ability to manage prisoners. The power of a guard to "write up" an inmate for an infraction is a large factor in the length of time that inmate will serve. Parole boards give heavy weight to an inmate's behavioral record, and of course they have only the official records of infractions to go by. Prison officials have always argued that they need these carrots and sticks in order to maintain control over the prison population.[59]

At the same time, parole serves as a safety valve for the prison population. Prisons have always been overcrowded, and parole has permitted some leeway in keeping the problem from getting completely out of hand. One of the interesting new developments in the 1980s is a series of prison overcrowding laws. Michigan and Iowa require the automatic release of prisoners (by the speeding up of parole eligibility dates) whenever their prison populations exceed a certain limit. This innovation simply makes explicit what has long been one of the latent functions of parole.

Whither Parole?

The question remains: What to do about parole? Can it be improved substantially, or should it be abolished altogether? The main argument in its defense has a curiously negative thrust: we need it to correct other problems. Parole is necessary to shorten excessively long sentences and to allow us to manage the behavior and size of the inmate population. This is hardly a principled defense of one of the cornerstones of our criminal justice policy.

Our focus in this inquiry is crime control. Putting aside other problems related to parole for the moment, we need to ask: Could we reduce crime by either improving or abolishing parole? My answer is no.

—————————————— **PROPOSITION 25** ——————————————
Neither the improvement nor the abolition of parole will reduce serious crime.

Does Parole Work?

Does parole work? This question really encompasses two others. The first relates to the length of prison terms. Do longer prison terms effectively deter and incapacitate criminal offenders? Or do longer terms impose high societal and personal costs without reducing crime? The second question involves the nature of parole supervision. Does more intensive supervision, or some other variant of parole, reduce recidivism?

Recidivism, the traditional measure of success, is a very elastic concept. A parolee can fail in at least four ways: by a technical violation of one of the conditions of parole, by absconding, by committing a relatively minor offense, and by committing a serious offense. You can manipulate your success rate by counting some items and discounting others. Another problem involves the length of the follow-up period. A one-year follow-up will obviously produce a much higher success rate than an eight-year follow-up. Finally, recidivism rates vary according to the type of crime. Murderers have a low recidivism rate; drug dealers have a high one.

The most thorough study of persons released on parole is the report *4,000 Lifetimes,* by the National Council on Crime and Delinquency (NCCD), which studied 104,182 adult male felons paroled between 1965 and 1970. A smaller sample of 1,810 parolees was studied for a period of eight years.

Table 11.1   Reasons for "failure" on parole, eight-year follow-up

Performance	Number of men	Percent of sample (N = 1,810)
Minor conviction	225	12.43
Absconding	22	1.22
Parole violator returned (no convictions)	214	11.82
Parole violator returned (minor convictions)	82	4.53
Major offense (California)	626	34.59
Major offense (elsewhere)	103	5.69
Total	1,272	70.28

SOURCE: Michael R. Gottfredson and Don M. Gottfredson, *Decision-Making in Criminal Justice: Toward the Rational Exercise of Discretion* (Cambridge, Mass.: Ballinger, 1980), p. 262.

Table 11.1 indicates the success and failure rates for the latter group. About 30 percent had no problems at all and can be counted as complete successes (although admittedly some may have committed crimes but were never arrested). But to say that 70 percent failed is a little misleading. The most significant figure is the 40 percent representing persons who failed because they committed another major offense. The 12 percent who failed by virtue of a conviction on a minor offense are a problem but a less serious one.[60]

Regardless of the reason, most failures occur in the first two years. At the end of the first year, 25 percent of the original 1,810 had failed, and at the end of the second year, 43 percent had failed. From that point on, the number of new failures each year drops off considerably.

Improving Parole

Have we any hope of improving parole? Can we design a program that will cause people to commit fewer crimes after they leave prison? Proposals for improving parole fall into three general categories: improve the quality of parole supervision; improve parole release decision making; and finally, the most drastic approach of all, abolish parole altogether.

Programs designed to improve the quality of parole supervision are essentially identical to probation reforms. California maintained a Special Intensive Parole Unit (SIPU) for ten years and subjected it to in-house evaluation. When Robert Martinson reviewed the SIPU evaluations, he found that three of the four phases produced no meaningful improvement in the behavior of parolees. The phase involving smaller case loads did appear to yield some positive results. Martinson concluded that parolees in this phase appeared to be more successful because they were returned to prison more often for technical violations. He concluded that this was a deterrent rather than a rehabilitative effect. Parolees behaved themselves a little better when they knew that they faced a real prospect of being sent back to prison.[61] With only ambiguous success in one of its four components, SIPU is hardly an overwhelming endorsement of the rehabilitative effect of parole.

None of the researchers who have surveyed evaluations of rehabilitation programs have found much evidence that one form of parole is more effective than any other. A major reason is the inherent superficiality of parole supervision. As in the case of probation, the "supervision" is largely a bureaucratic formality. The parolee reports in once a month and the parole officer fills out the required reports. Despite all the rhetoric, no "correctional treatment" is being given.[62]

Martinson himself concludes that the best argument in favor of parole is simply that parolees do no worse than their colleagues who stay in prison. That, of course, is an argument not for parole supervision but for shorter prison terms. Releasing prisoners relatively early would be much cheaper and no less effective. Andrew von Hirsch and Kathleen Hanrahan recommend that release on parole be maintained for the purpose of shortening sentences, but that parole supervision be abolished.[63]

A second approach to parole reform focuses on improvement in parole decision making. Liberals and conservatives have different objectives in this regard. Liberals want to structure decision making to eliminate arbitrariness and discrimination. Conservatives want to improve the predictive quality of decisions to make sure that fewer chronic recidivists are released early.

Criminologists and correctional officials have sought to develop effective guidelines for parole release for more than fifty years. E. W. Burgess, at the University of Chicago, developed the first predictive device in 1928. Over the next half century, the search for better diagnostic and predictive tools was one of the major concerns of academic criminology. The California correctional system, which invested far more resources in research than did any other system, developed the most elaborate tools. Yet, as Martinson and others found, there is no evidence that California's procedures in fact yield accurate predictions of offenders' behavior after they are released.[64]

Parole release decisions, of course, represent another variant of the prediction problem. The task is to identify those prisoners who represent a low risk, so they can be released early, and those who represent a high risk, so they can be held in prison longer. We do not need to review the prediction problem in detail again at this point. Suffice it to say that criminologists and parole authorities have available to them the same basic set of data about offenders: the offenses for which they were convicted, their prior records, evidence of violent behavior, and such relevant personal data as employment history and drug or alcohol abuse. The most recent and most sophisticated attempts to derive effective predictions from these data have not been impressive. Parole authorities have traditionally used an even less sophisticated approach.

Peter Hoffman compared the success and failure rates of prisoners released on parole and those who served their full terms (in prisoner jargon, they "jammed out" or "maxed out"). Of the 1,135 adult male offenders released in 1968 who had been convicted of robbery, burglary, or manslaughter, the parolees did better than those who served their full terms. Only half as many parolees as full-termers were arrested for a new offense. Many of the offenders who served their full terms, however, were "false positives." Parole authorities held them in prison in the erroneous belief that they would be recidivists. Many of those who were paroled, meanwhile, were false negatives. They were deemed ready for release (rehabilitated) when in fact they did commit new crimes.[65]

One recent innovation is the formulation of more formal parole decision-making guidelines. (The same idea underlies the recent development of sentencing guidelines, such as the ones Minnesota has constructed.) Parole guidelines structure discretion and provide a greater degree of consistency and fairness. These are worthy objectives, given the general arbitrariness of most parole decision making. But to devise guidelines is not to address the question of effectiveness in controlling crime. The presumptive release dates are derived from averages of past practice. Because armed robbers have served an average of x months in prison, x becomes the presumptive sentence length. While this formula adds a degree of consistency, it does not answer the basic question: How much time is enough for an armed robber?

The final proposal is not to improve parole but to abolish it altogether. California took a big step in this direction with its determinate sentencing law in 1976. Release dates are mandatory once a prisoner has served the sentence imposed by the judge and good time has been deducted. The federal sentencing guidelines that took effect on November 1, 1986, also abolish parole and replace it with presumptive sentences. Many liberals continue to argue that parole should be retained because it shortens otherwise excessively long sentences. It is too early to evaluate the impact of the abolition of parole in the federal system.[66]

Abolition of parole is essentially irrelevant to crime control. It may or may not be advisable to abolish parole in order to eliminate the discretionary problems it often raises. But abolition would not in any way affect crime rates. Whether prison terms should be longer or shorter is also a separate question. With or without parole, sentences could be shortened or lengthened. Whether any change would enhance either the rehabilitative, deterrent, or incapacitative effect of prison is not clear.

Rehabilitation Reaffirmed?

Can rehabilitation ever work? Rehabilitation has been the whipping boy of the correctional community for nearly fifteen years now. It is important to point out, however, that despite all the rhetorical attacks, rehabilitation remains the dominant aim of American criminal justice policy. Most convicted offenders receive a sentence of probation. Virtually all prisoners secure early release on parole. Probation and parole continue to exist for both legitimate and illegitimate reasons. Part of the explanation is sheer bureaucratic inertia. The correctional bureaucracy has a vested interest in maintaining itself, and the alternatives do not command sufficient political support. Most important, however, the alternatives are simply unrealistic. We simply cannot afford to imprison everyone convicted of a felony—nor would we want to as a matter of justice or humanity. Thus the existing system continues to muddle along. Is there any hope for improvement?

The best argument raised in defense of rehabilitation is that the charge that "nothing works" has been overstated. Ted Palmer, director of research with the California Youth Authority, correctly points out that the Martinson report did not find that absolutely nothing works. Some positive results were evident in 48 percent of the studies Martinson surveyed. The other surveys of the rehabilitation literature drew similar conclusions. The most accurate thing we can say about rehabilitation, then, is that some programs work for some offenders. Selecting the right program for the right offender—ah, now there's the problem.[67]

Tailoring just the right kind of program for selected offenders calls for a high degree of diagnostic precision. Practical application requires discriminating judgments about who is a good candidate for probation and who is not, or who "deserves" a long prison sentence and who deserves only a short one. As our discussions of the prediction problem have repeatedly shown, this is the Achilles' heel of many conservative and liberal programs. Our diagnostic tools are not adequate for this task and there is no reason to believe they will improve in the near future. The real world of American criminal justice does not allow for such fine tuning. Judges base their sentences on gross categories—primarily the seriousness of the offense and the offender's prior record.

Palmer's defense—that some programs work for some offenders—is a truism that offers little practical help. The bad news is that we probably have to continue to muddle along. Many of our predictions will prove to be accurate. Many offenders granted probation will not go on to become career criminals. Many prisoners released on parole will cease their criminal activity. But we will also make many mistakes. We will release into the community some people who go on to commit many serious crimes. It is easy to indict this system. Political grandstanding is cheap. Designing a practical alternative, however, is the real challenge.

The defenders of rehabilitation have also raised moral and humanitarian arguments. Palmer asserts that "society still has a responsibility for making at least some assistance available to offenders as human beings." Francis Cullen and Karen Gilbert make the same point. In their view, "rehabilitation is the only justification of criminal sanctioning that obligates the state to care for an offender's needs or welfare." Furthermore, "rehabilitation has historically been an important motive underlying reform efforts that have increased the humanity of the correctional system."[68]

The last statement ignores the major findings of the excellent histories of American corrections. David Rothman's two books on the history of the prison and correctional treatment make a persuasive case for the proposition that good intentions do not necessarily produce good results. Quite the contrary, the historical evidence appears to indicate that good intentions often produce bad results. In important respects, correctional reforms have actually increased the savage and punitive aspects of our penal system while masking them in humanitarian rhetoric. Prison conditions may be more brutal than the corporal punishments they were designed to replace. Prison terms lengthened under the allegedly more enlightened indeterminate sentence.[69] Diversion, intended to channel people out of corrections system, seems to bring more people under social control. Sound criminal justice policy, then, requires more than good intentions.

Palmer is indeed right about society's responsibility for providing assistance to offenders. But this is a social justice question that is independent of the entire issue of rehabilitation. We should provide employment for people who do not have it. At present we don't provide full employment for offenders or nonoffenders. A genuine full-employment program, as a matter of national policy, could coexist with traditional rehabilitation-oriented criminal justice programs (probation, the indeterminate sentence, parole, and the rest) or with a strictly punishment-oriented system of determinate sentencing. The humanitarian gloss of rehabilitation only deludes people into thinking we are doing good when in fact those programs are not doing anyone much good. The evidence seems to indicate that the supervision provided to probationers and parolees is a relatively meaningless form of bureaucratic record keeping that does not address the real needs of the people under supervision.

Elliot Currie argues persuasively that rehabilitation programs often work in the short run but are undermined by larger social problems. Some programs make positive changes in the behavior of offenders but then send them back into a community environment that leads (or drives) them back into criminality. Currie cites an evaluation of graduates of the Wiltwyck School in New York. During the 1950s the Wiltwyck School was seen as a very advanced rehabilitation program for delinquent youths. It offered what it called "disciplined love": a structured environment that avoided punitive treatment and sought to foster self-control and self-esteem. Wiltwyck had some famous graduates: the noted writer Claude Brown and the former heavyweight boxing champion Floyd Patterson.[70]

The evaluators of Wiltwyck compared it with the Lyman reform school, a traditional punishment-oriented institution, and traced comparable groups of graduates into the 1980s, when most were in their thirties or forties. The Wiltwyck graduates had a low rate of recidivism during the first five years after their release—much lower than that of the Lyman graduates. In short, it appeared that Wiltwyck's rehabilitation-oriented "treatment" was far more successful than Lyman's punishment-centered program. After five years, however, the Wiltwyck graduates began to have serious problems with the law. Criminality among the Lyman graduates, meanwhile, began to drop. How do we explain these seemingly contradictory trends? Currie argues that the increased recidivism among the Wiltwyck youths was confined almost exclusively to the black and Hispanic graduates. Most of the Lyman graduates were white—Irish, Italian, or French-Canadian in background. The white youths had more success finding work and a stable place in society (one former delinquent of Irish descent became a cop). The black and Hispanic graduates of Wiltwyck faced higher barriers of prejudice and lack of job opportunities, and consequently slid back into lives of crime. Wiltwyck successfully "rehabilitated most of its boys," only to send its minority graduates back into a criminogenic environment.

The final argument in defense of rehabilitation is the call for more research. The National Academy of Science's Panel on Research on Rehabilitative Techniques has called for "more systematic, long-term, and focused research that will have a substantial probability of improving techniques and programs that can be evaluated in ways that will produce more definitive conclusions." John Conrad replies to this suggestion by pointing out the most obvious question of all: "Why was it that rehabilitation never worked as a system with a goal to achieve?"[71] The accumulated research on correctional institutions and programs is rather persuasive. These institutions appear to have some inherent problems that undermine the basic goal of successfully intervening and reducing recidivism rates. It is wishful thinking to believe that additional research is going to uncover a magic key that has somehow been overlooked for 150 years.

Notes

1. Lee B. Sechrest, Susan O. White, and Elizabeth Brown, *The Rehabilitation of Criminal Offenders: Problems and Prospects* (Washington, D. C.: National Academy of Sciences, 1979), pp. 18–19.

2. Robert Martinson, "What Works? Questions and Answers about Prison Reform," *Public Interest* 35 (Spring 1974): 22–54.

3. American Friends Service Committee, *Struggle for Justice* (New York: Hill & Wang, 1971).

4. The state of California made the most serious effort to evaluate its correctional programs systematically. But see the criticism in Robert Martinson, "California Research at the Crossroads," *Crime and Delinquency* 24 (April 1976): 180–191.

5. Sechrest et al., *Rehabilitation of Criminal Offenders*, pp. 14, 31, 102.

6. Walter Bailey, "Correctional Outcome: An Evaluation of 100 Reports," *Journal of Criminal Law, Criminology, and Police Science*, 57 (June 1966): 153–160; William E. Wright and Michael Dixon, "Community Prevention and Treatment of Juvenile Delinquency: A Review of Evaluation Studies," *Journal of Research*

in Crime and Delinquency, 14 (January 1977): 35–67; Charles Logan, "Evaluation Research in Crime and Delinquency: A Reappraisal," *Journal of Criminal Law, Criminology, and Police Science*, 63 (September 1972): 378–387; Robert Martinson, "New Findings, New Views: A Note of Caution Regarding Sentencing Reform," *Hofstra Law Review* 4 (Winter 1979): 254.

7. Ted Palmer, *Correctional Intervention and Research* (Lexington, Mass.: Lexington Books, 1978).

8. Susan E. Martin, Lee B. Sechrest, and Robin Redner, *New Directions in the Rehabilitation of Criminal Offenders* (Washington, D. C.: National Academy Press, 1981), p. 23; John P. Conrad, "News of the Future: Research and Development in Corrections," *Federal Probation* 46 (June 1982): 66–69.

9. Eugene Doleschal, "The Dangers of Criminal Justice Reform," *Criminal Justice Abstracts* 14 (March 1982): 133–152.

10. Raymond T. Nimmer, *Diversion: The Search for Alternative Forms of Prosecution* (Chicago: American Bar Foundation, 1974).

11. Edwin M. Schur, *Radical Nonintervention: Rethinking the Delinquency Problem* (Englewood Cliffs, N. J.: Prentice-Hall, 1973).

12. Nimmer, *Diversion*.

13. Ibid.

14. Vera Institute of Justice, *The Manhattan Court Employment Project: Final Report* (New York, 1972).

15. U. S. Department of Justice, *Diversion of Felony Arrests: An Experiment in Pretrial Intervention* (Washington, D. C.: U. S. Government Printing Office, 1981).

16. Thomas G. Blomberg, "Widening the Net: An Anomaly in the Evaluation of Diversion Programs," in *Handbook of Criminal Justice Evaluation*, ed. M. W. Klein and K. S. Teilman (Beverly Hills, Calif.: Sage, 1980), pp. 572–592.

17. Ibid.

18. Ibid., p. 592.

19. Jamie S. Gorelick, "Pretrial Diversion: The Threat of Expanding Social Control," *Harvard Civil Rights–Civil Liberties Law Review* 10 (1975): 180–214.

20. Kathleen B. Brosi, *A Cross-City Comparison of Felony Case Processing* (Washington, D. C.: INSLAW, 1979), chap. 7.

21. Joan Petersilia, Susan Turner, James Kahan, and Joyce Peterson, *Granting Felons Probation: Public Risks and Alternatives* (Santa Monica, Calif.: Rand Corporation, 1985): *New York Times*, April 3, 1987.

22. Petersilia et al., *Granting Felons Probation*, pp. 20–26.

23. Kevin Krajick, "Probation: The Original Community Program," *Corrections Magazine* 6 (December 1980): 7–15.

24. John P. Conrad, *Justice and Its Consequences* (Lexington, Mass.: Lexington Books, 1981), chap. 9.

25. Palmer, *Correctional Intervention and Research*.

26. U. S. National Institute of Justice (NIJ), *New Dimensions in Probation: Georgia's Experience with Intensive Probation Supervision (IPS)*, Research in Brief (Washington: U. S. Government Printing Office, 1987).

27. Ibid.

28. J. Banks, A. L. Porter, R. L. Rardin, T. R. Silver, and V. E. Unger, *Evaluation of Intensive Special Probation Projects*, National Evaluation Program, Phase I (Washington, D. C.: U. S. Government Printing Office, 1977).

29. Bailey, "Correctional Outcome"; James Robison and Gerald Smith, "The Effectiveness of Correctional Programs," *Crime and Delinquency* 17 (January 1971): 67–80.

30. Charles A. Murray and Louis A. Cox, Jr., *Beyond Probation: Juvenile Corrections and the Chronic Delinquent* (Beverly Hills, Calif.: Sage, 1979).

31. David McDowall, Richard McCleary, Andrew C. Gordon, and Michael Maltz, "Regression Artifacts in Correctional Program Evaluations," in *Corrections at the Crossroads: Designing Policy*, ed. Sherwood E. Zimmerman and Harold D. Miller (Beverly Hills, Calif.: Sage, 1981), pp. 27–47.

32. Peter W. Greenwood, *Selective Incapacitation* (Santa Monica, Calif.: Rand Corporation, 1982).

33. NCCD, "Nondangerous Offender."

34. Michael Sherman and Gordon Hawkins, *Imprisonment in America: Choosing the Future* (Chicago: University of Chicago Press, 1981), pp. 44–45.

35. Paul J. Hofer et al., *Home Confinement: An Evolving Sanction in the Federal Criminal Justice System* (Washington, D. C.: Federal Judicial Center, 1987).

36. Elliott Currie, *Confronting Crime*, p. 235.

37. Hofer et al., *Home Confinement.*

38. Bonnie Berry, "Electronic Jails: A New Criminal Justice Concern," *Justice Quarterly* 2 (March 1985): 1–22; J. Robert Lilly, Richard A. Ball, and W. Robert Lotz, Jr., "Electronic Jail Revisited," *Justice Quarterly* 3 (September 1986): 353–361, and Berry's reply on pp. 363–370.

39. Gary Marx, *Undercover: Police Surveillance in America* (Berkeley: University of California Press, 1988).

40. Rand Corporation, cited in *Omaha World Herald*, December 15, 1987.

41. Warren Burger, address at Lincoln, Nebraska, December 16, 1981, in *Criminal Justice Newsletter*, January 1, 1982.

42. Gordon Hawkins, "Prison Labor and Prison Industries," in *Crime and Justice: An Annual Review of Research*, ed. Michael Tonry and Norval Morris, vol. 5 (Chicago: University of Chicago Press, 1983), pp. 85–127.

43. Samuel Walker, *Popular Justice: A History of American Criminal Justice* (New York: Oxford University Press, 1980), pp. 83–84, 149, 156.

44. Robert Sommer, *The End of Imprisonment* (New York: Oxford University Press, 1976), pp. 42–48.

45. Andrew von Hirsch, *Doing Justice* (New York: Hill & Wang, 1976).

46. Michael R. Gottfredson and Don M. Gottfredson, *Decision-Making in Criminal Justice: Toward the Rational Exercise of Discretion* (Cambridge, Mass.: Ballinger, 1980), pp. 250–257; Daniel Glaser, *The Effectiveness of a Prison and Parole System* (Indianapolis: Bobbs-Merrill, 1964): Martinson, "What Works?"

47. American Friends Service Committee, *Struggle for Justice.*

48. Norval Morris, *The Future of Imprisonment* (Chicago: University of Chicago Press, 1974); David Rothman, *The Discovery of the Asylum* (Boston: Little, Brown, 1971). See also David Rothman, *Conscience and Convenience* (Boston: Little, Brown, 1980).

49. Walker, *Popular Justice.*

50. Hawkins, "Prison Labor and Prison Industries."

51. Michael Fedo, "Free Enterprise Goes to Prison," *Corrections Magazine* 7 (April 1981). The system also receives an endorsement in Hawkins, "Prison Labor and Prison Industries."

52. U. S. Department of Justice, *Analysis of Prison Industries and Recommendations for Change* (Washington, D. C.: U. S. Government Printing Office, 1978).

53. Ibid.; General Accounting Office, *Improved Prison Work Programs Will Benefit Correctional Institutions and Inmates*, Report no. GGD-82-37 (Washington, D. C.: U. S. Government Printing Office, June 29, 1982).

54. Hawkins disagrees with this view: "Prison Labor and Prison Industries," p. 103.

55. President's Task Force on Victims of Crime, *Final Report* (Washington, D. C.: U. S. Government Printing Office, 1982), pp. 83–85.

56. Andrew von Hirsch and Kathleen J. Hanrahan, *Abolish Parole?* (Washington, D. C.: U. S. Government Printing Office, 1978).

57. For the best summary of the liberal view on these issues, see Edna McConnell Clark Foundation, *Overcrowded Time: Why Prisons Are So Crowded and What Can Be Done* (New York, 1982).

58. American Friends Service Committee, *Struggle for Justice*.

59. Rothman, *Conscience and Convenience*.

60. Gottfredson and Gottfredson, *Decision-Making in Criminal Justice*, pp. 250–257.

61. William P. Adams, Paul M. Chandler, and M. G. Neithercutt, "The San Francisco Project: A Critique," *Federal Probation* 35, no. 4 (1971): 45–53; Robert Martinson and Judith Wilks, "Save Parole Supervision," *Federal Probation* 41 (September 1977): 23–27.

62. Bailey, "Correctional Outcome"; Robison and Smith, "Effectiveness of Correctional Programs"; John P. Conrad, "Who Needs a Doorbell Pusher?" in *Justice and Its Consequences* (Lexington, Mass.: Lexington Books, 1981), chap. 9.

63. Von Hirsch and Hanrahan, *Abolish Parole?*

64. Von Hirsch, *Doing Justice*, chap. 3.

65. Peter B. Hoffman, "Mandatory Release: A Measure of Type II Error," *Criminology* 11 (February 1974).

66. Von Hirsch and Hanrahan, *Abolish Parole?* U. S. Sentencing Commission, *Sentencing Guidelines and Policy Statements* (Washington, D. C.: Government Printing Office, April 13, 1987).

67. Palmer, *Correctional Intervention and Research*.

68. Ibid., p. 109; Francis T. Cullen and Karen E. Gilbert, *Reaffirming Rehabilitation* (Cincinnati: Anderson, 1982); pp. 247, 261.

69. Rothman, *Discovery of the Asylum*; Rothman, *Conscience and Convenience*.

70. Currie, *Confronting Crime*, pp. 241–244.

71. Martin et al., *New Directions in the Rehabilitation of Criminal Offenders*; Conrad, "News of the Future," pp. 66–69.

Chapter 12

Reform the Law: Decriminalization

The "first principle" advanced by Norval Morris and Gordon Hawkins in their 1970 book, *The Honest Politician's Guide to Crime Control*, involved removal of a broad range of crimes from the statutes. Decriminalization of certain types of behavior has long been a major item on the liberal crime control agenda. In his book *Crime and Punishment: A Radical Solution*, Aryeh Neier, then executive director of the ACLU, offered decriminalization as his primary crime-reduction proposal.[1]

For liberals the problem is what Morris and Hawkins call the "overreach" of the criminal law. It covers too wide a range of human behavior. Too much of it reflects the moralistic concerns of particular groups that are offended by the behavior of others. Morris and Hawkins urge us to "strip off the moralistic excrescences on our criminal justice system so that it may concentrate on the essential." They propose decriminalization in seven general areas:

1. *Drunkenness.* Public drunkenness shall cease to be a criminal offense.
2. *Narcotics and drug abuse.* Neither the acquisition, purchase, possession, nor use of any drug will be a criminal offense. The sale of some drugs other than by a licensed chemist (druggist) and on prescription will be criminally proscribed; proof of possession of excessive quantities may be evidence of a sale or of intent to sell.
3. *Gambling.* No form of gambling will be prohibited by the criminal law; certain fraudulent and cheating gambling practices will remain criminal.
4. *Disorderly conduct and vagrancy.* Disorderly conduct and vagrancy laws will be replaced by laws precisely stipulating the conduct proscribed and defining the circumstances in which the police should intervene.

5. *Abortion.* Abortion performed by a qualified medical practitioner in a registered hospital shall cease to be a criminal offense.
6. *Sexual behavior.* Sexual activities between consenting adults in private will not be subject to the criminal law. In adultery, fornication, illicit cohabitation, statutory rape and carnal knowledge, bigamy, incest, sodomy, bestiality, homosexuality, prostitution, pornography, and obscenity the role of the criminal law is excessive.
7. *Juvenile delinquency.* The juvenile court should retain jurisdiction only over conduct by children which would be criminal were they adult.

The Rationale

Decriminalization has three principal rationales. First, many laws are criminogenic. This is a particularly important point for our inquiry. Laws actually create crime in three ways: by labeling, by encouraging secondary deviance, and by creating a "crime tariff." According to labeling theory, the criminal justice process enhances or "amplifies" criminality. The person who is arrested, prosecuted, convicted, and incarcerated internalizes the label of "criminal" and proceeds to act out the role, committing additional and more serious crimes. Advocates of decriminalization argue that laws covering essentially harmless behavior should be abolished.[2] The laws also create what is known as "seconday deviance." A person becomes addicted to heroin and then, because the drug is illegal and expensive, must turn to crime to support the habit. If addiction were handled as a medical problem, with appropriate treatment or maintenance programs, addicts would not have to rob and steal. Thus we would reduce much of the drug-related crime. Secondary deviance is closely related to the crime tariff problem. Making a product illegal only drives up the price. The high price increases the amount of money the person needs to obtain illegally and encourages the development of criminal syndicates that control the market. It is generally recognized that existing gambling laws help sustain organized crime.

Overly broad criminal statutes also undermine respect for the law. Prohibition is the classic example. The Eighteenth Amendment, which outlawed the sale of alcoholic beverages in 1919, made criminals out of millions of people who simply wanted a recreational drink. Today it is argued that the illegal status of marijuana, a relatively harmless recreational drug, causes many young people to lose respect for the law and the legal system.

Overcriminalization also places serious burdens on the criminal justice system. Morris and Hawkins argue that the police waste far too much time enforcing statutes prohibiting vagrancy, disorderly conduct, and public intoxication when they could be concentrating on serious crimes against people and property. Moreover, insofar as the gambling statutes sustain

"Looks like a nice liberal neighborhood."

organized crime, they are responsible for the most serious patterns of corruption in the criminal justice system.

The final decriminalization argument is that the laws violate individual rights. Much of the behavior that has been covered by criminal statutes is a private matter: one's sexual preference or the decision to have an abortion, for example. As long as the behavior harms no one, it should not be considered a crime. Most of the items on Morris and Hawkins's list are referred to as "victimless crimes."

There is room for debate on many of these issues. The extent to which gambling should be legalized is an important social policy question, involving many considerations. Abortion is certainly the most politically controversial moral issue in the United States today. Whether or not the drug addict is a "victim" is arguable. The debate between the libertarians, who wish to restrict the scope of the criminal law in order to enhance individual liberty, and the legal moralists, who argue that the law can and should reflect fundamental moral principles, has been going on for over a hundred years and is likely to continue.

Here we are concerned with the control of serious crime. On the question of decriminalization, my position is:

PROPOSITION 26

Decriminalization of essentially private behavior, with the possible exception of the sale of heroin, is simply irrelevant to the control of robbery and burglary.

To place decriminalization at the center of a crime control policy, as Morris, Hawkins, and Neier do, is to evade the issue. There are no easy answers to the problem of serious crime. Conservatives and liberals respond to this dilemma in different ways. Conservatives focus on serious crime but tend to propose unworkable solutions. Liberals tend to shift the subject and talk about social reforms that are not directly related to serious crime at all.

The one possible exception to the general irrelevance of decriminalization involves heroin. The connection between heroin addiction and crime is clear, although experts disagree about the nature and extent of that connection. Nonetheless, as we shall see, there is no consensus on the effective solution to the heroin problem. Decriminalization is only one possible alternative, and its efficacy is not clearly established.

Victimless Crimes and Serious Crimes

The lack of connection between most victimless crimes and robbery and burglary becomes very evident when we examine the items on Morris and Hawkins's list.

Public drunkenness, disorderly conduct, and vagrancy are public nuisances rather than predatory crimes. While they may offend the sensibilities of many people, they do not inflict serious harm. Traditionally, these three crimes have consumed the bulk of the police's time and energy.[3] In the nineteenth century as many as 80 percent of all arrests were in these three categories, and they still make up the largest single group of arrests. In 1981 they accounted for 18.5 percent of all arrests, or as many as all eight of the Index crimes and three times as many as robbery and burglary.

Public nuisance arrests are indeed a burden on the police, the lower courts, and city jails. There are many good reasons for decriminalizing the behaviors in all three categories. From our standpoint, the question is whether or not this step would help reduce serious crime, as it potentially could in two different ways.

The most direct effect would take the form of more efficient police work. In theory, police would be freed from about 20 percent of their arrest work load and would be able to concentrate on the more serious crimes against people and property. There are two reasons why this shift in police priorities would not significantly reduce serious crime. We have already found that the capacity of the police to control crime has some basic limits. Decriminalization is simply the liberal's device for adding more cops. In poorly managed police departments the savings in officer time will not be effectively used. In well-managed departments, as we have already learned, more patrol and more detectives will not lower the crime rate.

To a great extent, public nuisances have already been decriminalized over the past fifteen years. In *Easter* v. *District of Columbia,* a U.S. district court ruled that chronic alcoholism was a condition and not a crime. Meanwhile, a number of states have repealed their public intoxication statutes and some cities have replaced arrest with referral to detoxification programs. These steps reflect a growing consensus that criminalization is not the appropriate response to social and medical problems. The arguments of the decriminalization advocates, in other words, have found some acceptance.[4]

The police have shifted their priorities away from public nuisance offenses. The percentage of all arrests in the categories of public intoxication, disorderly conduct, and vagrancy fell from 39.7 percent in 1969 to 15 percent by 1984. It is unlikely that the number of drunks and unemployed vagrants declined in those years. If anything, their numbers probably increased. Instead, the police simply shifted their priorities in order to devote more time to serious crime. The redirection of effort was probably not the result of a formal policy directive from the chief. Rather, individual patrol officers, perhaps in consultation with their sergeants, made a common-sense judgment about what was important.[5]

Not everyone, however, supports this reordering of police priorities. George L. Kelling and James Q. Wilson argue that the police should devote more attention to the little nuisance problems that define the quality of life at the neighborhood level. Police should be more aggressive in keeping drunks off the street (or at least out of the neighborhood), for example, as a way of maintaining a sense of public safety among law-abiding residents. The police neglect of the small quality-of-life issues, according to Kelling and Wilson, contributes to neighborhood deterioration.[6]

There is a serious question about whether labeling has any effect on serious crime. Labeling theory is generally applied to juvenile delinquents— and even then its validity remains a matter of debate. The people who are arrested for public intoxication and vagrancy are not the kind who graduate to predatory crime. For the most part they are the chronic alcoholics and the chronically unemployed. Often in a helpless condition, they are commonly the victims of crime. Police frequently arrest them, in fact, in order to provide them with some protection from either the elements or potential muggers. Arrest does not encourage them to become predatory criminals. They are not the young, healthy, and aggressive males who become career criminals. Decriminalization of public intoxication, disorderly conduct, and vagrancy may well be sound social policy; but it is not a solution to the problem of serious crime.[7]

Much has happened since Morris and Hawkins recommended the decriminalization of abortion in 1970. Three years later the Supreme Court declared abortion to be a fundamental right in *Roe* v. *Wade*. One can debate the morality of abortion and the wisdom of the *Roe* decision as social policy. But it is hard to establish a connection between serious crime and the old policy on abortion as a criminal act. There is nothing to suggest that a person is transformed into a robber or burglar because he or she performs or has an abortion. By the same token, the argument of many right-to-life advocates that abortion undermines the moral fabric of the nation and thereby contributes to crime is without foundation. Abortion is a supremely important social policy question but it has no bearing on serious crime.

The same may be said for the proposal to decriminalize various sexual activities between consenting adults. The laws in many states still make crimes of adultery, fornication, cohabitation, statutory rape, homosexuality, and prostitution. Whether or not these activities are acceptable is an important question of morality and social policy. For the most part, however, police and prosecutors have accommodated themselves to changing moral standards by simply not enforcing such laws. When was the last time two unmarried adults were arrested for sleeping together? Even the sodomy laws that make homosexual activity a crime are not enforced. The Supreme Court upheld the constitutionality of Georgia's sodomy law in its controversial decision in *Bowers* v. *Hardwick*, but the law is rarely if ever enforced.[8] Police may target gay men who engage in public solicitation but essentially ignore the behavior of consenting adults in private. To a great extent all of these behaviors are already decriminalized. Further changes will not affect the level of predatory crime one way or the other. The one possible exception is prostitution. A certain amount of ancillary crime accompanies this activity. Customers are occasionally mugged and robbed before or after their transactions with prostitutes. But those instances represent only a minor part of the total robbery picture. Prostitutes themselves are often beaten, either by customers or by their pimps.

A good case can be made for the proposition that gambling sustains organized crime in the Unites States. Most experts on the subject agree that the major part of the revenues that flow to criminal syndicates, certainly their steadiest and most secure revenues, are generated by gambling. Our social policy of making many forms of gambling illegal creates a potentially lucrative area of enterprise for anyone willing to assume the risks of providing the necessary goods and services. The pernicious effects of criminal syndicates on our society are well known. Organized crime money is the major corruptive force in the criminal justice system and in politics generally. Criminal syndicates also invest their money in legitimate businesses and, using their accustomed methods, pervert the free enterprise system. Organized crime does generate some violent crime, but these murders and assaults are directed against other members of the criminal syndicates. To be sure, some threats and actual violence are directed against nonmembers, such as owners of legitimate businesses that the syndicates are attempting to take over. But this category represents at most a tiny fraction of the violent crimes in this country. Decriminalization of gambling may or may not be a wise social policy. It may or may not strike at the roots of organized crime, as many people believe. But it will not reduce the incidence of robbery and burglary.

The Heroin Problem

Heroin is the one area in which decriminalization might help reduce crime. There is no question that heroin is a terrible problem in our society and that a lot of predatory crime is committed by heroin addicts. Decriminalization is one possible remedy but many serious questions remain unanswered. There is great disagreement over three central points: the number of heroin addicts, the amount of crime committed by addicts, and whether methadone maintenance or some other form of treatment effectively reduces addiction and crime.

The drug problem, unfortunately, has attracted more than its share of crusaders and quacks. Much of the information put out by drug crusaders is grossly wrong. Sorting our way through the misinformation is a difficult task by itself.

The first question concerns the number of heroin addicts in the United States. Official estimates range from 200,000 to 900,000, with about half of them in New York City. Use of the term "addict" is part of the problem. Not everyone who uses heroin is physically addicted to it. Antidrug propagandists created the myth that even the smallest use results in addiction. But there are large numbers of "weekend chippers" who use heroin occasionally as just another recreational drug. There are also many regular users who are not truly addicted. Even among addicts, the intensity of the addiction and the amount of heroin needed vary greatly. As we shall see, these differences play an important part in efforts to estimate the amount of crime committed by heroin addicts. For the sake of argument, let us accept the lower estimates and assume that there are between 200,000 and 300,000 regular users of heroin, including addicts, in the country, and that 40 percent to 50 percent of them are in New York City.[9]

The second question is the amount of crime that is the direct result of heroin addiction. Or, to put it another way, how much crime could be eliminated by an effective heroin-control policy (we'll leave the exact policy open for the moment)? On this issue we must sort our way through some truly fantastic estimates. The Rand Corporation estimated in 1969 that heroin addicts were responsible for $2 billion to $5 billion worth of crime in New York City. Frightening estimates of this sort are routine in the drug-control business but they often bear little relation to reality.

In a devastating critique, Max Singer found that the Rand heroin/crime estimates were pure fantasy. If in fact there were 100,000 addicts in New York City who needed $30 every day to maintain their habit, they would have to raise more than $1 billion over the course of a year (100,000 × $30 × 365). But criminals must sell their stolen goods to fences, who give them at most 25 percent of actual value (Singer may have been overly generous; some goods yield only 10 percent of their value from fences). Thus the total value of stolen property would be in the neighborhood of $4 to $5 billion in New York City alone. By looking at the figures for particular crimes, Singer found that amount to be utterly absurd. Retail sales in New York City totaled $15 billion annually, and if addicts were responsible for half of the estimated 2 percent inventory loss, they would realize only $150 million during the year. Likewise, 500,000 burglaries at an average loss of $200 would yield the addicts only another $100 million. In 1969, however, there were only

196,397 reported burglaries in New York City (or about 400,000 total burglaries, if we assume that only half were reported). The same absurdity applies to robbery. At an average take of $100 (high by most recent estimates), 800,000 robberies would yield the addicts $8 million. Unfortunately, there were only 61,209 reported robberies, or an estimated 120,000 actual robberies, in New York City in 1969. Singer concludes that addicts are responsible for, at most, only one-tenth of the amount of crime attributed to them by the Rand report.[10]

How could the Rand report and most of the other drug experts be so wrong? Easily. You begin with a high estimate of heroin users and assume that all users are addicts. Then you multiply the result by a relatively high estimate of the price of satisfying an intense level of addiction each day. This calculation ignores some well-known facts about heroin use. Not all users are addicts. Neither regular users nor addicts have the same daily need. Some addicts can meet their needs through lawfully gained income. The cases of addicted physicians and musicians are well known. Some blue-collar and now even white-collar workers can continue to work while addicted. Many addicts meet their financial needs through prostitution, pimping, and drug dealing. Only some heroin addicts, then, must turn to predatory crime to feed their habits. They are indeed responsible for a lot of crime, but it is much less than most of the sensational estimates lead us to believe.

A realistic estimate of the amount of crime committed by heroin addicts must take into account the fluctuating intensity of addiction. An addict/criminal may rob or steal six times as much during a "run," or a period of heavy addiction, as during a period of less intense addiction.[11] Estimates based on interviews with addicts who report their needs during peak periods will inevitably result in gross exaggerations of the total heroin/crime picture. In short, there is no such thing as an "average" heroin addict (even if we forget, for the moment, about the nonaddicted users); and as we saw in relation to the problem of estimating average offense rates for career criminals, there is no meaningful "average" amount of crime committed by addicts.

The question of whether heroin causes predatory street crime has been hotly debated. The drug crusaders traditionally paint a picture of the addict driven to crime by the need to supply his or her habit. In this scenario, heroin causes crime. Criminologists tend to take a different view. Research has indicated that among addicts/criminals, the first arrest preceded the first use of heroin by about a year and a half. Crime and heroin use are seen as two parts of a deviant lifestyle, without a strong causal relationship working in either direction. Many factors lead people into this deviant lifestyle, but criminologists have yet to isolate any one of them as taking priority over the others. From our perspective, this lack of established causality signifies that the effective control of heroin (by whatever means) would not in and of itself keep substantial numbers of people from entering lives of crime.[12]

Several alternative strategies are available for dealing with heroin-related crime. It is useful to divide them into two classes: "supply reduction" and "demand reduction."[13] Advocates of the former strategy want to reduce the amount of heroin available on the streets, either by interdicting importation or by cracking down on major dealers. Decades of law enforcement effort have proven this approach to be a will-o'-the-wisp. The potential sources of supply are simply too numerous, and too many people are willing to take the risks of becoming importers and major dealers. A number of supply-reduction campaigns may actually have backfired. When the supply of any commodity is reduced, of course, its price rises. Thus this strategy may only force current addicts to increase their criminal activity to meet the higher price. Or it may cause drug users to turn to other drugs to meet their recreational or physical needs.

Demand reduction does not appear to be any more promising. The most notable effort in this regard is the 1973 New York drug law, which we examined earlier. Despite its draconian penalties, the law did not reduce the level of drug use in New York City. Deterring people from wanting heroin is not a realistic goal.[14]

These lines of reasoning bring us to decriminalization. Many thoughtful observers have argued, quite persuasively, that the criminalization of heroin use has done incalculable damage to our society and our criminal justice system. Criminal penalties have brought suffering to addicts, sustained criminal syndicates, corrupted the criminal justice system, and brought the law and law enforcement into disrepute by exposing their helplessness. As a policy, decriminalization does not mean a total legalization of and disregard for heroin. Advocates of decriminalization acknowledge that the drug is a terribly destructive commodity that requires control. Decriminalization usually means the removal of criminal penalties for the *use* of heroin but not for its sale and distribution. Thus the individual addict would not face criminal penalties. Heroin trafficking, however, would remain a crime. At the same time, most decriminalization proposals call for some form of treatment or maintenance for the addict. Methadone is the most popular form of maintenance, although some experts propose that addicts be maintained through medically prescribed heroin.

The story of methadone maintenance describes a syndrome familiar in the treatment literature: a new treatment is announced, its proponents claim amazing success rates amid great publicity, independent evaluations reveal that the successes are greatly exaggerated, and a powerful backlash sets in. In the case of methadone maintenance, Drs. Vincent Dole, Marie Nyswander, and Alan Warner claimed, in the pages of the December 1968 issue of the *Journal of the American Medical Association*, a 90 percent success rate in treating heroin addicts. After four years of treatment through methadone maintenance, 88 percent of their 750 addicts with criminal records remained arrest-free. By comparison, 91 percent of the group had had some jail experience before entering treatment. Only 5.6 percent of the group were arrested and convicted while in methadone treatment. Dole, Nyswander, and Warner professed to have saved New York City over $1 million per day in prevented crime. A year later, Dr. Francis Gearing, of Columbia University School of Public Health, asserted that after three years of methadone maintenance his group of heroin addicts had an arrest rate lower than that of the general population.[15]

The backlash was not long in coming. A reevaluation of the Dole, Nyswander, and Warner data showed that while only 6 percent of the addicts were arrested in the year following treatment, only 20 percent had been arrested the year before entering the program. This represents some improvement, but only a modest one. Further studies indicated that the people who ran many methadone programs were not careful to ensure enrollment of true addicts rather than occasional heroin users. Some provided methadone but no other treatment services. Levels of dosage varied widely. Not all programs monitored the behavior of their clients carefully to ensure that they were not selling their methadone. As is the case with so many evaluations of other forms of correctional treatment, evaluators failed to use adequate controls, and the resulting findings are not reliable. Arnold Trebach concludes that there are "no definitive answers in the 'scientific' studies." The backlash reached its apogee with Edward Jay Epstein's 1974 article, "Methadone: The Forlorn Hope." Appearing in *The Public Interest* in the same year that the magazine published Martinson's "What Works?" Epstein's article denounced methadone as a complete failure. Not only was there no evidence of its success but in many respects it was as damaging as heroin itself.[16]

The truth is that methadone maintenance is partially but not completely successful. John Kaplan estimates that it achieves permanent success with about 40 percent of the addicts who receive treatment. That may not seem like a terribly high success rate, but, Kaplan argues, it is "about as well as we can do." Methadone maintenance is "the most cost-effective treatment we have today" for this destructive drug that has resisted every form of control and treatment. With respect to crime, it appears that methadone maintenance reduces but does not eliminate criminal activity. In one California experiment, income from criminal activity dropped from $3,900 to $400 a year for one group of former addicts, and from $7,200 to $1,700 for another group. Another study by Dr. Paul Cushman found that arrest rates for addicts fluctuated from 3.1 per 100 person-years before addiction to 35.1 per 100 during addiction (confirming other data indicating that addicts do indeed commit large numbers of crimes). During methadone maintenance, arrest rates dropped to 5.9 per 100 and then rose to 9.0 per 100 after the clients were discharged from the program. We can view this "success" from different perspectives. Discharged clients were committing about three times as much crime after treatment as before addiction, but less than during their addiction period.[17]

As John Kaplan suggests, heroin is indeed "the hardest drug." It is the hardest not just in terms of its addictive powers but also because it has resisted all our attempts to control it. Kaplan suggests that decriminalization is the wisest approach to this terrible problem. But he has no illusions about its being a total cure. Decriminalization, with methadone maintenance and accompanying treatment, might make some difference. But it will neither completely reduce addiction nor eliminate heroin-related crime.

Notes

1. Norval Morris and Gordon Hawkins, *The Honest Politician's Guide to Crime Control* (Chicago: University of Chicago Press, 1970), chap. 1; Aryeh Neier, *Crime and Punishment: A Radical Solution* (New York: Stein & Day, 1976).
2. Edwin M. Schur, *Crimes without Victims* (Englewood Cliffs, N.J.: Prentice-Hall, 1965).
3. Raymond T. Nimmer, *Two Million Unnecessary Arrests* (Chicago: American Bar Foundation, 1971).
4. Ibid.
5. David E. Aaronson, C. Thomas Dienes, and Michael C. Musneno, "Changing the Public Drunkenness Laws: The Impact of Decriminalization," *Law and Society Review* 12 (Spring 1978): 405–436.
6. George L. Kelling and James Q. Wilson, "Broken Windows: The Police and Neighborhood Safety," *Atlantic Monthly* 249 (March 1982), reprinted in James Q. Wilson, *Thinking about Crime*, rev. ed. (New York: Basic Books, 1983), chap. 5.
7. Nimmer, *Two Million Unnecessary Arrests*, chap. 2.
8. Bowers v. Hardwick, 478 U.S. _____, 92 L. Ed. 2d 140, 106 S. Ct. _____ (1986).
9. John Kaplan, *The Hardest Drug: Heroin and Public Policy* (Chicago: University of Chicago Press, 1983).
10. Max Singer, "The Vitality of Mythical Numbers," *Public Interest* 23 (Spring 1971): 3–9.
11. Kaplan, *Hardest Drug*, pp. 55–57.
12. Ibid., p. 55.
13. Mark H. Moore, "Controlling Criminogenic Commodities: Drugs, Guns, and Alcohol," in *Crime and Public Policy*, ed. James Q. Wilson (San Francisco: ICS Press, 1983), pp. 125–144.
14. U.S. Department of Justice,*The Nation's Toughest Drug Law: Evaluating the New York Experience* (Washington, D.C.: U.S. Government Printing Office, 1978).
15. Arnold Trebach, *The Heroin Solution* (New Haven: Yale University Press, 1982), pp. 259–260.
16. Edward Jay Epstein, "Methadone: The Forlorn Hope," *Public Interest* 36 (Summer 1974).
17. Kaplan, *Hardest Drug*, p. 222; Trebach, *Heroin Solution*, p. 261.

Chapter 13

Reform the System: Eliminate Injustice

Reform of the criminal justice system is accorded high priority by liberals. The major problem is discrimination against racial minorities, the poor, women, and people of all descriptions who exhibit a nonconventional political or cultural lifestyle. The President's Crime Commission's 1967 report, *The Challenge of Crime in a Free Society*, devotes most of its pages to proposals for improving the criminal justice system. Improve the quality of justice, this approach assumes, and we will reduce crime.[1]

The nature and extent of system injustice is a question that separates liberals from radical criminologists, including Marxists. Liberals operate on the assumption that the criminal justice system, despite its many problems, is basically sound. They seek to eliminate the worst problems so that the system can fulfill its legitimate role of controlling crime and ensuring public safety. Marxists, in contrast, question the basic legitimacy of the system. In their view, criminal justice institutions serve the interests of an economic ruling class and maintain the suppression of politically and economically powerless groups. The Marxists' aim is not to reform the criminal justice system but to change the basic economic institutions of society. Indeed, radical leftists criticize liberal reforms as efforts to camouflage the fundamentally oppressive nature of the criminal justice system—to put a velvet glove on the iron fist.[2]

Liberals differ from conservatives in the priority they give to system injustices. While some conservatives acknowledge the problem of discrimination, they do not give it top priority and certainly do not see it as a cause of criminality. Indeed, conservatives direct their harshest criticisms at policies that put more stress on justice than on crime control.

Crime Control vs. Due Process

The best analysis of the issues that divide liberals and conservatives is Herbert Packer's famous article "Two Models of the Criminal Process." On

"Freddie likes sticking it to the liberals."

one side is the crime control model, which gives precedence to the efficient and effective repression of crime. The control of crime is essential to the maintenance of an orderly society. On the other side is the due-process model, which gives top priority to the protection of individual rights. The greater harm to society occurs when an innocent person is swept into the system, or when two people guilty of the same offense are treated differently, or when punishment far exceeds the bounds of decency. Both sides emphasize the importance of rules, but they focus on different sets of rules. The crime control model stresses the criminal law as a set of rules governing the behavior of all citizens. The due-process model stresses criminal procedure as a set of rules governing the behavior of criminal justice officials.[3]

We can see the distinction between the two most clearly by focusing on their respective worst nightmares. The crime-control-oriented people envision the total collapse of civilization if the laws are not fully and effectively enforced. They see the streets completely controlled by predatory criminals. Due-process-oriented people imagine a totalitarian society in which officials are unrestrained by any rules. Recent exposées of FBI spying on and harassment of such public figures as Martin Luther King, Jr., suggest that "it can happen here."[4]

It is necessary to emphasize that the distinction between these two positions is one of *priority*. Liberals are not uninterested in crime control, nor are conservatives unconcerned about fairness and procedural regularity. The difference lies in which issue receives top priority. The exclusionary rule illustrates the point perfectly. In the interests of effective crime control, conservatives would admit evidence that has been obtained by methods not altogether regular. In the interests of due process, however, liberals would assign preeminence to the rights of the individual and exclude the evidence. Conservatives argue that we best protect society as a whole by apprehending and convicting criminals rather than by insisting on "perfect justice."[5] Liberals reply that proper methods are just as effective in bringing about the arrest, prosecution, and conviction of people who are in fact engaged in crime.

The debate between the crime control and due-process positions is a debate over fundamental values. It will not be resolved, nor should it be. It is an ongoing dialogue over the nature of justice and the good society. We have examined the crime control position in considerable depth in our inquiry. We have considered its argument that such things as the exclusionary rule, the *Miranda* warning, and the right to bail contribute positively to crime, and we have found no evidence to support that assertion. Let us now turn our attention to the liberal/due-process argument that system injustice contributes to crime. My position is that it does not.

―――――――――――――――― **PROPOSITION 27** ――――――――――――――――

Elimination of injustices from the criminal justice system will not reduce serious crime.

In the first edition of his widely read book *Thinking about Crime*, James Q. Wilson indicted liberals for having ignored the problem of crime. In his view, they had lost touch with the people for whom they purported to speak when they refused to address the problem of predatory crime, which was causing increasing suffering and fear among a major segment of their constituents. Moreover, liberal policy makers listened only to their criminological advisers, who pressed on with a futile search for the "root causes" of crime.[6]

Wilson's indictment was wide of the mark. Liberal Democrats accorded a low priority to crime in the early 1960s because their constituents did not see it as a major concern. Wilson simply forgets that the overriding social issue in the early 1960s was civil rights. Other issues revolved around it. The War on Poverty, for example, was initiated in part as a means of providing economic opportunity for disadvantaged blacks. Bail reform succeeded because it addressed the related problems of economic and racial discrimination. In the mid-1960s the issue of "crime in the streets" was raised only by people who opposed the landmark pieces of civil rights legislation. When predatory crime did become an issue for a majority of white Americans by the late 1960s, the Democrats dutifully followed by trimming their commitment to social reform.

Nor is it true that the Democrats ignored the problem of crime. Lyndon Johnson made a stronger commitment to an effort to deal with the problem than any previous president had done. His Crime Commission was the first such effort since Herbert Hoover's Wickersham Commission (1929–1931). Johnson first established the Office of Law Enforcement Assistance (OLEA) in 1965 and then sponsored what became LEAA, both of which represented the first concerted investment of federal dollars in assistance to criminal justice.[7] What Wilson really means is that he disagrees with the particular crime policy advanced by Johnson and the Democrats. Johnson's policy consisted of three anticrime initiatives: rehabilitation, system improvement, and economic opportunity. In its own way, each was designed to reduce crime. We have considered the efficacy of rehabilitation at length. In Chapter 14 we will look at the question of crime reduction through expanded economic opportunity. Here we focus on the issue of system improvement.

System Reform and Crime Reduction

The argument that system improvement will reduce crime is based on the assumption that discrimination is in fact criminogenic. Nowhere has this point been proven in any persuasive way. Let there be no misunderstanding on this point. Discrimination should be eliminated because it is wrong. To treat people less than fairly because of race or income or sex is to violate the most cherished values of our society. But it has not been proven that discrimination by criminal justice agencies actually increases the number of crimes committed.

Labeling theory advanced the idea that the criminal justice process is itself criminogenic. That theory holds that black and poor kids are swept up into the system more often than others and as a consequence more of them are launched on careers of crime. This argument is based on two assumptions: first, that the labeling phenomenon does occur, and second, that a greater proportion of black and poor kids are in fact swept into the system.[8]

Considerable effort has gone into research on these points. The very first research on police arrest patterns focused on juvenile arrests. The initial studies did find a pattern of racial discrimination. Subsequent studies, which controlled more effectively for the relevant variables, found no systematic pattern of racial discrimination (see the discussion on pp. 50–52). Police officers do exercise discretion in making arrests, allowing many offenders to go free. Arrest is more likely when the suspected offense is more serious, when the suspect and the victim are strangers, and when the victim expresses a desire for arrest. Race is not the significant determinant of arrest decision making that many critics of the criminal justice system believe it to be.[9]

Recent research has generally brought into question many of the earlier assumptions about racial discrimination in the criminal justice system. There is some discrimination, but not nearly as much as many people had believed. The most thorough survey of the topic, a report by the Rand Corporation, found discrimination at two major points. Oddly, the first represented discrimination against whites. After arrest, whites were more often held for prosecution than blacks. The report also found, however, that convicted blacks were more likely to be incarcerated than whites, and in two of the three states examined they served longer prison terms. On average, blacks served 2.4 months longer than whites in California and 7.7 months longer in Texas. While significant, these differences are nowhere near so great as those suggested by the fact that the national prison population is disproportionately black (48 percent, whereas blacks comprise 12 percent of the general population).[10]

The prisons are disproportionately black not primarily because of racial discrimination in sentencing for particular crimes but because of a bias against crimes committed by lower-class persons. As we have seen several times in the course of this inquiry, our criminal justice system deals rather harshly with certain types of serious crime. Armed robbers do not get off easy. They are prosecuted on robbery charges, are usually convicted, and when convicted go to prison for relatively long terms. We have also seen that criminal justice officials, as a matter of standard practice, make distinctions involving the social circumstances of crimes. Some crimes, those that fall into the second layer of our wedding cake, are serious matters and are prosecuted fully. Others are deemed to be not so serious—the crimes between people who know each other, the private disputes—and are disposed of through nonarrest, dismissal, plea to a lesser charge, or probation at worst. These offenses fall into the third layer of the wedding cake.

Criminal justice officials make distinctions between offenses in the same crime category, between different robberies and different assaults. On an even broader scale, distinctions are made between different crime categories. We reserve our severest treatment, and most of our resources, for the so-called street crimes—the Index crimes, or the predatory crimes. Public policy reflects the general public preoccupation with the robber, the burglar, and the rapist.

Public policy does not give anything like the same emphasis to white-collar crimes, even though in dollar terms they cost us about ten times as much as all the robberies and burglaries combined. The "leakage" of these offenses occurs throughout the criminal justice system. Many are never detected in the first place. The fraud is so successful that the victim does not know it has occurred. Even when a crime is suspected, proving it is extremely difficult. This is especially true of the more extensive price-fixing arrangements and elaborate embezzlements. Prosecutors simply do not have the resources to investigate thoroughly and bring indictments. Because many of those offenses are crimes of conspiracy, they require the most intrusive law enforcement techniques, as the FBI's ABSCAM operation illustrates. The FBI's tactics may well have crossed over into the area of entrapment in some of the ABSCAM investigations. The white-collar criminal, even if convicted, enjoys the benefit of prejudice in his or her behalf. The crime does not carry the same social stigma as a crime of violence; the offender does not "look like a criminal" (that is, does not look like an armed robber). Almost by definition, the white-collar criminal is a substantial member of the community. Few convicted white-collar criminals are sent to prison. The three-year prison sentence given the noted Wall Street trader Ivan Boesky in 1987 for "insider trading" surprised many people. It is rare for a wealthy white-collar criminal to be given a stiff prison sentence. In many respects, Boesky is the exception that proves the general rule.

The bias that affects the prosecution of white-collar crimes also applies to many of the "victimless" crimes. If the gambling and adultery statutes were fully enforced, most adult Americans would find themselves behind bars at one time or another. These laws are not enforced precisely because the gamblers and adulterers are regarded as "otherwise law-abiding" people. The same problem has long bedeviled crackdowns on drunk driving. Drinking and driving are too commonly linked. Enforcement strikes too close to home, and, as we have seen, the system has a great capacity to mitigate the prescribed punishment. The vagrancy laws, meanwhile, have always been reserved as a means of controlling poor persons when they wander into places where other people don't want them to be.

If all of our criminal statutes were enforced, the composition of the prisons would not be so heavily black. Prisons would be filled with vast numbers of additional white offenders. The differential treatment given perpetrators of different types of crimes represents a form of discrimination based on social class. This is undoubtedly the most consistent pattern of bias within the criminal justice system. Because of the economic status of the majority of black Americans, it is often indistinguishable from racial discrimination. The street crimes that receive the harshest treatment are those committed almost exclusively by young males who are primarily from low-income backgrounds and who are disproportionately black. The recent research on system discrimination seems to indicate that armed robbers are treated relatively equally. White robbers do not receive substantially more lenient treatment. The problem is that robbery is disproportionately a black activity.

It is not the criminal justice system but society as a whole that is criminogenic. People commit the crimes that are available to them. Business executives commit white-collar crimes. Unemployed black kids do not have the same opportunity; burglary and robbery are the most readily available crimes. Moreover, one does not need to be an economic determinist to recognize that other social factors contribute to predatory criminality among low-income males. Poverty and lack of economic opportunity hardly endear one to the prevailing social system. For black kids, racism adds a powerful destructive element. Charles Silberman has written imaginatively and persuasively in *Criminal Violence, Criminal Justice* on the social roots of the explosion of black crime in the 1960s.[11]

There is persuasive new evidence that we can significantly reduce systematic racial discrimination in the criminal justice system. Between 1971 and 1984, for example, the number of citizens shot and killed by the police declined by 51 percent, from 353 to 172. Moreover, the disparity between blacks and whites was cut in half. In 1971 the police shot seven black citizens for every white. By 1984 the ratio was 2.8 to 1. This change reflects the impact of the new rules on the use of deadly force by the police. In short, rules work. Carefully drafted rules based on principles of equal protection and due process influence police behavior in a positive direction.[12]

Wolfgang's second delinquency birth cohort study reveals substantial improvement in the behavior of the Philadelphia police. They arrested 44 percent of the black juveniles in the first cohort (representing essentially the years 1955 through 1963) and only 23 percent of the whites. In the second cohort (representing the years 1968 through 1976), the police arrested 60 percent of the black juveniles and 51 percent of the whites. It is significant that arrest rates went up for all juveniles but the point here is that the racial disparities narrowed considerably. The change was undoubtedly the result of police sensitivity to court rulings on due process and political pressure from civil rights groups. Keep in mind that during these years the Philadelphia police force was widely regarded as one of the worst big-city departments in the entire country. If racial disparities narrowed there, it is safe to assume that similar improvements occurred in other cities.[13]

This evidence leads to a hopeful proposition:

PROPOSITION 28

Carefully drafted rules reflecting the principles of due process and equal protection of the laws can enhance the quality of justice.

Rules can originate in any of three places. The courts can require them. That is essentially what the Supreme Court did in *Mapp, Miranda, Terry,* and the other landmark cases related to police procedures. The Court stepped into a vacuum and imposed a set of rules. Legislatures can also impose rules by statute. Even before the Supreme Court ruled in *Tennessee v. Garner,* about two-thirds of the states had rules placing relatively strict limits on the circumstances in which the police could use deadly force. Some of these statutes were more restrictive than others. Legislative bodies can impose rules in other areas of criminal justice administration— regulation of high-speed chases by police, for example. The Seattle city council passed an imaginative ordinance outlawing police spying on political and religious groups and imposing regulations on the use of undercover agents. Finally, police departments can develop their own rules. In fact, most big-city police departments were unaffected by *Garner* because they had adopted rules restricting the use of deadly force years before the case ever reached the Supreme Court.[14]

Discrimination should be eliminated because it violates our basic values. Its elimination will not, however, reduce serious crime. That is a separate problem.

Notes

1. President's Commission on Law Enforcement and Administration of Justice, *The Challenge of Crime in a Free Society* (Washington, D. C.: U. S. Government Printing Office, 1967).
2. Center for Research on Criminal Justice, *The Iron Fist and the Velvet Glove: An Analysis of the U. S. Police* (Berkeley: Center for Research on Criminal Justice, 1977).
3. Herbert Packer, "Two Models of the Criminal Process," in Packer, *The Limits of the Criminal Sanction* (Stanford: Stanford University Press, 1968), chap. 8.
4. David J. Garrow, *The FBI and Martin Luther King, Jr.* (New York: Norton, 1981).
5. Macklin Fleming, *The Price of Perfect Justice* (New York: Basic Books, 1974).
6. James Q. Wilson, *Thinking about Crime* (New York: Basic Books, 1975), chaps. 3, 4.
7. Samuel Walker, *Popular Justice: A History of American Criminal Justice* (New York: Oxford University Press, 1980), chap. 9.
8. Edwin M. Schur, *Radical Nonintervention: Rethinking the Delinquency Problem* (Englewood Cliffs, N. J.: Prentice-Hall, 1973).
9. Donald M. Black, *Manners and Customs of the Police* (New York: Academic Press, 1980).
10. Joan Petersilia, *Racial Disparities in the Criminal Justice System* (Santa Monica, Calif.: Rand Corporation, 1983).
11. Charles Silberman, *Criminal Violence, Criminal Justice* (New York: Random House, 1978).
12. Lawrence W. Sherman and Ellen G. Cohn, *Citizens Killed by Big City Police, 1970–1984* (Washington, D. C.: Crime Control Institute, 1986).
13. Paul E. Tracy et al., *Delinquency in Two Birth Cohorts: Executive Summary* (Washington, D. C.: U. S. Department of Justice, September 1985).
14. Tennessee v. Garner, 471 U. S. 1 (1985); Samuel Walker, "The Politics of Police Accountability: The Seattle Police Spying Ordinance as a Case Study," in *The Politics of Crime and Criminal Justice*, ed. Erika S. Fairchild and Vincent J. Webb (Beverly Hills, Calif.: Sage, 1985), pp. 144–157.

Chapter 14

Reform Society: Provide Opportunity

L iberals have traditionally emphasized the social and economic influences on criminal activity. The bulk of criminological research since the 1920s has focused on the criminogenic effect of poverty, inadequate educational opportunities, racial discrimination, broken families, and the cultural values of low-income peer groups. The policy implications are simple: expand social and economic opportunities for disadvantaged people and we will reduce their tendency to commit crimes.

The liberal social policies of the 1960s reflected this view of crime. The War on Poverty and many of the recommendations of the President's Crime Commission were attempts to expand legitimate opportunities for disadvantaged youths, to reduce the stigmatizing effect of the criminal justice system on those who did fall into the hands of the law, and to assist convicted offenders in establishing productive, law-abiding lives through community-based rehabilitation programs. At the same time, improvement in the criminal justice system would reduce the criminogenic effect of discriminatory arrest, prosecution, and punishment. Social reform was only one part of a crime-reduction package that included diversion, correctional treatment, and system improvement. All were based on the same assumptions about the causes of crime.[1]

It is fashionable among conservatives today to mock the liberal view of crime. James Q. Wilson points out that the great social experiments of the 1960s coincided with the greatest increase in crime in American history. He dismisses the entire mainstream of American criminology with a wave of the hand, saying he never saw a "root cause" of crime. The challenge thrown down by Wilson and other conservatives is a serious one. Why did the greatest increase in crime in our history go hand in hand with our most concerted effort yet to eliminate the causes of crime? The 1960s also represented the most sustained period of prosperity in this century. How do we explain what Wilson calls the "paradox" of crime amidst prosperity?[2]

Four explanations are possible. First, the theory may be wrong: social and economic deprivation may not be the principal cause of crime. Second, the theory may be sound but the programs it inspired were flawed and did not fulfill their goals. The third possibility is that some of the programs were effective but were not implemented on a broad enough scale to make a significant difference. Finally, government programs to help individuals may be irrelevant in the face of massive economic dislocation. What may be needed is a truly radical restructuring of economic opportunity. Somewhat surprisingly, even the conservative James Q. Wilson leans toward this view. Referring to Marxist criminologists, he observes that "in a sense, the radical critics of America are correct. If you wish to make a big difference in crime rates, you must make a fundamental change in society."[3]

Social Theory and Social Policy

Where exactly did the ambitious social programs of the 1960s go wrong? We should begin by examining their theoretical roots, which can be found in a 1960 book titled *Delinquency and Opportunity*, by Richard Cloward and Lloyd Ohlin.[4] This enormously influential book summarized the dominant themes in American theoretical criminology. Appropriately, the authors dedicated it to Robert K. Merton and Edwin H. Sutherland, two giants in the field of social theory and criminology. *Delinquency and Opportunity* inspired most of the War on Poverty and many of the recommendations of the President's Crime Commission. Ohlin had ample opportunity to put his ideas into practice as one of the four associate directors of the Crime Commission.

As the title of their book suggests, Cloward and Ohlin found the primary causes of delinquency in lack of social and economic opportunity. They began with Robert Merton's argument that deviant behavior results from "a breakdown in the relationship between goals and legitimate avenues of access to them." Delinquents are not abnormal or sick people. They share the same values and aspirations as other people. In the United States, most people aspire to "success," measured by material well-being. People who cannot achieve success through legitimate means turn to illegitimate means. Elliot Liebow's classic study of ghetto life, *Tally's Corner*, also painted a picture of people continually trying to fulfill the conventional values of successful Americans (job, family, etc.) but repeatedly failing.[5]

Refining Merton's ideas, Cloward and Ohlin identified three delinquent subcultures, each reflecting a different choice of illegitimate means. The *criminal* subculture involves illicit activity as a career, often through organized criminal syndicates. The individual is socialized into a relatively disciplined, though illegal, lifestyle. The *conflict* subculture involves violent antisocial behavior as a way of life. Unlike members of the criminal subculture, the delinquents in this group lead lives that are highly disorga-

"Listen, Mac, if I had the skills, I'd prefer taking this money from you in a more socially acceptable and profitable way, like plumbing or auto repair."

nized. The *retreatist* subculture involves absorption in drug use and a retreat from any purposive behavior (criminal or otherwise) not related to drugs.

Cloward and Ohlin's point is that delinquents begin with normal and legitimate values and aspirations (although by the time they fall into the hands of the law they may be very seriously damaged). It is the lack of legitimate opportunities, not some inherently "sick" personality or willful free choice, that leads them into delinquency and lives of crime. The solution to this problem is obvious: expand the opportunities for legitimate advancement. The specific policies include reducing unemployment, expanding educational opportunities, and eliminating the barriers of racism.

Crime and Unemployment

Not everyone accepts the basic premise that unemployment causes predatory street crime. Liberals, noting that predatory crime is concentrated in low-income neighborhoods and that most offenders have marginal employment records at best, regard the premise as self-evident fact, while conservatives question it. James Q. Wilson points out the paradox of rising crime during the great prosperity of the 1960s. Conservatives find somewhat more self-evident the failure of the criminal justice system to deter criminals effectively through meaningful punishment. Just as we have examined this conservative assumption, so we should take a close look at the liberal view that unemployment generates crime.

Research on the relationship between crime and unemployment resembles research on the death penalty in two respects. First, the proposition is inherently difficult to test scientifically, given the multitude of factors that influence human (and thus criminal) behavior. Even though the economic formulas are increasingly sophisticated, we may never be able to isolate the critical variables with precision. Second, the findings of the research to date are highly ambiguous. Some researchers claim to find a direct relationship between crime and unemployment, while others do not.

Oddly enough, Isaac Ehrlich has made one of the stronger cases for the connection between crime and unemployment by using the same approach he subsequently took in his research on the deterrent effect of the death penalty. (Ehrlich's work poses a dilemma for liberals. If his death-penalty research is deeply flawed, mustn't they reject his research on crime and unemployment as well?) Ehrlich's article "Participation in Illegitimate Activities" is one of the cornerstones of the econometric theory of crime. It begins with the assumption that individuals make rational choices, weighing the relative costs and benefits of each action. Thus, if the risks of punishment are slim and the relative monetary gains are high, people will be more inclined to commit crimes. (Despite the apparent differences, Ehrlich's perspective is remarkably similar to the Merton-Cloward-Ohlin view. They too see people choosing crime as a rational alternative in the face of blocked legitimate alternatives.) The costs and benefits will differ with a person's circumstances. The unemployed person has more to gain by a successful robbery than the employed person and less to lose in social status by apprehension and conviction.[6]

Analyzing cross-sectional data on crime, income levels, and unemployment for the years 1940, 1950, and 1960, Ehrlich found a correlation between economic status and crime. His data indicate "that the rates of all felonies, particularly crimes against property, are positively related to the degree of a community's income inequality." The higher the level of unemployment and the greater the proportion of people below the median income level, the higher the crime rate. In the same analysis, however, Ehrlich found that the risk of punishment was also correlated with crime: the lower the risk, the higher the crime rate. Given the economic view of human behavior, these two factors are opposite sides of the same coin. One measures relative gain, the other relative cost.

Sheldon Danziger and David Wheeler also concluded that economic opportunity and deterrence are interrelated. They examined the rates of aggravated assault, burglary, and armed robbery between 1949 and 1970, in conjunction with cross-sectional data on urban areas in 1960. Their variables included the unemployment rate, the distribution of income, the percentage of the population in the crime-prone ages of fifteen to twenty-four, the probability of imprisonment, and the expected sentence for those imprisoned. They concluded that crime could be reduced either by an increase in the level of punishment or by a reduction of economic disparities. According to their data, however, income redistribution produced the greater reduction in crime.[7]

Does Crime Pay? A Skeptical Look

In passing, we should give a thought to the widespread belief that "crime pays." Certain crimes do pay, but robbery and burglary are not among them. Organized or syndicated crime may provide a living wage (and in some cases an upscale lifestyle), but only in special cases. Those who reap the greatest financial rewards from such criminal enterprises are always careful to insulate themselves from any direct involvement in street-level activity. They are usually the managers or financiers of criminal syndicates. The people who actually handle the illegal goods (the drugs, the stolen cars, and so on) not only reap the smallest rewards but bear the greatest risk of arrest and prosecution. In this respect, criminal activity resembles legitimate business enterprise in America. The wealthiest are the most secure. Those who do the actual hands-on work in the factories bear the greatest social and financial insecurity.

Max Singer's devastating analysis of the fantastic figures bandied about on the heroin problem provides a good model for analyzing the question of whether street crime pays.* The average robbery yields only about $50. Thus it would require five robberies a week (let's assume that our hypothetical offender takes two days off each week) to produce $250 per week or $12,500 a year. That income is hardly enough to finance an upscale lifestyle. More to the point, it requires a tremendous amount of work. A robbery a day, over the course of a year, is a tremendous pace. Moreover, such an intense level of activity, in what would have to be a relatively confined geographical area, would lead to an arrest before several months had elapsed. You can perform the same calculation with respect to burglary, taking into account the average loss (between $50 and $200) and discounting it to what the offender gets from the fence (at most 25 percent and usually closer to 10 percent).

Predatory street crime simply does not pay, in the sense that a person could make a steady living at it (which is another reason that the term "career criminal" is misleading). An offender who is really serious about a life of crime graduates to the more lucrative and secure syndicated criminal activity. Those who confine themselves to street crime do so intermittently (even though their annual rate is fairly high) and are periodically arrested and imprisoned.

* Max Singer, "The Vitality of Mythical Numbers," *Public Interest* 23 (Spring 1971): 3–9.

The research on crime and unemployment suffers from the same problems that plague the death-penalty research. Aggregate data on income, unemployment, crime, and other variables inevitably mask the behavior of individuals. We simply may not be able to specify the impact of the relevant variables on the crime-prone individuals who are our primary concern. Furthermore, there are serious problems with the data. As we saw earlier, the official data on crime rates are highly suspect, and the further back in time we extend our analysis, the more suspect they become. Without a reliable estimate of the amount of crime, we cannot accurately measure the risks of apprehension, conviction, and imprisonment. Our economic data are not much better. The official unemployment rate is as fictitious as the FBI's crime rate. The official figures grossly understate unemployment among teenagers, and among black teenagers in particular—precisely the groups we are most concerned with in our efforts to understand the sources of crime.

Given these problems, other analysts have concluded that the evidence in support of the idea that unemployment causes crime is weak at best. In a skeptical review of the subject, Thomas Orsagh and Anne Witte point out that aggregate data on income, unemployment, and crime conceal fundamental differences among types of offenders. They identify four distinct categories of criminals, each with a different relation to economic status. Some offenders, by definition, must be employed in order to commit their offenses (employee theft and embezzlement, for example). Other offenders combine employment with crime, while a third group moves back and forth between full-time employment and full-time criminal activity. Finally, there is a group of offenders who are only marginally employed at best and commit offenses at a very high rate.[8] The fourth group, the marginally employed, is the proper object of our attention, and we may gain a better understanding of the relationship between crime and unemployment if we think of this group as an "underclass."

Orsagh and Witte's findings have broad implications. They set out to determine the extent to which different kinds of offenders would respond to rehabilitation programs. Their conclusions are relevant to other crime control strategies as well. Just as some kinds of offenders are more amenable to rehabilitation programs, so offenders respond dissimilarly to the deterrent threat posed by prosecution and imprisonment. The traditional discussions of rehabilitation, deterrence, and incapacitation are flawed by the habit of regarding criminal offenders as an undifferentiated group. A more sensible approach is to recognize that different kinds of people will respond positively, in varying degrees, to alternative crime control strategies.

The Underclass

The most disturbing economic trend in the United States is the emergence of a permanent underclass. The sociologist William Julius Wilson, in an illuminating discussion of the subject, prefers to call this group "the truly disadvantaged." Whatever the term we use, we are concerned here with a group of people who are enmeshed in a set of interrelated social and economic problems. The critical new factor is not the incidence or degree of poverty and unemployment; we have experienced both throughout our history. The new phenomenon is a condition that permanently traps people at the bottom of the social heap. The result is the emergence of a class line unlike any we have known before in American history.[9]

The idea of an underclass is closely associated with the concept of the "culture of poverty." Unfortunately, this concept has been grossly misunderstood and applied in a way that leads us far from its original point. It originated with the anthropologist Oscar Lewis, who argued that the special conditions of advanced capitalist societies trap some of the poor at the bottom of the social heap and reinforce attitudes and behavior that make it difficult or impossible for those individuals to escape from poverty.[10] Some analysts, instead of being encouraged to examine the larger economic system, transformed his idea by focusing on the attitudes and behavior of the poor themselves. This is a classic instance of the phenomenon of "blaming the victim."

The driving force behind the creation of the underclass in the United States has been the steady disappearance of manufacturing jobs and, in particular, of entry-level jobs. Between 1953 and 1984 New York City lost nearly 600,000 manufacturing jobs. It gained 700,000 white-collar service jobs, but those are beyond the reach of young people at the bottom of society. Over the same period, Philadelphia lost 280,000 manufacturing jobs and St. Louis lost 127,000. Virtually every industrial city in the Northeast and Midwest had the same experience.[11] The best index of this development is the steady rise of teenage unemployment, as table 14.1 indicates. Black teenagers have always borne the brunt of the unemployment problem. White teenage unemployment rose slightly between 1950 and 1979, while black teenage unemployment more than doubled. Throughout the course of the past thirty years, black unemployment has been consistently double the rate for whites, and the gap between white and black teenagers has been growing. Moreover, the data in the table do not reflect the devastating impact on both races of the 1980–1982 recession.

These figures shed some light on the so-called paradox of crime in the 1960s. Although the economy as a whole was prosperous, young blacks did not share in the prosperity and in fact were becoming steadily worse off in relation to young whites. The baby boom only aggravated the long-term economic trends. Not only were there more kids in the high-crime age group but their economic condition was far worse than that of any previous teenage group.

The researchers who examined crime and unemployment may have been looking in the wrong place. Fluctuations in the unemployment rate measure the number of people moving in and out of employment. As far as

Table 14.1   Unemployment rates, white and black males, 1950–1979 (percent)

	Total, 16 years and over		16 and 17 years		18 and 19 years		20 to 24 years	
	White	Black	White	Black	White	Black	White	Black
1950	4.7	9.4	13.4	12.1	11.7	17.7	7.7	12.6
1951	2.6	4.9	9.5	8.7	6.7	9.6	3.6	6.7
1952	2.5	5.2	10.9	8.0	7.0	10.0	4.3	7.9
1953	2.5	4.8	8.9	8.3	7.1	8.1	4.5	8.1
1954	4.8	10.3	14.0	13.4	13.0	14.7	9.8	16.9
1955	3.7	8.8	12.2	14.8	10.4	12.9	7.0	12.4
1956	3.4	7.9	11.2	15.7	9.7	14.9	6.1	12.0
1957	3.6	8.3	11.9	16.3	11.2	20.0	7.1	12.7
1958	6.1	13.8	14.9	27.1	16.5	26.7	11.7	19.5
1959	4.6	11.5	15.0	22.3	13.0	27.2	7.5	16.3
1960	4.8	10.7	14.6	22.7	13.5	25.1	8.3	13.1
1961	5.7	12.8	16.5	31.0	15.1	23.9	10.0	15.3
1962	4.6	10.9	15.1	21.9	12.7	21.8	8.0	14.6
1963	4.7	10.5	17.8	27.0	14.2	27.4	7.8	15.5
1964	4.1	8.9	16.1	25.9	13.4	23.1	7.4	12.6
1965	3.6	7.4	14.7	27.1	11.4	20.2	5.9	9.3
1966	2.8	6.3	12.5	22.5	8.9	20.5	4.1	7.9
1967	2.7	6.0	12.7	28.9	9.0	20.1	4.2	8.0
1968	2.6	5.6	12.3	26.6	8.2	19.0	4.6	8.3
1969	2.5	5.3	12.5	24.7	7.9	19.0	4.6	8.4
1970	4.0	7.3	15.7	27.8	12.0	23.1	7.8	12.6
1971	4.9	9.1	17.1	33.4	13.5	26.0	9.4	16.2
1972	4.5	8.9	16.4	35.1	12.4	26.2	8.5	14.7
1973	3.7	7.6	15.1	34.4	10.0	22.1	6.5	12.6
1974	4.3	9.1	16.2	39.0	11.5	26.6	7.8	15.4
1975	7.2	13.7	19.7	39.4	17.2	32.9	13.2	22.9
1976	6.4	12.7	19.7	37.7	15.5	34.0	10.9	20.7
1977	5.5	12.4	17.6	38.7	13.0	36.1	9.3	21.7
1978	4.5	10.9	16.9	40.0	10.8	30.8	7.6	20.0
1979	4.4	10.3	16.1	34.4	12.3	29.6	7.4	17.0

SOURCE: Adapted from U. S. Department of Labor, *Handbook of Labor Statistics, 1980* (Washington, D. C.: U. S. Government Printing Office, 1981), pp. 63–64.

crime is concerned, most of these people are not our primary concern. Middle-management executives and sales representatives who lose their jobs do not become career criminals. The fluctuating unemployment rate does not reflect the true size or nature of the underclass. The unemployment rate was cut in half between the 1982 recession and 1987 (from 10 percent to 5 percent), yet this economic achievement had only a marginal effect on the underclass. Crime continued to decline, but not at a rate equal to the reduction in unemployment. The economic boom of the mid-1980s left the criminogenic milieu of the underclass untouched.

The emerging underclass was not totally unaffected by the civil rights movement. In *Criminal Violence, Criminal Justice,* Charles Silberman tackles the sensitive question of black crime in an imaginative and thought-provoking manner. The extremely high rates of criminal violence among blacks cannot be ignored. Although crime increased in all groups in the

1960s, much of that increase was produced by a veritable explosion of violence among black Americans. And since violent crime is overwhelmingly an intraracial phenomenon, most of the victims were black as well. In 1972, deaths of black males by homicide in the United States reached the astounding level of 83.1 per 100,000. This was ten times the rate for white males (8.2) that year and more than 100 times higher than the national rate for England and some other European countries. Murder was the leading cause of death among young black men.[12]

Silberman explains the explosion of violence by reference to the history of blacks in this country. Racial oppression not only generated powerful sources of anger but turned that anger inward, in the direction of self-hatred and intergroup violence. The civil rights movement challenged and dismantled the structure of power that had created and focused black anger. As the constraints fell, that anger poured out in all directions. Much of it was channeled into organized political protest, particularly the mass protests of the early 1960s. Some of it found expression in the riots of the mid-1960s. And much of it took the form of aggressive criminal violence. Silberman's point is that criminal violence in the United States cannot be understood solely as an outgrowth of poverty. The history of racism has given the black component of criminal violence an especially volatile character. The deteriorating economic condition of the black teenage underclass added further fuel to this explosive situation.

The nature of the underclass also suggests that there are limits to the decline in criminal violence which can be expected to flow from demographic trends. I have already argued that the aging of the baby-boom generation and the relative decline in the proportion of people in the fourteen-to-twenty-four-year-old age group is probably the major reason for the fall in crime rates since the mid-1970s. Aggregate population figures, however, mask important distinctions. The overall birth rate declined through the 1960s and even approached zero population growth in the early 1970s. The decline was greatest among middle-class whites. Among low-income people, and low-income blacks in particular, the birth rate dropped only moderately and thus remained substantially higher than that of middle-class whites. The number of low-income, inner-city males between fourteen and twenty-four has declined as well, but not so much as the national average. One can argue that the modest decline that is occurring in this group is offset by the continuing deterioration of its economic prospects. All indicators suggest that unemployment and family breakdown are increasing rather than improving for people in the underclass. This segment of our population, permanently trapped at the bottom of our society, will probably remain as significant a generator of predatory crime as before. Demographic trends do not offer the relief from crime that some observers have anticipated.

One final comment on economic trends is in order. It is now obvious that the American economy is in the midst of a historic transition, one that rivals the Industrial Revolution 150 years ago. Manufacturing jobs have been moving to the Third World (first to Japan and now to Korea, Singapore, etc.). There has been an enormous and perhaps permanent erosion of jobs in the basic industries of steel, automobiles, and machine tool production. Service industries have been the major source of new jobs since the 1970s. The social impact of these developments on the industrial cities of the Northeast is still uncalculated. With the collapse of the basic industries, thousands of blue-collar workers have become economically irrelevant. Not only have they lost their own jobs but their children can no longer expect to step into similar jobs, as they themselves once took their places in the factories next to their parents, older siblings, and other relatives. In short, what happened to black teenagers in the 1950s is now happening to white adults in the 1980s. Both groups are rendered economically superfluous by long-term economic trends.

From the Dangerous Class to the Underclass: A Historical Note

At this point the skeptic (and most conservatives) may well raise a serious objection to the underclass argument. Haven't we been through this before? Didn't we always have an urban underclass consisting of the most recent arrivals to the city? And didn't they all eventually succeed in achieving upward mobility? Isn't it really just a matter of time?

Almost exactly one hundred years ago, the social reformer Charles Loring Brace published a widely read book titled *The Dangerous Classes*. Brace's account has a familiar ring: the inner city was filled with a new and "dangerous" element, people mired in poverty whose lives were characterized by alcoholism, unemployment, family breakdown, and crime. Worse, many of the young men seemed to be completely amoral, with no respect for law and order.[13] Sound familiar? The people Brace was talking about were primarily Irish immigrants. Fifty years later, other reformers would write the same things about the new Italian and Jewish immigrants. Yet each of these groups has managed to be assimilated by the mainstream of American society. Their communities are no longer characterized by the cycle of unemployment and crime.

The idea that every immigrant group encountered difficulty at first but then succeeded is extremely attractive. It was first advanced more than twenty years ago by Nathan Glazer and Daniel Moynihan (the current senator from New York) in *Beyond the Melting Pot*. Black Americans are simply the latest in a long line of immigrant groups and they too will eventually succeed. More recently, the noted black conservative economist Thomas Sowell has made the same argument in *Ethnic America*.[14]

There are several problems with this view, however. First, and most important, it ignores the structural changes occurring in the American economy. Previous immigrant groups arrived at a time of extraordinary industrial growth. There was a demand for unskilled labor. Today we face a serious shrinkage of those same kinds of jobs. This process began slowly in the 1950s and, as table 14.1 indicates, had a devastating effect on black teenage employment. Second, it ignores the special quality of American racial discrimination. The historian Herbert Gutman has challenged the popular view that the problems of the black family can be traced back to slavery. His research indicates that the black family emerged from slavery in remarkably strong condition. The current problems with the black family are a result of more recent economic conditions in the urban North. Finally, Moynihan himself repudiated the central thesis of *Beyond the Melting Pot* twenty years later. In a remarkable act of intellectual courage, he admitted he had been wrong. The experience of the previous immigrant groups was not a viable model for our current problems. Moynihan now claims that since the 1960s the gap between rich and poor has been dramatically widening. We are closer to becoming a truly class-divided society now than at any earlier time in our history.[15]

In short, the combination of new economic forces and long-standing racial discrimination has led us into a historically unique situation. The so-called lessons of the past about other immigrant groups do not apply.

Economic Reconstruction

Virtually everyone agrees that in the long run, economic opportunity will reduce crime by allowing ordinary people to establish productive lives and stable families. The real dispute between liberals and conservatives is over the means to achieve that end. Conservatives put their hopes in a market-place free of government intervention. Liberals, on the other hand, want the government to assume an active role both in stimulating growth and in providing assistance to people in need.

The social programs of the 1960s failed because they did not address the need to create massive numbers of jobs. The Vietnam War did that job better by stimulating production and channeling hundreds of thousands of young men out of the work force and into military service. But even the war-induced prosperity failed to stem the rising tide of teenage unemployment and the growth of the underclass. The education and job-training programs of the War on Poverty were irrelevant in the face of the structural changes in the economy. The criticisms published in *The Public Interest* and other neoconservative journals are probably fair: the programs never demonstrated their effectiveness and many were counterproductive. But those criticisms are beside the point. Even if the programs had been effective, they would not have served enough people to reduce unemployment significantly and certainly would not have halted the steady erosion of entry-level jobs and the growth of the underclass.

If in fact unemployment breeds crime, we will not solve that problem by social tinkering. Job training for a few thousand unemployed, or a 30 percent or even 50 percent reduction in the official unemployment rate, will not in any way touch the underclass, which is the core of our predatory crime problem. Yet neither liberal Democrats nor conservative Republicans have offered a realistic program for the creation of massive numbers of jobs.

Beyond Race?

William Julius Wilson makes a persuasive argument about the kinds of social programs that are politically feasible in today's political environment. The problems of unemployment, family breakdown, and crime are disproportionately concentrated in a relatively small group—the truly disadvantaged, the underclass, call it what you want. In the political arena, however, the majority will not support programs designed just for this group. To obtain the necessary political support, effective programs will need to be presented as beneficial to all racial and economic groups. As Wilson puts it, "The hidden agenda is to improve the life chances of groups such as the ghetto underclass by emphasizing programs in which the more advantaged groups of all races can positively relate." In short, the fate of the underclass is tied up with the fate of all the rest of us. To deal with crime we should target not just the hard-core career criminals, Wolfgang's famous 6 percent, but the social policies that affect society as a whole.[16]

Notes

1. Samuel Walker, *Popular Justice: A History of American Criminal Justice* (New York: Oxford University Press, 1980), pp. 232–239.
2. James Q. Wilson, *Thinking about Crime*, rev. ed. (New York: Basic Books, 1983), chap. 1.
3. James Q. Wilson, "Thinking about Crime," *Atlantic Monthly*, September 1983, pp. 86, 88.
4. Richard A. Cloward and Lloyd E. Ohlin, *Delinquency and Opportunity* (New York: Free Press, 1960), p. 83.
5. Elliot Liebow, *Tally's Corner* (Boston: Little, Brown, 1967).
6. Isaac Ehrlich, "Participation in Illegitimate Activities: A Theoretical and Empirical Investigation," *Journal of Political Economy*, May–June 1973, pp. 521–565.
7. Sheldon Danziger and David Wheeler, "The Economics of Crime: Punishment or Income Distribution," *Review of Social Economy* 33 (October 1975): 113–131.
8. Thomas Orsagh and Anne D. Witte, "Economic Status and Crime: Implications for Offender Rehabilitation," *Journal of Criminal Law and Criminology* 72 (1981): 1055–1071.
9. Ken Auletta, *The Underclass* (New York: Vintage, 1983); William Julius Wilson, *The Truly Disadvantaged: The Inner City, the Underclass, and Public Policy* (Chicago: University of Chicago Press, 1987).
10. Oscar Lewis, *Five Families: Mexican Case Studies in the Culture of Poverty*

(New York: Basic Books, 1959), and *The Children of Sánchez* (New York: Random House, 1961).

11. Wilson, *Truly Disadvantaged*, pp. 157–158.

12. Charles Silberman, *Criminal Violence, Criminal Justice* (New York: Random House, 1978).

13. Charles Loring Brace, *The Dangerous Classes of New York* [3rd ed., 1880] (New York: Patterson Smith, 1967).

14. Nathan Glazer and Daniel Patrick Moynihan, *Beyond the Melting Pot* (Cambridge: MIT Press, 1963); Thomas Sowell, *Ethnic America: A History* (New York: Basic Books, 1981).

15. Herbert G. Gutman, *The Black Family in Slavery and Freedom, 1750–1925* (New York: Pantheon, 1976); Moynihan, *New York Times*, November 9, 1985.

16. Wilson, *Truly Disadvantaged*, p. 120.

PART FIVE

CONCLUSION

What Have We Learned?

We began this inquiry with a single-minded objective: to discover some practical strategies for reducing serious crime. We set certain ground rules for ourselves. Any crime-reduction strategy had to promise to be able to reduce the level of robbery or burglary and to do so at an acceptable social cost. We would entertain no strategy that would entail an unreasonable dollar cost or do violence to established standards of constitutionality and human decency.

Along the way we have learned a lot about criminal justice in the United States. We have a much better understanding of how our criminal justice system works. The most important things we have learned include the following:

1. We already punish rather severely those major offenders whom we succeed in catching;
2. the chances of catching more criminals are very slim;
3. our criminal justice institutions resist major change; the individuals who administer justice day in and day out have an enormous capacity to absorb, blunt, evade, or frustrate new policies designed to change the way the criminal justice system works;
4. criminal offenders are also very uncooperative; they don't respond to our attempts to manipulate their behavior through either deterrence or rehabilitation.

In Search of a New Paradigm

The January 4, 1988, issue of *Newsweek* grandly announced the "end of the 1980s." This pronouncement may have seemed a little premature, since almost two full years remained in the decade. With respect to crime policy, however, *Newsweek* may have been right. The ideas that have dominated crime control thinking during the decade (actually the last fifteen years) are no longer viable. The evidence is clear that "getting tough" won't reduce crime. Many of the get-tough policies now stand exposed as useless political rhetoric. Some have been implemented and they have either made no difference or created serious new problems (such as prison overcrowding). Liberals are in no position to gloat over the conservatives' failure. They have offered no realistic alternatives. Most of their ideas are warmed-over versions of old programs.

We head toward the end of the twentieth century in search of a new paradigm. A paradigm is described as a governing set of assumptions that shapes thinking about a particular subject. A liberal paradigm reigned during the 1960s and early 1970s. A conservative paradigm has ruled during the past fifteen years. In retrospect, we can say that neither responded adequately to the crime problem. That is, neither met the criteria established at the beginning of this book: realistic policies that would effectively reduce serious crime at an acceptable social cost. Where do we go from here?

Is Criminal Justice Policy Irrelevant?

Perhaps criminal justice policy is irrelevant. This is a serious challenge and we have to face it squarely. Changing the criminal justice system—the criminal law, criminal procedure, the way the police, prosecutors, judges, and prison officials work—may have absolutely no effect on serious crime. This is a bitter pill for criminal justice experts to swallow. After all, how many doctors would be willing to admit that they had no solutions to the problems of public health? How many economists would want to admit that their profession had no answers for the problem of economic growth? And there is good evidence to suggest they don't. Over the past fifteen years the economists have resembled the criminal justice experts in a disturbing fashion: instead of reasonable and effective programs, they have given us either stale old ideas (the liberals) or reckless new proposals that have done long-term economic damage (the conservatives).

Unpleasant as it may be, this conclusion may be true. As I suggested in Chapter 14, the real solution to the crime problem probably lies in the area of economic policy. Given genuine long-term economic opportunity, most people can take care of themselves. They will fulfill their aspirations of finding meaningful work, raising families, acquiring possessions, and establishing a comfortable lifestyle. To do this they don't need either the threat of punishment or a treatment program. The creation of real economic opportunity, however, depends on political choices that have little to do with criminal justice policy.

Where does this leave the criminal justice expert? Should we all just hang up our badges (our Ph.D.'s, that is) and look for honest work?

There are many important things for the criminal justice expert to do. The primary responsibility—the responsibility of all intellectuals—is to speak truth to power. There are things we know with reasonable certainty. I have tried to discuss many of them in this book. The expert's responsibility is to provide the best wisdom, without fear or favor. If some new crime control program is utterly crazy, we should say so. We should say so even when we upset our friends and political allies by doing so. If the evidence clearly suggests that a major overhaul of economic policy is the key to reducing our high levels of crime, that is what the expert should say.

The expert also has an important role in helping establish justice. Too often we forget that the criminal justice system has two objectives: to control crime *and* to establish justice. We have given too much attention to the former and not enough to the latter. Improving the fairness of our system is a worthy goal. There is persuasive evidence that we have already made some important gains in this direction and that more are possible. Reducing police shootings, establishing standards of fairness in our courts, creating decent and humane conditions in our prisons—these are important and worthy goals.

In the end we need to change the terms of the criminal justice debate. Crime control is an elusive goal. Justice is elusive too, but the goal of eliminating many of the injustices we have perpetuated is within our grasp.

Index